An Islamic Reformation?

An Islamic Reformation?

Edited by
Michaelle Browers and Charles Kurzman

LEXINGTON BOOKS
Lanham • Boulder • New York • Toronto • Oxford

LEXINGTON BOOKS

Published in the United States of America
by Lexington Books
An imprint of The Rowman & Littlefield Publishing Group, Inc.
4501 Forbes Boulevard, Suite 200, Lanham, Maryland 20706

PO Box 317
Oxford
OX2 9RU, UK

British Library Cataloguing in Publication Information Available

Library of Congress Cataloging-in-Publication Data

An Islamic reformation? / edited by Michaelle Browers and Charles Kurzman.
    p. cm.
    Includes bibliographical references and index.
    ISBN 0-7391-0554-X (cloth: alk. paper)
    1. Islam—21st century. 2. Islamic renewal. 3. Islamic modernism. I. Browers,
Michaelle, 1968– II. Kurzman, Charles.

BP161.3.I75 2003
297'.09'051—dc22   2003060464

Printed in the United States of America

♾™ The paper used in this publication meets the minimum requirements of American
National Standard for Information Sciences—Permanence of Paper for Printed Library
Materials, ANSI/NISO Z39.48–1992.

Contents

Acknowledgments

The editors gratefully acknowledge Gabriel Morris' assistance in pulling together the bibliography and dedicate this work to Dominic and Zoë Marazita, and Max and Sam Barrett Kurzman.

Note on Transliteration

The transliteration of Arabic names and terms generally conforms to a simplified version of the format used in the *International Journal of Middle East Studies*. Persian names and terms are generally transliterated according to the *Encyclopaedia Iranica* system. Diacritical marks are not used except for ' for the *'ayn* and ' for the *hamza* when it occurs in the middle of a word. The *hamza* is omitted when at the beginning or end of words, as well as after the definite article.

In cases of proper names that have common English spellings—such as places (e.g., Cairo, Beirut, Morocco) and individuals whose names have a consistent transliteration (e.g., Abdolkarim Soroush, Nasser)—we usually opted for the more familiar spelling.

Introduction

Comparing Reformations

Charles Kurzman and Michaelle Browers

The Christian Reformation is a hot topic in many Muslim societies. In Iran, for example, author Hashem Aghajari became an international celebrity after speaking on this theme in June 2002. Aghajari argued that, like medieval Christianity, religion in the Islamic Republic of Iran had become bureaucratized and hierarchical. Iranian Muslims of the fifteenth Islamic century ought to embark on a "project of Islamic Protestantism," just as fifteenth century Christians had done. He described "Islamic Protestantism" as "a rational, scientific, humanistic Islam. It is a thoughtful and intellectual Islam, an open-minded Islam."[1]

Aghajari was arrested soon thereafter, and sentenced to death by the religious establishment that he had criticized, becoming an icon for Islamic reform around the world. In Malaysia, columnist Matahati Mazeni Alwi wrote that Aghajari stuck a "dagger into the heart of the theocratic Islamic state" and worried that Malaysia's Islamic opposition might also be harboring theocratic designs.[2] In California, web-editor Shahed Amanullah hoped that Aghajari "has brought the conservative ruling class to their knees."[3]

Aghajari's case was unusual in its setting: a Shi'i country with a constitution placing religious scholars at the head of state. But his argument was far from unique. Around the world, numerous Muslim authors make use of the analogy with the Christian Reformation, and have done so since the nineteenth century, as have Western observers of Islamic reform movements.

This volume examines the analogy from several perspectives, asking: What are some of the most significant transformations and developments taking place in the contemporary Middle East? Do the various reformist individuals and movements in the Middle East today constitute a reformation of Islamic society as such? To what extent are changes or prospects in Muslim societies similar to the Christian Reformation? How useful is such a comparison? The last section of this chapter introduces these analyses. Meanwhile, the first section examines the historical usage of the analogy itself: When did it emerge, what forms does it take, and what purpose does it serve, for Muslims and non-Muslims?

Historical Usages of the Reformation Analogy

It is impossible to trace the origins of the Reformation analogy with any certainty. Nonetheless, it is clear that the theme was visible by the beginning of the twentieth century, both among Muslims and among Western, typically Protestant Christian, observers of Islam. On the Western side, the analogy grew out of the long-standing polemical tradition that treated Islam and other religions as inferior to Christianity.[4] It was only with the rise of modern intellectuals, trained outside of the seminary, that a new form of comparative religious studies emerged, one less explicitly intended to discredit other people's faiths. Certain Enlightenment thinkers of the eighteenth century, for example, "tended to make Mohammed almost a good Protestant and in any event a perceptive enemy of the Curia Romana"[5]—though other Enlightenment thinkers continued the older tropes of hostility.[6] In the late nineteenth century, the founder of the "scientific" study of religion urged researchers to adopt a scholarly identity distinct from theology, to compare faith traditions while "claim[ing] no privilege, no exceptional position of any kind, for his own religion, whatever that religion may be."[7] The field of religious studies never fully resolved the tension between theological and nontheological approaches,[8] but the appeal to "scientific" standards, at least in some quarters, opened a space for creative comparisons across faith traditions.

It was in this context that the Reformation analogy emerged. In 1881, for example, British poet and publicist Wilfred Scawen Blunt (1840-1922) likened "Wahhabism"—an outsiders' term for the Muwahhidun (Unitarian) revivalist movement founded by Muhammad ibn 'Abd al-Wahhab in eighteenth century Arabia—with Protestant Christianity: "Just as the Lutheran reformation in Europe, though it failed to convert the Christian Church, caused its real reform, so Wahhabism has produced a real desire for reform if not yet reform itself in Mussulmans."[9] Another author used the same analogy in 1916 to make the opposite point: "Just as the Protestant Reformation was followed by a counter-reformation in Roman Catholicism, so Wahabism [sic] was the instrument for arousing the Sunni Moslems."[10] Numerous observers have likened Islamic revivalism to Christian Puritanism, focusing on shared features such as asceticism, simple garb, a work ethic, restrictive sexual mores, opposition to secularism, and a foregrounding of religion in everyday life.[11] An early example appears in a Turkish newspaper in 1924: "Wahabism [sic] in its relation to Islamism [sic] is like Protestantism as compared with Catholicism. It does not admit the Moslem faith except when purged of certain practises and symbolic manifestations. No beautiful mosques, no ornamental tombs!"[12] As Islamic radicalism has become increasingly prominent in world politics, mass media commonly describe it as "puritanical," using the analogy implicitly.[13]

On the Muslim side, "Wahhabis" have remained uninterested in comparisons with the West—their writings focus exclusively on Islamic precedents. The first Muslims to take up the analogy, rather, were Islamic modernists seeking to reconcile Islamic faith with Western values and institutions.[14] As in Christianity, Islamic scholarship has a long prehistory of polemical comparative religious studies.[15] Also as in Christianity, this tradition shifted with the emergence of a new class of intellectuals who adopted an identity distinct from, and hostile to, that of the traditional seminarians. Enthusiastic about Western-style learning—in combination with Islamic education—these new intellectuals were open to cross-religious analogies such as the Islamic Reformation.

If Western observers saw developments in Islam that resembled Christian history, however, Islamic modernists saw the reverse: developments in Christian history that resembled Islam. Their prime use of the analogy held that the Reformation moved Christianity closer to the values and practices of the pure, initial Islam, and "Martin Luther was often considered [by Islamic modernists of this period as] a latter-day Muslim anxious to combat superstitions and restore religion to its original progressive nature."[16] The most prominent Islamic modernist of the period, Muhammad 'Abduh of Egypt (1849-1905), was one of many authors to make this argument:

> In the west the desire for knowledge intensified and concern grew to break the entail of obscurantism. A strong resolve was generated to curb the authority of religious leaders and keep them from exceeding the proper precepts of religion and corrupting its valid meanings. It was not long after that a party made its appearance in the west calling for reform and a return to the simplicities of the faith—a reformation which included elements by no means unlike Islam.[17]

Similarly, the most prominent South Asian Islamic modernist, Muhammad Iqbal (India, 1877-1938), suggested that the West had come to resemble Islam not just through the Reformation, but also through democratic political theory:

> Luther, the enemy of despotism in religion, and Rousseau, the enemy of despotism in politics, must always be regarded as the emancipators of European humanity from the heavy fetters of Popedom and absolutism, and their religious and political thought must be understood as a virtual denial of the Church dogma of human depravity. The possibility of the elimination of sin and pain from the evolutionary process, and faith in the natural goodness of man, are the basic propositions of Islam, as of modern European civilization, which has, almost unconsciously, recognized the truth of these propositions in spite of the religious system with which it is associated.[18]

In Iqbal's view, Luther and other Christian reformists realized Islamic values independently, even "in spite of" their Christianity. A leading Turkish modernist, Ziya Gökalp (Turkey, 1876-1924), took the comparison even further, claiming that the Protestant Reformation was in fact inspired by Islamic ideals:

> When we study the history of Christianity, we see that, following the Crusades [eleventh-thirteenth centuries], a new movement started in Europe, which was then acquainted with Islamic culture. This movement aimed at imitating Islamic civilization and religion. It penetrated Europe with time, and finally culminated in Protestantism as a new religion entirely in contra-distinction to the traditional principles of Christianity. This new religion rejected the priesthood, and the existence of two kinds of government, spiritual and temporal. It also rejected the papacy, the Councils, the Inquisition—in short, all institutions which had existed in Christianity—as contrary to the principles of Islam. Are we not justified if we look at this religion as a more or less Islamicized form of Christianity?[19]

This approach seems to have dwindled as the twentieth century proceeded. It often contained an implicit call for Muslims to imitate the Christian Reformation and return to the pure roots of Islam, but some made this call for imitation explicit. In so doing, they adopted the Western version of the Reformation analogy: comparing Islam with Christianity rather than Christianity with Islam. Today, it sounds peculiar to hear the equation of Protestantism and Islam, as though Islam were the yardstick against which other religious traditions might be measured. But it has become generally acceptable to equate certain Islamic trends with Protestantism, taking Christian history as the point of reference.

Sayyid Jamal al-Din al-Afghani (Iran, 1838-1897), for example, said he "cannot keep from hoping that Muhammadan society will succeed someday in breaking its bonds and marching resolutely in the path of civilization after the manner of Western society."[20] The sole cause of Western civilizational progress, Afghani argued, was "the religious movement raised and spread by Luther."[21] Indeed, the idea that "Islam needed a Luther . . . was a favourite theme of al-Afghani's," and Afghani may have seen himself as that Luther.[22] Similarly, the Indian reformer Sayyid Ahmad Khan (1817-1898) proclaimed that "the fact is that India needs not merely a Steele or an Addison, but also, and primarily, a Luther."[23] This sentiment was echoed by Fath 'Ali Akhundzadah (1812-1878) in the Russian Empire[24] and Abdullah Cevdet (1869-1932) in the Ottoman Empire,[25] both of whom used the reformation analogy as a cover for atheism. More devout was Musa Jarullah Bigi (Russian Tatarstan, 1875-1949), who argued that the Christian Reformation was responsible for civilization itself:

> through reformers like Martin Luther, the Christian world entered on the path of progress; meanwhile, through religious scholars and leaders such as Ibn Kemal [Kemalpasazâde, Turkish scholar, circa 1468-1534] and Abu al-Sa'ud

[Ebussu'ud Efendi, Turkish religious leader, circa 1491-1574], the Muslim world went into decline. That is, while the civilized world progressed through the freedom of reason, through the captivity of reason the Muslim world declined.[26]

Writing in 1925, Habib Allah Pur-i Riza (Iran) argued that Shi'i Islam needed a "sacred revolution" with "thinkers like Luther and Calvin."[27] Muhammad Rashid Rida (Syria-Egypt, 1865-1935) cited the need to combine "religious renewal and earthly renewal, the same way Europe has done with religious reformation and modernization."[28] Iqbal, who identified Islamic elements in Protestantism in 1909, as quoted above, identified Protestant elements in Islam two decades later: "We are today passing through a period similar to that of the Protestant revolution in Europe, and the lesson which the rise and outcome of [Martin] Luther's movement teaches should not be lost on us."[29]

Optimistic supporters of the modernist Islamic movement felt that it heralded the beginning of a Protestant-style Reformation. Hadi Atlasi (Tatarstan, circa 1875-1940) claimed that "there was an urgent need for a Muslim 'Luther' in order to save the Muslim world, but whatever the reason was, no such person appeared until . . . the 'Muslim Luther,' the renewer [Shihabuddin] Marjani [Tatarstan, 1818-1889] appeared among the northern Muslims, at the end of the thirteenth century [nineteenth century A.D.]."[30] Marjani was widely hailed as the founder of Islamic modernism in Russia. Similarly, Wilfred Scawen Blunt noted that Muslim reformers, including his friend 'Abduh, "stand in close resemblance to the 'Reformers' of Christianity; and some of the circumstances which have given them birth are so analogous to those which Europe encountered in the fifteenth century that it is impossible not to draw in one's mind a parallel, leading to the conviction that Islam, too, will work out for itself a Reformation."[31] By the late twentieth century, at least one author, the secularist Syrian thinker Sadiq Jalal al-'Azm, suggested that enough of an Islamic Reformation had taken place to have generated a "counterreformation," led by the Muslim Brotherhood and similar movements.[32] In contrast, some conservative Muslims have employed the analogy disparagingly in accusing various reformists and radicals, including the Muslim Brotherhood, of acting like Muslim Luthers.[33]

But the Islamic Reformation analogy is constantly reinvented. A century after the analogy first emerged, sociologist Jose Casanova identified Reformation-like changes occurring in "the very recent past": "if there is anything on which most observers and analysts of contemporary Islam agree, it is that the Islamic tradition in the very recent past has undergone an unprecedented process of pluralization and fragmentation of religious authority, comparable to that initiated by the Protestant Reformation."[34] It is interesting—perhaps ironic—that this most recent and widespread use of the analogy by Western observers occurs amidst doubts in historical studies that the Reformation forms a coherent or discrete period at all. A recent textbook, entitled *The European*

Reformations, explains the plural in its title by stating that "In more recent scholarship this 'conventional sense' of the Reformation [as a unified period] has given way to recognition that there was a plurality of Reformations which interacted with each other: Luther, Catholic, Reformed, and dissident movements."[35]

Nonetheless, by the late twentieth century, observers identified a new crop of Muslim Luthers, as previous candidates failed to fulfill the role of generating a full-blown Reformation. Anthropologist Dale Eickelman has argued that a best-selling 1990 book by Syrian author Muhammad Shahrour (born 1938) "may one day be seen as a Muslim equivalent of the 95 Theses that Martin Luther nailed to the door of the Wittenberg Castle church in 1517."[36] Journalist Robin Wright reported in 1995 that "both supporters and critics now call [Abdolkarim Soroush, Iran, born 1945] the Martin Luther of Islam."[37] Another journalist has attached the label to Tariq Ramadan (Switzerland, born 1962), the grandson of Muslim Brotherhood founder Hassan al-Banna (1906-1949) and author of the book *To Be a European Muslim*.[38] A third has singled out a female scholar in Egypt, Su'ad Salah, who heads the Islamic law department of the al-Azhar's women's college.[39] Yet another maintains that an Islamic political party, Turkey's Justice and Development Party, "could usher in an Islamic version of the Protestant Reformation."[40] A recent critique of Middle East and Islamic Studies argues that these fields "were so preoccupied with 'Muslim Martin Luthers' that they never got around to producing a single serious analysis of bin Laden and his indictment of America."[41] The point may or may not be accurate, but it is worth noting that conservative journalists have been as eager as liberal academics to search for Muslim Luthers.[42]

While there seem to be a growing tendency to analyze the Islamic Reformation as a present fact,[43] most studies treat the subject in the conditional rather than the present tense. Numerous authors have suggested that Islam is on the verge of a Reformation. For example, the jurist Asaf Ali Asghar Fyzee (India, 1899-1981) maintained that "if the complete fabric of the *shari'a* is examined in this critical manner [in the interest of social justice and social well-being], it is obvious that . . . a newer 'protestant' Islam will be born in conformity with conditions of life in the twentieth century, cutting away the dead wood of the past and looking hopefully at the future." Fyzee calls this new "protestant" Islam, "Liberal Islam."[44]

Similarly, the famous Iranian reformer, 'Ali Shari'ati (1933-1977), held that Islam "is living at the end of the Medieval period," comparable to the position of Christian thinkers who "found their new destiny by destroying their old faith, and transforming traditional Catholicism to a protesting, world-minded, political, and materialist Protestantism."[45] Shari'ati urged Muslims to embrace "an Islamic Protestantism similar to that of Christianity in the Middle Ages, destroying all the degenerating factors which, in the name of Islam, have stymied and stupefied the process of thinking and the fate of the society, and giving birth to new thoughts and new movements."[46] Hashem Aghajari's speech of June 2002, quoted at the start of this chapter, amplified these themes on the occasion of the twenty-fifth anniversary of Shari'ati's untimely death. Similarly, Abdullahi Ahmed An-Na'im (Sudan, born 1946) has suggested that "today, Islam is in a period of pre-Reformation," arguing that Islamic fundamentalism is "our counter-Reformation [that] is the prelude to the Islamic Reformation"[47]—though he has stressed that "an Islamic reformation cannot be a belated and poor copy of the European Christian model. . . . It will have to be an indigenous and authentically Islamic process if it is to be a reformation at all."[48] Ahmad Bishara maintains that the aim of the liberal political group in Kuwait he heads, the National Democratic Movement, is "to reform Islam the way Martin Luther reformed the Catholic church."[49] Ali Mazrui (Kenya-U.S., born 1933) and Alamin Mazrui (Kenya-U.S., born 1948) muse that "It would be particularly fitting if the Martin Luther of the Islamic Reformation turned out to be a woman, posting her 95 theses of reform not on the door of a Wittenberg mosque but universally on the Internet."[50]

The British newsweekly, *The Economist*, has been particularly active in promoting this theme of an impending Islamic Reformation, which appears in numerous articles since the 1980s. In 1994, for example, the magazine wrote:

> It is now, in the moon-regulated calendar of Muslims, the year 1415. In the Christians' year 1415, at the Council of Constance, the conservatives who were trying to stamp out the beginnings of the Reformation burnt Jan Hus at the stake, and arranged for John Wycliffe's bones to be dug out of their English grave and tossed onto a fire. And yet, by 1436, a Hussite army had forced a first concession out of the conservatives; by the 1470s the printed bibles made possible by Gutenberg's press were spreading through Europe; by 1506 Zwingli was preaching in Switzerland; and in 1517 Martin Luther nailed his theses to the church door at Wittenberg. And, remember, things go much faster now.[51]

The same article went so far as to create a "Reformation check-list" of similarities between "Islam's 15th century, which on the Muslim count began a few years ago," and "the Christian 15th century, the period Europe went through shortly before the Reformation." The items included: 1) "disillusionment with both the religious and the political apparatus of the old order"; 2) "an almost cosmic sense of despair"; 3) "a powerful desire to put things right by going back to the roots of the faith"; and 4) "an enriching stimulus from outside."[52] The *Economist*'s use of the analogy was amplified amidst the furor over Salman Rushdie's *Satanic Verses* and the death sentence imposed on him: "Since the Reformation the western world has got used to hearing such things said, for each listener to agree of disagree with as he wishes. The Muslim world has not yet gone through a Reformation."[53] "Reformation" in this context seems to refer to a reconsideration of the religion's doctrine and practice that not only sets into motion a process of fragmentation of religious authority, but also an increasing privatization of religious belief.

In his influential work *The Clash of Civilizations*, Samuel Huntington argues that while "in its political manifestations, the Islamic Resurgence bears some resemblance to Marxism, . . . [a] more useful analogy . . . is the Protestant Reformation":

> Both are reactions to the stagnation and completion of existing institutions; advocate a return to a purer and more demanding form of their religion; preach world order, and discipline; and appeal to emerging, dynamic middle-class people. Both are also complex movements, with diverse strands, but two major ones, Lutheranism and Calvinism, Shi'ite and Sunni fundamentalism, and even parallels between John Calvin and the Ayatollah Khomeini and the monastic discipline they tried to impose on their societies. The central spirit of both the reformation and the Resurgence is fundamental reform.[54]

While Huntington points out many of the same indicators as the *Economist* and sees similar levels of conflict resulting from this Reformation, he is less willing to posit secularism—or the privatization of religion—as an outcome. Among the important legacies he predicts are an increased awareness of religio-cultural distinctiveness and commitment to Islam; a "network of Islamist social, cultural, economic, and political organizations" and, possibility further in the future, "disillusionment with political Islam, a reaction against it, and a search for alternative 'solutions.'"[55] Like other societies that Huntington sees as grappling with modernity, the primary outcome of this Islamic Resurgence-Reformation will be "indigenization"—that is, a form of cultural assertiveness, where actors reject Western sources of development and "find the means of success within their own society, and hence accommodate the values and culture of that society." In the case of Muslim majority societies, "indigenization" means a "re-Islamicization" that "is not a rejection of modernity," but rather "a rejection of the West and of the secular, relativistic, degenerate culture associated with the West."[56]

Some authors, by contrast, feel that an Islamic Reformation is not just around the corner. Typically, this argument appears in a context of hostility towards Islam, where the inability to undergo a Reformation is presented as a condemnation of the religion. For example, Syed Kamran Mirza of the Institute for the Secularization of Islamic Society (ISIS) likens contemporary Islam to "a raging fever in its most acute phase," badly in need of Reformation through "sustained critical scrutiny," and laments that "the prospect for such a Muslim reformation is currently remote."[57] As a U.S. newspaper columnist wrote in 1978: "Christianity came to terms with modern science, industry and society only after the Protestant Reformation and a thousand lesser shocks. Islam, however, has not had a Reformation—and probably will not."[58] However, in 1992 the foreign editor of the same newspaper entertained the more "hopeful view" expressed by a French official: "It is possible, [the French official] said, that the fundamentalists [in Algeria] will play the same purifying—and ultimately modernizing—role that the Protestant Reformation played in Europe. [The official] cited Max Weber's famous argument, in 'The Protestant Ethic and the Spirit of Capitalism,' that the 17th-century Protestant fundamentalists paved the way for the development of modern political and economic institutions in Europe."[59] Another author has commented on the repeated failures of Reformation predictions: "Since the Enlightenment broke the lock of medieval prejudice against Islam, the reform of Islam had been declared inevitable, even imminent, by a parade of visionaries and experts. The current representation of Islamic fundamentalism as a portent of democracy has opened another chapter in this cyclical saga of hope and disillusionment."[60]

And then there are those who reject the Reformation analogy entirely. Some view the analogy with suspicion, maintaining as Tareq al-Suwaidan, a Muslim Brotherhood leader and host of popular Islamic programs on Arab satellite TV does, that "from [liberal Muslims calling for a Reformation's] point of view, reformation means dropping Islam."[61] Another common trope holds that Islam has no clergy in the Catholic Christian sense of divine representatives and shepherds of souls. As a result, Muslims have no target against which to stage a Reformation, so the analogy fails. In a famous debate between Muhammad 'Abid al-Jabiri (Morocco, born 1936) and Hassan Hanafi (Egypt, born 1935), for example, both thinkers agreed, despite their many differences, that "Islam is not a church that we can separate from the state."[62] Some authors have contended that Western "Orientalists, and more particularly those who are Protestants, cannot free themselves from what might be called the inevitability of the Reformation."[63] Indeed, all teleologies that view other cultures as recapitulating the history of one's own culture—including modernization theory and Marxian historical materialism—remain vulnerable to similar criticism.

Nonetheless, the Reformation analogy continues to be proffered, both by Muslims and non-Muslims, with even greater frequency since the terrorist attacks of September 11, 2001. One year later, for example, the Center for the Study of Islam and Democracy hosted a panel discussion in Washington, D.C., on the question "Does Islam Need a Reformation?" Six days later and less than half a mile away, the newly established Global Policy Exchange convened "A Conversation on the Theme, An Islamic Reformation?" at the National Press Club. More recently, the editor of the *American Journal of Islamic Social Sciences* has asserted the distinctiveness of Islam's Reformation, while calling for a Reformation, nonetheless: "the Muslim East should be allowed to undertake its own reformation, which would inevitably result in the reorientation and rationalization of religious values and beliefs of Muslims, and must hence, take the form of an Islamic reformation."[64]

Assessing the Analogy

"Reformation" is usually employed to refer to a transformation linked with recognition of the need to overhaul institutions, practices, and ideas of religious authority. As such, reformation suggests both social and intellectual dimensions. Both dimensions are dealt with in the chapters that follow, but the authors differ in their assessments of how this characterization might best be applied to Islamic societies. The widespread and longstanding usage of the Reformation analogy makes an examination of the subject worthwhile. However, to understand to what extent the analogy is accurate and useful, let us draw out three themes in the Reformation analogy, each of which is both found in the history of the use of the comparison and employed by various contributors to this volume.

The first theme might be termed "contextualist" and maintains that it is neither possible nor productive to compare transformations that are occurring the Islamic region. This view is articulated by Abdelwahab El-Affendi in an essay entitled "The Elusive Reformation." According to El-Affendi, many social scientists who attempt to account for the lack of democracy in Muslim countries by pointing to "prepolitical" factors such as Islam reach the conclusion that what is then necessary is a "Reformation" or "radical intellectual and ethical orientation of Islam."[65] Yet, in regard to the issue of liberal democracy, the Reformation of Islam is neither the problem, nor the solution: "an 'Islamic Reformation' is neither necessary nor sufficient for enabling Muslims to build stable and consensual political institutions."[66] The task for social scientists is, in his view, to understand not the extent to which a broad-based consensus exists among members of a community which allows for "consensual popular rule" (his definition of liberal democracy).

In this volume, the contextualist view is best represented by the contribution from Salwa Ismail (chapter 4). Despite the fact that revisionist writings working in both Western and Muslim traditions have questioned accounts of the lives and missions of Jesus and Muhammad, Ismail maintains that the Muslim revisionist thinkers she highlights are best understood through reference to the historical and discursive context out of which they arose. Only then can one accurately determine the aims of Islamic reformists, assess their relative importance, and gauge the response they have generated. In Ismail's view, using an analogy with the European reformation as a point of reference tends to create totalizing views of Islam and place Islamic societies on an anachronistic historical trajectory. Comparison with the Reformation period in Europe detracts from and, in this case, serves to obscure the unique negotiations between secular and sacred taking place in the reformist projects of contemporary Egyptian historical revisionists.

A second view, which might be termed "critical comparativist," holds that the European Reformation is useful as a point of comparison, but only in very specific ways. For example, in her contribution, Michaelle Browers (chapter 3) argues that the analogy is only productive in a very limited sense and, in the end, the comparison may call into question more about the popular view of the Protestant Reformation than it reveals about the Reformation emerging in Islamic societies. Focusing on contemporary Islamic thinkers whose training does not place them among the traditional 'ulama and whose thought builds upon but is distinct from the modernists of the eighteenth and early nineteenth centuries, Browers discusses the similar hermeneutical focus of reformers in contemporary Islamic and sixteenth century Christian contexts.

Charles Kurzman (chapter 4) is considerably less hesitant about the comparison when applied to one particular case. According to Kurzman, the 1979 revolution in Iran has had the effect of transforming Shi'i religious scholars into a hierarchal institution with administrative authorities that even many Iranians regularly compare to the "church" and "clergy" in Catholic Christianity. Specifically, Iran's jurist-ruler (vali-ye faqih) and his followers have sought a monopoly of interpretative authority such that to cast themselves as the sole legitimate interpreters of the true faith and have become the focus for contemporary Iranian reformists.

Most of the chapters presented here represent a third theme, which might most properly be termed "comparativist." This view is both more convinced that an Islamic reformation is either well under way or has already occurred, and the most adamant in deeming the example of the Protestant Reformation as a productive basis for understanding recent transformations in Islamic societies. In an updated version of an article that was very influential in generating the current interest in the comparison among American and European scholars, Dale Eickelman (chapter 1) points to "the combination of mass education and mass communications" as an important material factor that is transforming both the means and manner of challenging, bypassing, and recreating traditional religious authority in the Muslim world. Eickelman describes how increasing literacy, satellite television, audio and video cassettes, and the Internet are contributing in various ways to an expanding marketplace of views and an emboldened public sphere.

Felicitas Opwis (chapter 2) looks at the changes advocated by leading Sunni jurists in the area of legal theory in the late nineteenth and early twentieth centuries and the conditions that inspired them and finds strong parallels with the Reformation of sixteenth century Western Christianity. Although, like Eickelman, Opwis emphasizes the importance of educational reforms and the printing press as contexts for reform, the legal basis of the Islamic Reformation that Opwis identifies seems much less dramatic, slower, and harder to pinpoint— and at times more reactionary—than that characterized by Eickelman. In contrast to Browers' focus on contemporary interpreters, Opwis places most significance on an earlier generation of Islamic reformists, such as Muhammad Abduh, Rashid Rida, Jamal al-Din al-Qasimi, and Mahmud Shaltut, who used a concept of social interest (*maslaha*) as the basis of their *ijtihad*. Thus, for Opwis, the Islamic Reformation has already occurred.

Mark Sedgwick (chapter 6) also points to the increasing emphasis on various forms of *ijtihad* at the expense of *taqlid* as indicative of the diminished authority of the traditional schools of Islamic jurisprudence. However, Sedgwick finds greater evidence for a process of reformation in the nineteenth century in the consequences of that reformation. According to Sedgwick, the eclipsing of Sufi beliefs and practices in Muslim societies holds parallels with the eclipse of central elements of Catholic beliefs and practices in early Protestantism. Sedgwick finds the eclipsing of Sufi authority most apparent in the response of the Budshishiyya, a Moroccan Sufi order that has enacted what Sedgwick characterizes as an important, albeit limited, counterreformation. Since the 1960s, the Budshishiyya's counterreformation has met success in confronting the anti-Sufi stereotypes generated by the Islamic reformation—stereotypes similar in many respects to early Protestant stereotypes of Rome—and reestablishing Sufi practices and beliefs among elites.

The contributions of Ernest Tucker (chapter 7) and Nader A. Hashemi (chapter 8) are most explicitly built upon a comparison between the Reformation in Europe and transformations under way in Muslim countries. In a comparison of the Anabaptists of Münster in the 1530s and the Talibans of Afghanistan in the 1990s, Tucker finds that, despite the very different outcomes of these two movements, each group displayed a similar "primitivism" in their response to a period of religious crisis. Münsterites and Talibans both dealt with change by attempting to "purify" and "cleanse" religious truth of worldly elements, both articulated religious doctrine in "consciously naïve and extremist" ways, and each dealt similarly with women and with other religious forces that opposed them.

Hashemi also uses the sixteenth century as the focus of his comparison for the lessons he argues it provides for Muslim societies dealing with modernization and religio-political conflict. Like the Reformation in Europe, the Reformation taking place in the Middle East promises to be complicated, with reformist trends emerging among counterreformation forces. But Hashemi's longer view of history suggests that trends like "fundamentalist" Islamic should not be seen as antimodernization or regressive, but as genuine response to social transformations and as part of a process that in the long-term effect may portend significant political development for the region.

Notes

1. Ayelet Savyon, "The Call for Islamic Protestantism: Dr. Hashem Aghajari's Speech and Subsequent Death Sentence," *The Middle East Media Research Institute Special Dispatch Series* 445, 2 December 2002, www.memri.org/bin/

articles.cgi?Page=subjects&Area=reform&ID=SP44502 (24 March 2003).

2. Matahati Mazeni Alwi, "The Case of Hashem Aghajari: Islamic State Vision Comes Full Circle," *Malaysiakini*, 30 November 2002, www.malaysiakini.com/columns/20021130013683.php (24 March 2003).

3. Shahed Amanullah, "Human Rights in the Muslim World: Still a Long Way to Go," *alt.muslim*, 9 December 2002, www.altmuslim.com/world_comments.php?id=843_0_22_0_C (24 March 2003).

4. Norman Daniel, *Islam and the West: The Making of an Image* (Edinburgh, Scotland: Edinburgh University Press, 1960); R. W. Southern, *Western Views of Islam in the Middle Ages* (Cambridge: Harvard University Press, 1962).

5. Kenneth M. Setton, *Western Hostility to Islam, and Prophecies of Turkish Doom* (Philadelphia: American Philosophical Society, 1992), 54.

6. Perhaps most famously, Voltaire's *Mahomet, or Fanaticism* (1745). Other examples can be found in Edward Said, *Orientalism* (New York: Vintage Books, 1978).

7. Donald Wiebe, *The Politics of Religious Studies: The Continuing Conflict with Theology in the Academy* (New York: St. Martin's Press, 1999), 19.

8. Wiebe, *The Politics of Religious Studies*, Parts II-III; Eric J. Sharpe, "Religious Studies, the Humanities, and the History of Ideas," *Soundings* 71 (1988): 245-58. On Islamic studies in particular, see Jean-Jacques Waardenburg, *L'Islam dans le Miroir de l'Occident: Comment Quelques Orientalistes Occidentaux se Sent Penchés sur l'Islam et se Sont Formés une Image de Cette Religion* (Islam in the Mirror of the West: How Several Western Orientalists Felt Inclined Toward Islam and Formed an Image of that Religion) (Paris: Mouton & Co., 1963).

9. Wilfred Scawen Blunt, "The Future of Islam," *The Fortnightly Review* 30 (1881): 223; reprinted in *The Future of Islam* (London: Kegan Paul, Trench & Co., 1882), 46.

10. Samuel Graham Wilson, *Modern Movements among Moslems* (New York: Fleming H. Revell Company, 1916), 57.

11. James L. Peacock, *Muslim Puritans: Reformist Psychology in Southeast Asian Islam* (Berkeley: University of California Press, 1978); Jacques Waardenburg, "The Puritan Pattern in Islamic Revival Movements," *Schweizerische Zeitschrift für Soziologie* (Swiss Journal of Sociology) 3 (1983): 687-702; Jean-Claude Vatin, "Popular Puritanism Versus State Reformism: Islam in Algeria," in *Islam in the Political Process*, ed. James P. Piscatori (Cambridge, England: Cambridge University Press, 1983); Katie Platt, "Island Puritanism," in *Islamic Dilemmas*, ed. Ernest Gellner (Berlin: Mouton Publishers, 1985), 169-86; Ellis Goldberg, "Smashing Idols and the State: The Protestant Ethic and Egyptian Sunni Radicalism," in *Comparing Muslim Societies: Knowledge and the State in a World Civilization*, ed. Juan R.I. Cole (Ann Arbor: University of Michigan Press, 1992), 195-236.

12. *Stamboul* (22 October 1924), tr. in a U.S. diplomatic document of 23 October 1924, in *Documents on the History of Saudi Arabia, Volume 1*, ed. Ibrahim al-Rashid (Salisbury, N.C.: Documentary Publications, 1976), 196.

13. Jonah Goldberg, "Islamic Rites: Why Muslims Need a Pope," 4 April 2002, *National Review Online*, www.nationalreview.com/goldberg/goldberg040302.asp (24 March 2003).

14. See selections in Charles Kurzman, ed., *Modernist Islam, 1840-1940: A Source-Book* (New York: Oxford University Press, 2002).

15. Aziz Al-Azmeh, "Barbarians in Arab Eyes," *Past and Present* 134 (1992): 3-18.

Relatively nonpolemical exceptions also existed, such as Muhammad al-Biruni (973-1051) and Muhammad Shahrastani (d. 1153)—see Chandra Muzaffar, "Multi-Civilisational Asia: the Promise and the Peril," *International Movement for a Just World*, 8 July 2001, www.just-international.org/multi-civilisational.asia.htm (24 March 2003).

16. Youssef M. Choueiri, *Islamic Fundamentalism* (Boston: Twayne Publishers, 1990), 32.

17. Muhammad 'Abduh, *The Theology of Unity (Risalat al-Tawhid)*, tr. Ishaq Masa'ad and Kenneth Cragg (London: Allen & Unwin, 1966), 149.

18. Muhammad Iqbal, "Islam as a Moral and Political Ideal," *The Hindustan Review* (July 1909): 34; reprinted in *Modernist Islam*, 306-7.

19. Ziya Gökalp, "Islam and Modern Civilization," in *Turkish Nationalism and Western Civilization: Selected Essays of Ziya Gökalp*, tr. Niyazi Berkes (London: George Allen and Unwin, 1959), 222.

20. Nikki R. Keddie, *An Islamic Response to Imperialism: Political and Religious Writings of Sayyid Jamal ad-Din "al-Afghani"* (Berkeley: University of California Press, 1968), 87.

21. Afghani, as reported by 'Abd al-Qadir al-Maghribi and cited in Nikki R. Keddie, *Sayyid Jamal ad-Din al-Afghani: A Political Biography* (Berkeley: University of California Press, 1972), 391-92, see also 95, 142, 178, and 359.

22. Albert Hourani, *Arabic Thought in the Liberal Age, 1798-1939* (Cambridge, England: Cambridge University Press, 1983), 122. See also Keddie, *An Islamic Response to Imperialism*, 82.

23. Mazheruddin Siddiqi, *Modern Reformist Thought in the Muslim World* (Islamabad, Pakistan: Islamic Research Institute, 1982), 5.

24. Mirza Fath 'Ali Akhunduf, *Alifba-yi Jadid va Maktubat* (The New Alphabet and Letters) (Baku, USSR: Nashriyat-i Farhangistan-i 'Ulum-i Jumhuri-yi Shuravi-yi Azarbayjan, 1963), 354.

25. M. Sükrü Hanioglu, *Bir Siyasal Düsünür Olarak Doktor Abdullah Cevdet ve Dönemi* (Doctor Abdullah Cevdet: A Political Thinker and His Era) (Istanbul, Turkey: Üçdal Nesriyat, 1981), 335.

26. Musa Jarullah Bigi [Bigiyef], *Khalq Nazarïna Bir Nichä Mäs'älä (Several Problems for Public Consideration)* (Kazan, Tatarstan, Russia: Äliktro-Tipografiyä Ümid, 1912), 35, tr. Ahmet Kanlidere, in *Modernist Islam*, 255.

27. Mohamad Tavakoli-Targhi, "Frontline Mysticism and Eastern Spirituality," *ISIM Newsletter* 9 (January 2002): 13.

28. Muhammad Rashid Rida, "al-Tajdid wa al-Tajaddud wa al-Mujaddidun" (Renewal, Renewing, and Renewers), *al-Manar* (The Beacon), Cairo, Egypt, 31 (1931): 775, tr. Emad Eldin Shahin, in *Modernist Islam*, 80.

29. Muhammad Iqbal, *The Reconstruction of Religious Thought in Islam* (Oxford, England: Oxford University Press, 1930), 139-70, reprinted in *Liberal Islam: A Source-Book*, ed. Charles Kurzman (New York: Oxford University Press, 1998), 262.

30. Ahmet Kanlidere, *Reform within Islam: The Tajdid and Jadid Movements among the Kazan Tatars (1809-1917)* (Istanbul, Turkey: Eren, 1997), 57.

31. Wilfred Scawen Blunt, "The Future of Islam," 586-87; The *Future of Islam*, 136. Blunt makes a similar claim in his *Secret History of the English Occupation of Egypt, Being a Personal Narrative of Events* (London: T. F. Unwin, 1907), 77.

32. Saqir Abu Fakhr, "Trends in Arab Thought (Interview with Sadek Jalal al-

Azm)," *Journal of Palestine Studies* 27 (1998): 70.

33. Kanlidere, *Reform within Islam*, 56; Mohammed Al-Abbasi, "Protestant Islam," n.d., 65.39.144.73/ISLAM/misc/pislam.htm (24 March 2003).

34. The quote continues: "Unlike the sectarian tendency of Protestantism to garment into separate communities, however, Islam has been able to preserve its identity as an 'imagined community.'" Jose Casanova, "Civil Society and Religion: Retrospective Reflections on Catholicism and Prospective Reflections on Islam," *Social Research* 68 (2001): 1041-81.

35. Carter Lindberg, *The European Reformations* (Oxford: Blackwell), 9.

36. Dale F. Eickelman, "Mass Higher Education and the Religious Imagination in Contemporary Arab Societies," *American Ethnologist* 19 (1992): 643-55. Similar claims are made in Dale F. Eickelman, "Islamic Liberalism Strikes Back," *MESA Bulletin* 27 (1993): 163-8; "Inside the Islamic Reformation," *The Wilson Quarterly* 22 (1998): 80-89; "The Coming Transformation of the Muslim World." *MERIA Journal* 3 (1999): 78-81; "Islamic Religious Commentary and Lesson Circles: Is There a Copernican Revolution?" *Commentaries = Kommentare: Aporemat* 4 (1999): 121-46; "Islam and the Languages of Modernity," *Daedalus* 129 (2000): 119-35; and "Muhammad Shahrour and the Printed Word," *ISIM Newsletter* 7 (2001): 7. See also Dale Eickelman and Jon W. Anderson, "Print, Islam, and the Prospects for Civic Pluralism: New Religious Writings and their Audiences," *Journal of Islamic Studies* 8 (1997): 43-62; "Redefining Muslim Publics," in *New Media in the Muslim World: The Emerging Public Sphere*, ed. Eickelman and Anderson (Bloomington: Indiana University Press, 1999), 1-18.

37. Robin Wright, "Islam's Theory of Relativity," *Los Angeles Times*, 27 January 1995: 1, 10-11. Wright makes similar claims in "Islam and Liberal Democracy: Two Visions of Reformation," *Journal of Democracy* 7 (1996): 64-75; "Iran's New Revolution," *Foreign Affairs* (January-February 2000): 133-45; and *The Last Great Revolution: Turmoil and Transformation in Iran* (New York: A. A. Knopf, 2000), 33. Others have contested the analogy, arguing that Soroush is more like Islam's Erasmus than its Luther, remaining within the system even as he criticizes it. See L. Carl Brown, "Review: Reason, Freedom, and Democracy in Islam," *Foreign Affairs* 79 (2000): 148; Mahmoud Sadri, "Attack from Within: Dissident Political Theology in Contemporary Iran," *The Iranian*, 13 February 2002, www.iranian.com/Opinion/2002/February/Theology (24 March 2003).

38. Paul Donnelly, "Tariq Ramadan: The Muslim Martin Luther?" *Salon.com*, 15 February 2002, www.salon.com/people/feature/2002/02/15/ramadan/index_np.html (24 March 2003). Peter Ford quotes Ramadan using the phrase "Islamic Reformation" in describing what is required for Islam to modernize and embrace scientific and social changes in "Listening for Islam's Silent Majority," *Christian Science Monitor*, 5 November 2001. Tariq Ramadan is author of *To Be a European Muslim* (Markfield, U.K.: The Islamic Foundation, 1998).

39. Gretel C. Kovach and Carla Power, "Changing the Rule of Law," *Newsweek* (30 December 2002): 66.

40. Robert D. Kaplan, "Reform Party: Can Turkish Islamists Save Islam?" *The New Republic* 227 (16 December 2002): 13.

41. Martin S. Kramer, *Ivory Towers on Sand: The Failure of Middle Eastern Studies in America* (Washington, D.C.: Washington Institute for Near East Policy, 2001), 56.

42. Rod Dreher, "Inside Islam: A Brave Muslim Speaks," *National Review Online*, 8

January 2002, www.nationalreview.com/dreher/dreherprint010802.html (24 March 2003); Thomas Friedman, "An Islamic Reformation," *New York Times*, 4 December 2002: A31.

43. This is the premise of *Shaping the Current Islamic Reformation*, ed. Barbara Allen Roberson, (London: Frank Cass, 2003). The book's chapters were originally published in a special issue of *Mediterranean Politics*, 7:3 (2002).

44. Asaf A. A. Fyzee, "The Reinterpretation of Islam," in *Islam in Transition: Muslim Perspectives*, ed. John J. Donohue and John L. Esposito (New York: Oxford University Press, 1982), 189.

45. 'Ali Shari'ati, *Man and Islam*, tr. Fatollah Marjani (Houston: Free Islamic Literature, 1981), 106.

46. 'Ali Shari'ati, *What Is to Be Done?*, ed. and tr. Farhang Rajaee (Houston: Institute for Research and Islamic Studies, 1986), 25.

47. Abdullahi Ahmed An-Na'im, "The Islamic Counter-reformation," *New Perspectives Quarterly* 19 (2002): 31-2. This article was originally published in spring 1987 and then republished by *NPQ* after the events of September 11, 2001. An-Na'im's is author of *Toward an Islamic Reformation: Civil Liberties, Human Rights, and International Law* (Syracuse: Syracuse University Press, 1996).

48. "Blood and Irony," *Economist*, 11 September 1993: F34.

49. Quoted in Yaroslav Trofimov, "As Taliban Falls Inside Afghanistan, So Do Islamic Rules Beyond Order," *Wall Street Journal*, 31 December 2001: A10.

50. Ali Mazrui and Alamin Mazrui, "The Digital Revolution and the New Reformation," *Harvard International Review* 23 (2001): 55.

51. In a similar vein, John Esposito has suggested that "Reformation in Islam is inevitable. . . . But Muslims are faced with having to do it in a very compressed time." See Nicholas D. Kristof, "Stoning and Scripture," *New York Times*, 30 April 2002: A29. In a recent book W. R. Clement deemed an Islamic Reformation "imminent" and warned that it would continue to "affect the rest of the globe in nasty ways." See *Reforming the Prophet: The Quest for the Islamic Reformation* (Toronto: Insomniac Press, 2002), 11.

52. Brian Beedham, "It Is Now the Year 1415," *Economist*, 6 August 1994: 14-16.

53. "Islam's Arrow of Death," *Economist*, 11 March 1989: 42. An earlier use of the analogy in regard to the same issue is found in "If Rushdie is Killed," *Economist*, 25 February 1989: 12-13.

54. Samuel P. Huntington, *The Clash of Civilizations and the Remaking of World Order* (New York: Simon & Schuster, 1996), 111.

55. Huntington, *Clash of Civilizations*, 121.

56. Huntington, *Clash of Civilizations*, 94, 101.

57. Syed Kamran Mirza, "Why Critical Scrutiny of Islam Is an Utmost Necessity," *Free Inquiry* 22 (2002): 45-46.

58. Joseph Kraft, "The Limits of Islam," *Washington Post*, 5 December 1978: A21. Almost a quarter of a century later another writer for the same newspaper made the opposite claim: "Just as Gutenberg's printing press helped spread the ideas of the Protestant Reformation, the Internet, e-mail and jet travel are now giving Muslims unprecedented access to knowledge of their religion and the world." See Caryle Murphy, "In the Throes of a Quiet Revolution," *Washington Post*, 12 October 2002: B9.

59. David Ignatius, "Islam in the West's Sights: The Wrong Crusade?" *Washington Post*, 8 March 1992: C1.

60. Martin Kramer, "Islam vs. Democracy," *Commentary* 115 (January 1993): 35. More recently, Kramer has articulated similar sentiment, with considerably more sarcasm: "The reformers, who have always been a small minority, are today even worse off than they were a half-century ago: today, terrorists threaten to kill them. By all means, let us pray five times daily for an Islamic Reformation. But let us admit that there is no Luther in sight who could inspire them." See Kramer's remarks in Francis Fukuyama, Nadav Samin, and critics, "Controversy: Modernizing Islam," *Commentary* 114 (December 2002): 17.

61. Quoted in Trofimov, "As Taliban Falls": A10.

62. Hassan Hanafi and Muhammad 'Abid al-Jabiri, *Hiwar al-Mashriq al-Maghrib: Talih Silsila al-Rudud wa al-Munaqashat* (East-West Dialogue: Followed by a Series of Replies and Debates) (Casablanca: Dar Tubqal, 1990), 45.

63. A. L. Tabawi's "English-Speaking Orientalists: A Critique of their Approach to Islam and Arab Nationalism, Part I," *Islamic Quarterly* 1-2 (1964): 41.

64. Louay M. Safi, "Editorial: Overcoming the Cultural Divide," *American Journal of Islamic Social Sciences* 18, no. 1 (2002): vii.

65. Abdelwahab El-Affendi, "The Elusive Reformation," *Journal of Democracy* 14 (2003): 34.

66. El-Affendi, "Elusive Reformation": 38.

1

Who Speaks for Islam?
Inside the Islamic Reformation

Dale F. Eickelman

Like the printing press in sixteenth-century Europe, the combination of mass education, mass communications, and the greater ease of travel since the mid-twentieth century is transforming the Muslim majority world, a broad geographical crescent stretching from North Africa through Central Asia, the Indian subcontinent, and the Indonesian archipelago. In unprecedented numbers, the faithful—whether in the vast cosmopolitan city of Istanbul, the suburbs of Paris, or the remote oases of Oman's mountainous interior—are examining and debating the fundamentals of Muslim belief and practice in ways that their less self-conscious predecessors in the faith would never have imagined.

Buzzwords such as "fundamentalism" and catchy phrases such as Samuel Huntington's "West versus Rest"[1] or Daniel Lerner's "Mecca or mechanization"[2] are of little use in understanding this transformation. Indeed, they obscure or even distort the immense spiritual and intellectual ferment that is taking place today among the world's nearly one billion Muslims, reducing it in most cases to a fanatical rejection of everything modern, liberal, or progressive. To be sure, such fanaticism plays a part in what is happening—dramatically and violently— but it is not the entire story.

A far more important element is the unprecedented access that ordinary people now have to sources of information and knowledge about religion and other aspects of their society. Quite simply, in country after country, government officials, traditional religious scholars, and officially sanctioned preachers are finding it hard to monopolize the tools of literate culture.

Intellectual Monopolies Broken

No longer can governments control what their people know and what they think. The intellectual monopolies of the past have been irrevocably broken. What

18

distinguishes the present from previous eras is the large numbers of believers engaged in the "reconstruction" of religion, community, and society. In the past, one thought of profound changes in ideas and doctrines primarily in terms of "top-down" approaches and formal ideologies. Political or religious leaders would prescribe, and others were to follow. In the late twentieth century, the major impetus for change in religious and political values is coming from "below." It is not just changes in explicit ideologies that matter, but also the implicit background understandings against which beliefs and practices are formulated.[3] Thus, in one of the first major syntheses on the changing nature of the Muslim experience in Europe, Gilles Kepel's *Les banlieues de l'Islam: naissance d'une religion en France* (Islam's Suburbs: The Birth of a Religion in France) presaged the shift from being Muslim in France to being French Muslim.[4] In Turkey, this shift means that an increasing number of Turks, especially those of the younger generation, see themselves as European and Muslim at the same time, as do politicians in the Netherlands such as Oussama Cherribi, a Moroccan-born member of parliament. And some Iranians, such as political scientist Fariba Adelkhah, argue that the major transformations of the Iranian revolution occurred not in 1978-1979 but with the coming of age of a new generation of Iranians who were not even born at that time. These transformations include a greater sense of autonomy for both women and men and the emergence of a public sphere in which politics and religion are subtly intertwined, and not always as anticipated by Iran's formal religious leaders.[5]

Islam in the "Modern" Era

If "modernity" is defined as the emergence of new kinds of public space, including those not imagined by preceding generations, then developments in France, Turkey, Iran, and elsewhere suggest that we are living through a period of profound social transformation for the Muslim-majority world.

Distinctive to the modern era is that discourse and debate about Muslim tradition involve people on a mass scale. They also necessarily involve an awareness of other Muslim and non-Muslim traditions. Mass education and mass communication in the modern world facilitate an awareness of the new and unconventional. In changing the style and scale of possible discourse, these tools reconfigure the nature of religious thought and action, create new forms of public space, and encourage debate over meaning.

Mass education and mass communications are important in all contemporary world religions. However, the full effects of mass education, especially higher education, have only begun to be felt in much of the Muslim world since mid-century and in many countries considerably later. Morocco, for example, committed itself to universal schooling after gaining independence from France in 1956. Though in 1957 only 13,000 secondary school degrees were awarded, and university enrollments remained low, by 1965 there were more than 200,000 students in secondary schools and some 20,000 in universities. By 1992, secondary school enrollment topped 1.5 million, and university students numbered 240,000. While illiteracy rates in the general populace remain high—43 percent for men and 69 percent for women—a critical mass of educated people are now able to read and think for themselves.[6]

The situation in Oman is more dramatic because the transformation has taken place in a much shorter period. In 1975-1976, a mere 22 students graduated from secondary school. Little more than a decade later, in 1987-1988, 13,500 students were enrolled in secondary education institutions. In 1996-1997, 76,500 were enrolled, and more than 7,000 students were in postsecondary institutions, including the national university, which had opened in 1986.[7]

Elsewhere a similar picture emerges, although the starting dates and levels of achievement differ. In Turkey, mass education has reached every city, town, and village. Adult illiteracy rates as of 1995 were 8 percent for males and 28 percent for females, down from 65 percent and 85 percent, respectively, four decades earlier. Secondary schools are now ubiquitous, and both private and public universities have proliferated. In Indonesia, university enrollment, only 50,000 in 1960, reached 1.9 million in 1990.[8] Iran also has seen a significant expansion in education opportunities at all levels.

In Egypt, Morocco, and many other Muslim-majority nations, population growth has outpaced educational expansion; yet even so, the number of people able to question religious and political authorities, and not just listen to them, has increased dramatically. Women's access to education still lags behind that of men, although the gap is rapidly closing in many countries, including Turkey, Kuwait, and Malaysia.

Multimedia

Both mass education and mass communications, especially the proliferation of media and the means by which people communicate, have had a profound effect on how people think about religion and politics throughout the Muslim world. Multiple means of communication make the unilateral control of information and opinion much more difficult and foster, albeit inadvertently, a civil society of dissent. We are still in the early stages of understanding how different media—including print, satellite and broadcast television, radio, and audiocassettes—influence groups and individuals, encouraging unity in some contexts and fragmentation in others, but a few salient features may be sketched.[9]

At the high end of this transformation is the rise to significance of books such as *al-Kitab wa al-Qur'an* (The Book and the Qur'an), first published in 1990 and written by the Syrian civil engineer Muhammad Shahrour.[10] Although its circulation has been banned or discouraged in many places, it has sold tens of thousands of copies throughout the Arab world. The success of Shahrour's first book—regarded by legal scholar Wael Hallaq, as the "most convincing" of attempts to reformulate Islamic legal theory[11]—could not have been imagined before there were large numbers of people able to read it and understand its advocacy of reinterpreting ideas of religious authority and tradition and applying Islamic precepts to contemporary society.

Shahrour draws an analogy between the Copernican revolution and Qur'anic interpretation, which he says has been shackled for "too long" by the conventions of medieval jurists: "People believed for a long time that the sun revolved around the earth, but they were unable to explain some phenomena derived from this assumption until one person, human like themselves, said, 'The opposite is true: The earth revolves around the sun.' . . . After a quarter of a century of study and reflection, it dawned on me that we Muslims are shackled by prejudices [musallimat], some of which are completely opposite the [correct perspective]."[12]

On issues ranging from the role of women in society to rekindling a "creative interaction" with non-Muslim philosophies, Shahrour argues that Muslims should reinterpret sacred texts and apply them to contemporary social and moral issues: "If Islam is sound [salih] for all times and places," Shahrour writes, Muslims should not neglect historical developments, but must act as if "the Prophet just . . . informed us of this Book."[13]

Shahrour is not alone in attacking both conventional religious wisdom and the intolerant certainties of religious radicals and in arguing instead for a constant and open reinterpretation of how sacred texts apply to social and political life. Another Syrian thinker, the secularist Sadiq Jalal al-'Azm, for instance, does the same. A debate between al-'Azm and Qatari-Egyptian Shaykh Yusif al-Qaradawi, a conservative religious intellectual, was broadcast on Qatar's al-Jazeera satellite television on May 27, 1997, on the program "The Opposite Direction." For the first time in the memory of many viewers, the religious conservative came across as the weaker, more defensive voice.

Al-Jazeera is a new phenomenon in Arab-language broadcasting because its talk shows, such as "The Opposite Direction," feature live discussions on such sensitive issues as women's role in society, polygamy, Palestinian refugees, sanctions on Iraq, and democracy and human rights in the Arab world. Similar discussions are unlikely to be rebroadcast on state-controlled television in most Arab nations, where programming on religious and political themes is generally cautious. Nevertheless, satellite technology and videotape render traditional censorship ineffective.

Ideas Crossing Borders

Tapes of these satellite television broadcasts circulate from hand to hand in Morocco, Oman, Syria, Jordan, Egypt, and elsewhere. Al-Jazeera shows that people across the Arab world, like their counterparts elsewhere in the Muslim-majority world, want open discussion of the issues that affect their lives, and that new communications technologies make it impossible for governments and established religious authorities to stop them.

Other voices also advocate reform. Fethullah Gülen, Turkey's version of media-savvy American evangelist Billy Graham, appeals to a mass audience. In televised chat shows, interviews, and occasional sermons, Gülen speaks about Islam and science, democracy, modernity, religious and ideological tolerance, the importance of education, and current events. Gülen has the pulse of a wide spectrum of religious-minded Turks.[14] And religious movements such as Turkey's *Risale-i Nur* appeal increasingly to religious moderates. In stressing the link between Islam, reason, science, and modernity, and the lack of inherent clash between "East" and "West," they promote education at all levels and appeal to growing numbers of educated Turks.[15] As a sign of this sea change in public expression, Islamic political parties have incrementally moved to center stage in Turkey and, after a long process of trial and error and mutual adjustment, have become models of secular modernization legitimized by the ballot box.[16]

Iran's Abdolkarim Soroush argues that a proper understanding of Islam enjoins dialogue, a willingness to understand the opinions of others, adaptation, and civility. Indonesian and Malaysian moderates make similar arguments. To the annoyance of more conservative clerics, Soroush has captured the religious imagination of Persian speakers in Iran and abroad, and his work, in translation and on the Internet in several languages including Turkish, Arabic, and English, has a reach far beyond Iran.[17] In Pakistan, a 1997 book making an argument parallel to Shahrour's, *Qur'anic and Non-Qur'anic Islam*, by Nazir Ahmad, a retired military officer, quickly went into a second printing.[18]

Not all religious books are aimed at the intellectual elite. Mass schooling has created a wide audience of people who read but are not literary sophisticates, and there has been an explosive growth in what French scholar Yves Gonzalez-Quijano calls generic "Islamic books": inexpensive, attractively printed texts intended for such readers.[19] Many address practical questions of Muslim life in the modern world and the perils of neglecting Islamic obligations—and not all appeal to reason and moderation. Many of these books have bold, eye-catching covers and sensational titles such as *The Terrors of the Grave, or What Follows Death,* by Egyptian writer Ahmad al-Tahtawi, which informs readers of what awaits them if they do not prepare properly for Judgment Day.[20] Other, more subdued works offer advice to young women on how to live as Muslims today. Often based on the sermons of popular preachers, Islamic books are written in a breezy colloquial style instead of with the cadences of traditional literary Arabic, and are sold on sidewalks and outside mosques rather than in bookstores. While Egyptian Nobel Laureate Naguib Mahfouz is considered successful if he sells 5,000 copies of one of his novels in a year in his own country, Islamic books often have sales in six figures.

A Marketplace of Views

As a result of direct and broad access to the printed, broadcast, and taped word, more and more Muslims are individually interpreting the textual sources—

classical or modern—of Islam. Much has been made of the "opening up" (*infitah*) of the economies of many Muslim countries, allowing market forces to reshape economies, regardless of the painful short-term consequences. In a similar fashion, intellectual market forces support some forms of religious innovation and activity over others.

In Bangladesh, women's romance novels, once a popular specialty distributed in secular bookstores, now have Islamic counterparts that are distributed through Islamic bookstores, making it difficult to distinguish between "Muslim" romance novels and "secular" ones.[21] The result is a collapse of earlier, hierarchical notions of religious authority based on claims to the mastery of fixed bodies of religious texts. Even when there are state-appointed religious authorities—as in Oman, Saudi Arabia, Iran, and Egypt—no longer is there any guarantee that their word will be heeded, or even that they themselves will follow the lead of the regime.

Religious activists in Egypt, the West Bank, and elsewhere are more likely to be the products of mass higher education than of such traditional educational institutions as the *madrasa*, or mosque-school. The result of the "massification" of education, especially higher education, and the proliferation of means of communication is to challenge and collapse centralized and hierarchical claims to authority. No one group or type of leader in contemporary Muslim societies possesses a monopoly on the management of the sacred. Without fanfare, the notion of Islam as dialogue and civil debate is gaining ground. This new sense of public is emerging throughout Muslim-majority states and Muslim communities elsewhere. It is shaped by increasingly open contests over the use of the symbolic language of Islam.

Discourse Becomes Global

Increasingly, discussions in newspapers, on the Internet, on smuggled cassettes, and on television crosscut and overlap, contributing to a common public space. New and accessible modes of communication have made these contests increasingly global, so that even local issues take on transnational dimensions.

The combination of new media and new contributors to religious and political debates fosters awareness on the part of all actors of the diverse ways in which Islam and Islamic values can be created. This mixture feeds into new senses of a public space that is discursive, performative, and participative, and not confined to formal institutions recognized by state authorities.

This distinctly public sphere exists at the intersections of religious, political, and social life and contributes to the creation of civil society. With access to contemporary forms of communication that range from the press and broadcast media to fax machines, audio and video cassettes, from the telephone to the Internet, Muslims, like Christians, Hindus, Jews, Sikhs, and protagonists of Asian and African values, have more rapid and flexible ways of building and sustaining contact with constituencies than was available in earlier decades. New media in new hands are reversing the asymmetries of the earlier mass media revolution.

Muslims, of course, act not just as Muslims but also according to class interests, out of a sense of nationalism, on behalf of tribal or family networks, and from all the diverse motives that characterize human endeavor. Increasingly, however, large numbers of Muslims explain their goals in terms of the normative language of Islam. Muslim identity issues are not unitary or identical, but such issues have become a significant force in both Muslim-majority states and those in which Muslims form only a minority of the population. It is in this sense that one can speak of an emerging Muslim public sphere.

Ironically, from the perspective of governments whose Islamic credentials are often found wanting, the impact of modern mass education that they have fostered has been pervasive in developing this new public consciousness. Students are taught about the unity of Muslim thought and practice in a set national curriculum that includes Islamic studies as one subject among many. Instead of sitting at the feet of a recognized master of traditional learning, an impersonal relationship between students and teachers, who have become employees of the state, is stressed. Even while teaching that Islam permeates all aspects of life, the formal principles of Islamic doctrine and practice are compartmentalized and made an object of study. Most traditionally educated religious authorities sometimes adapt to this form of education, but some resist it. Without fanfare, the notion of Islam as dialogue, civil debate, and persuasion is gaining ground. Even if, for example, political institutions in the Arab world show less change than in any other major world region, Arab Muslims are now intensely aware of the political and religious unresponsiveness of their own societies.

A caution is in order. An expanding public sphere does not necessarily pose a direct challenge to authoritarianism, nor does it necessarily preclude appeals to violence such as those advocated by al-Qa'ida worldwide, Hamas in occupied Palestine, or the paramilitary Laskar Jihad in Indonesia, disbanded in the wake of the October 2002 terrorist attack in Bali. Authoritarian regimes are compatible with an expanding public sphere, although the latter offers wider avenues for awareness of competing and alternate forms of religious and political authority. Still, publicly shared ideas of community, identity, and leadership take new shapes in modern conditions, even as many communities and authorities claim an unchanged continuity with the past. Mass education, so important in the development of nationalism in an earlier era, and a proliferation of media and means of communication have multiplied the possibilities for creating communities and networks among them, dissolving prior barriers of space and distance, and opening new grounds for interaction and mutual recognition.

Conclusion

Thinkers such as Muhammad Shahrour and Fethullah Gülen are redrawing the boundaries of public and religious life in the Muslim-majority world by challenging religious authority, yet the replacement they suggest creates a constructive fragmentation. With the advent of mass higher education has come an objectification of Islamic tradition in the eyes of many believers, so that questions such as "What is Islam?" "How does it apply to the conduct of my life?" and "What are the principles of faith?" are foregrounded in the consciousness of many believers and explicitly discussed. These objectified understandings have irrevocably transformed Muslim relations to sacred authority. Of crucial importance in this process has been a "democratization" of the politics of religious authority and the development of a standardized language inculcated by mass higher education, the mass media, travel, and labor migration.

Like Martin Luther at the Diet of Worms in 1521, recent Muslim writers have "claimed to be attached to the authority of the Word of God alone and . . . in public asserted the relative unimportance of all who claimed to come between God and the believer's conscience."[22] This has led to an opening up of the political process and heightened competition for the mantles of political and religious authority.

Shortly before I completed an earlier version of this chapter, I visited Turkey's Fethullah Gülen. At the end of a spirited discussion on how the shift from face-to-face meetings to television had influenced his message, I told him of the title I had in mind, "Inside the Islamic Reformation." With polite amusement, he replied, "It's your title, not mine." Gülen explained that he saw his work—which includes the idea that there is no contradiction between an Islamic worldview and a scientific one—as an effort to persuade people to understand and live by the basic teachings of Islam. I pointed out that Martin Luther had said something very similar. Luther saw his work as returning to the fundamentals of belief, not creating anything new. Only later did others see his ideas and actions as instigating a "Reformation."

Any historical analogy is imperfect, and works only insofar as it is "good to think with," as Lévi-Strauss might say. Like the "Copernican revolution," the current challenge to established religious authority in the Muslim world is likely to be seen as significant only in retrospect—and the prospects for social and political violence cannot be underestimated. In addition, there is not any one central figure or hierarchy of authority to reject. Nonetheless, a new sense of public is emerging throughout Muslim-majority states and Muslim communities elsewhere, one shaped by increasingly open contests over the use of the symbolic language of Islam, and advocating a role for religion as moral authority in public life.

Notes

1. Samuel P. Huntington, "The Coming Clash of Civilizations—or, the West against the Rest," *New York Times* (June 6, 1993): E19.

2. See Daniel Lerner, *The Passing of Traditional Society: Modernizing the Middle East* (New York: Free Press, 1964), 405.

3. See Charles Taylor, "Modernity and the Rise of the Public Sphere," in the *Tanner Lectures on Human Values*, vol. 14, ed. Grethe E. Peterson (Salt Lake City: University of Utah Press, 1993), 217-19.

4. Gilles Kepel, *Les Banlieues de l'Islam: Naissance d'une Religion en France* (The Suburts of Islam: Birth of a Religion in Rance) (Paris: Éditions du Seuil, 1987).

5. Fariba Adelkhah, *Being Modern in Iran* (New York: Columbia University Press, 2000).

6. World Bank, *Knowledge for Development: World Development Report*, 1998-1999 (New York: Oxford University Press for the World Bank, 1999), table 2 and prior editions.

7. Sultanate of Oman, Ministry of Development, *Statistical Year Book, 1996* (Muscat: Ministry of Development, 1997), 541, and prior editions.

8. UNESCO, *Statistical Yearbook, 1998* (Latham, Md.: UNESCO Publishing and Bernan Press, 1998), table 3.7.

9. See Dale F. Eickelman and Jon Anderson, eds., *New Media in the Muslim World: The Emerging Public Sphere*, 2nd ed. (Bloomington: Indiana University Press, 2003).

10. Muhammad Shahrour, *al-Kitab wa al-Qur'an: Qira'a Mu'asira* (The Book and the Qur'an: A Contemporary Reading) (Beirut: Sharikat al-Matbu'at lil-Tawzi' wa al-Nashr, 1992).

11. Wael B. Hallaq, *A History of Islamic Legal Theories* (Cambridge: Cambridge University Press, 1997), 253.

12. Shahrour, *Kitab*, 29. Translations from *The Book and the Qur'an* are by Dale F. Eickelman.

13. Shahrour, *Dirasat Islamiyya al-Mu'asira fi al-Dawla wa al-Mujtama'* (Contemporary Islamic Studies on State and Society) (Damascus: al-Ahali lil-Taba'a wa al-Nashr, 1994), 23. As popular as Shahrour's views are in some circles, some conservative Muslims argue that he underestimates the ability of *madrasa*-trained religious scholars to adapt their version of authoritative religious learning to new contexts. See especially Muhammad Qasim Zaman, *The Ulama in Contemporary Islam: Custodians of Change* (Princeton: Princeton University Press, 2002).

14. See Bülent Aras, "Turkish Islam's Moderate Face," *Middle East Quarterly* 5, no. 3 (September 1998): 23-30.

15. The group's website, in both English and Turkish, can be found at www.nesil.com.tr.

16. Jenny B. White, *Islamist Mobilization in Turkey: A Study in Vernacular Politics* (Seattle: University of Washington Press, 2002).

17. See Abdolkarim Soroush, *Reason, Freedom, and Democracy in Islam: Essential Writings of Abdolkarim Soroush*, ed. Mahmoud Sadri and Ahmad Sadri (New York:

Oxford University Press, 2000). A website "dedicated to coverage and analysis of the ideas of Abdol Karim Soroush" can be found at www.seraj.org.

18. Nazir Ahmad, *Qur'anic and Non-Qur'anic Islam* (Lahore: Vanguard, 1997).

19. Yves Gonzalez-Quijano, *Les Gens du Livre: Édition et Champ Intellectuel dans l'Égypte Republicaine* (People of the Book: Publishing and Intellectual Field in Republican Egypt) (Paris: CNRS Éditions, 1998), 171-98.

20. Ahmad al-Tahtawi, *Ahwal al-Qubur wa Ma Ba'd al-Mawt* (*The Terrors of the Grave, or What Follows Death*) (Cairo: Dar al-Bashir, 1987).

21. See Maimuna Huq, "From Piety to Romance: Islam-oriented Texts in Bangladesh," in *New Media in the Muslim World: The Emerging Public Sphere*, 2nd ed., ed. Dale F. Eickelman and Jon W. Anderson (Bloomington: Indiana University Press, 2003), 129-57.

22. Marc Lienhard, "Luther and Europe," in *The Reformation*, ed. Pierre Chaunu (New York: St. Martin's Press, 1990), 96.

2

Changes in Modern Islamic Legal Theory: Reform or Reformation?

Felicitas Opwis

Efforts at renewal have been a constant feature of Islamic law (*shari'a*). An early example is provided by the transition from the "ancient schools of law" to more formal school affiliations.[1] The teachings attributed to Muhammad ibn Idris al-Shafi'i (767-820) reflect the desire to make Islamic law Islamic, in the sense of rooting law in the scriptural sources.[2] Shafi'i was probably not the first and certainly not the last jurist attempting to change the way laws were derived. Throughout the ages one finds scholars such as Abu Hamid al-Ghazali (1058-1111), Taqi al-Din ibn Taymiyya (1263-1328), Abu Ishaq al-Shatibi (d. 1388), Muhammad al-Shawkani (1760-1834), and Muhammad ibn 'Ali al-Sanusi (1787-1859) who emphasized that legal authority rests in the Qur'an and the *sunna* alone. The thought of these reformers is far from identical,[3] and even within one scholar's body of work inconsistencies exist, some the result of intellectual evolution, some of changed circumstances.[4] Yet, what these reformers have in common is a conviction that the status of Islam, and Islamic law in particular, in their respective times was not as it ought to be and that renewal was needed.[5]

While calls for reforming Islamic law and especially for returning to the scriptural sources of Islam abound, the religious reform movements of the late nineteenth and early twentieth centuries were in important respects exceptional. The particular historical context enabled reformers to have a profound effect on the interpretation of Islam ever since. But were the effects of the reforms advocated by figures such as Muhammad 'Abduh (1849-1905), Rashid Rida (1865-1935), and Mahmud Shaltut (1893-1963) analogous to the Reformation of Western Christianity in the sixteenth century? It is possible to draw an analogy to the Protestant Reformation, albeit in a limited way. As Germans say, "*der Vergleich hinkt*," meaning that it is an unequal comparison—and this not only because of the time lag. For one, there is no church in Islam with a unified authority structure. For another, the reform movements of the nineteenth and

28

early twentieth centuries were not concerned as much with theological issues as with the application of Islamic law in society, though of course any reformulation of religious law always relates to the theological underpinnings of the thought system. And, as pointed out in the introduction to this book, the last word on the assessment of the Protestant Reformation(s) has not yet been written, making a comparison dependent on which scholarly view one accepts as convincing. There are, however, certain features of similarity between the Protestant Reformation of the sixteenth century and the Islamic reformist movements of the end of the nineteenth century that warrant the analogy: both questioned the traditional authority of religious interpretation, both spread due to the print media, and both coincided with the growth of secular education.

In what follows, I elaborate on the environment in which the religious reform movements of the late nineteenth and early twentieth centuries flourished, concentrating mainly on the Middle East, with particular attention to how various government policies initiated fundamental changes in the societal position of the religious scholars. I present the content of the religious reform programs in the area of Islamic law; the question whether or not there has been a Reformation of Islamic theology is left to other scholars. Throughout the chapter I assess aspects of similarity between the Protestant Reformation and the reform of Islamic legal theory.

The Changing Environment

Europe

The thought of religious reformers of the nineteenth and early twentieth centuries differed from previous Islamic reformers in their concern with Europe. While the encroachment of the West was not perceived as a major threat to Muslim lands by reformers of the eighteenth century, it was central to reformist writings since the nineteenth century.[6] It is probably no exaggeration for Peters to say that "Islamic reformism as it came into existence by the end of the nineteenth century was a response to the challenge of the increasing Western impact in the Islamic world."[7] The political, military, commercial, and intellectual influence of Europe on the Middle East and North Africa took multiple forms in different areas and at various times. Likewise, the reaction of Muslim scholars to the European impact was far from uniform. For instance, Jamal al-Din al-Afghani (1838/9-1897) was foremost concerned with the military advances of European powers onto Muslim territories. He called for reforming Islam and Islamic law in order to unite and strengthen Muslims against the foreign threat. His thought greatly influenced other reformists, such as Muhammad 'Abduh and Rashid Rida. Their ideas, however, aimed less at defending Islam against Western political dominance than at responding to intellectual and cultural criticism as well as preserving Islam's relevance in the changing environment.[8] Moroccan religious scholars of the nineteenth century, in contrast, were more apprehensive of the commercial penetration of Europe and its negative effects on social mores than engaged in revitalizing Islam and Islamic law. Only toward the end of the nineteenth century did reformist ideas gain a hold on Morocco's *'ulama* (traditionally educated religious scholars)—and then it was closely connected with the emerging nationalist movement.[9]

Government Reform Programs in Education and Law

The political, cultural, and economic imperialism of Europe provoked reactions not only from religious scholars. More importantly, it led to reform programs by the political authorities. In the nineteenth and early twentieth centuries reforms of the administrative, military, legal, and educational sectors of the state were initiated throughout much of the Middle East and North Africa. The first attempts at reforming the Ottoman government and military started with Selim III (r. 1789-1807) in the late eighteenth century, and were continued under Mahmud II (r. 1808-1839) and in the Tanzimat era (1839-1876). In Egypt Muhammad 'Ali (r. 1805-1848) began implementing a reform program with wide-ranging effects. Syria first experienced modernization efforts during the period of Egyptian rule (1831-1841). Prior to French occupation in 1881, the Tunisian ruler had issued reform policies similar to the Ottomans. Likewise, Morocco's state bureaucracy underwent modernization in the nineteenth century.[10] Although neither the reform programs nor the resulting changes were the same everywhere[11]—nor did they happen all at the same time[12]—each took place in an intellectual atmosphere that perceived traditional religious law and its exponents largely as obstacles to progress and as antithetical to modernization. Enlightenment ideas, reason, and the rational sciences were held in high esteem, while adherence to traditional authority that could not stand the test of reason was rejected as obsolete.[13]

The reforms in the Ottoman Empire, Egypt, and other countries of the Middle East and North Africa had far-reaching effects on the position of the religious scholars in society. One area that was significantly affected was the educational system. The *'ulama* used to have almost exclusive control over education: from the primary education in the *kuttab* to the higher learning in mosques and *madrasa*s, they educated the high and low of the Muslim populations. Their educational hegemony gradually broke down, however, in the nineteenth century when the governments in Istanbul, Cairo, and other capitals founded state schools on Western models. In the Ottoman Empire the first secular schools for the military and bureaucracy opened their doors in the early nineteenth century, followed by foreign language schools, and then secondary schools during the Tanzimat era (1839-1876). Other parts of the Middle East followed suit. In Egypt under Isma'il (r. 1863-1879) new Western-type schooling introduced widespread changes in the educational system at all levels.[14] Sometimes the political authorities even attempted to interfere with the instruction given in the centers of religious learning, such as al-Azhar and the Qarawiyyin.[15] Moreover, graduates from the newly created state schools would compete with those from religious institutions for positions in the government services. A new elite was educated outside the purely religious curriculum and began to staff the government offices. The curriculum taught in these schools challenged the belief that religious knowledge alone was sufficient for work in the administrative, judicial, and military institutions of the state.[16] Yet, one should not imagine that secular institutions quickly replaced religious schools as the main provider of education. At the turn to the twentieth century, the majority of Egyptian Muslims were still receiving their education from religious schools.[17] The overall level of literacy, however, is hard to estimate. One authority calculated that by 1880 more than 500,000 Egyptians were literate, which puts it at 10 percent of the total population.[18] Regardless, changes in the educational sector led to a slow but steady increase in secular-educated Muslims, especially among the elite and in urban centers.

The gradual secularization of education in the Middle East and North Africa resembles the situation in Europe at the time of the Protestant Reformation. Over the course of the fourteenth and fifteenth centuries, European universities, sponsored by monarchs, princes, and wealthy merchants, helped raise the level of lay education. Conservative estimates place the literacy levels in the early sixteenth century for the overall population at 5 percent, with 30 percent of the urban population able to read.[19]

The other area where government reforms in Muslim countries directly affected religious scholars was the legal sphere. Efforts to centralize the state apparatus and make it more efficient included measures that interfered with the previously largely independent religious judiciary. Governments created new offices and incorporated many of the adjudicating functions of the 'ulama into the state structure, thereby weakening the positions of the religious scholars in the legal system administratively and economically. In the Ottoman Empire, the Seyhülislam and the Chief Mufti were drawn closer to the Sublime Porte under Mahmud II.[20] In Morocco, Hasan I (r. 1873-1894) appointed a second judge to share jurisdiction with the Chief Qadi over parts of Fez. Later, the sultan 'Abd al-'Aziz (r. 1894-1908) undermined the independent office of the Moroccan Chief Qadi by restricting his ability to appoint other judges and by renaming his title in a manner that made it clear that he was a representative of the government.[21] In the 1880s, the Egyptian shari'a courts were reorganized in a hierarchical system of tribunals.[22] A mainstay of 'ulama income, the administration of pious foundations (waqf, pl. awqaf), was either taken out of their hands completely, as in Morocco and Egypt, or brought under government control, as happened in the Ottoman Empire.[23]

In addition to administrative interference, the state began to expand its jurisdiction into areas previously reserved for religious law. European commercial activities brought with them the mixed court system; jurisdiction over disputes between native Muslims and Europeans was thus beyond the reach of the *qadi* (judge).[24] With the increase of European commercial penetration, the need for non-*shari'a* courts grew.[25]

More important than mixed courts for the gradual marginalization of Islamic law and its practitioners, however, was the introduction of legal codes. In the Ottoman Empire, special legislative councils and commissions became during the Tanzimat era a more common practice than before. The *'ulama* had little representation on these councils, which were dominated by the new secular-educated elite. These commissions drew up the Penal Code (1840 and 1858), the Commercial Code (1850), and the Imperial Land Code (1858) of the Ottoman Empire. The novelty of these codes derives from the fact that they were heavily influenced by Western, especially French, law or were a mixture of Western and Islamic laws adapted to the contemporary situation. Previously, nonreligious legislation in form of edicts used to accord at least theoretically with the *shari'a* and its spirit. With the new codes came a new system of secular courts (*nizamiyya*) with competence over all Ottoman civil jurisdiction.[26] Similarly, Egypt adopted French law in its Penal, Commercial, and Maritime Codes to be implemented in secular courts.[27] The new legal codes and secular court systems limited the sphere of religious law and the activities of the religious jurist. Lawyers from secular schools were better prepared than traditionally educated *'ulama* to adjudicate on the basis of these legal codes.[28] In addition, they created an institutionalized differentiation between "religious" and "worldly" affairs.[29]

The Ottoman government's intervention in religious jurisdiction reached its culmination in the *Mejelle*, intended as a civil code based on the *shari'a*. First promulgated in 1877, the *Mejelle* constituted a serious break from previous judicial practice in that it codified large areas of Islamic law, mainly concerning transactions (*mu'amalat*), in order to apply it in secular courts and make it binding on all subjects of the Empire, regardless of religion. The Ottoman Civil Code was "to provide the recently created (secular) tribunals with an authoritative statement of the doctrine of Islamic law and to obviate (without forbidding it) recourse to the works of Islamic jurisprudence which had proved difficult and impracticable."[30] The laws codified in the *Mejelle* were primarily based on the Hanafi school of law and did not necessarily represent the majority opinion of that school. Rather, the codifying commission eclectically chose interpretations that they saw as commensurate with the conditions of the time.[31]

The legal codification in the Ottoman Empire and Egypt began a continuous marginalization of Islamic law in the countries of the Middle East and North Africa. After the break-up of the Ottoman Empire and the creation of nation-states in the course of the twentieth century, most countries established legal codes based in full or part on Western models. Even family and personal status law, which in most countries remained grounded in Islamic law, was codified.[32] With the increase in secular legislation, the importance of Islamic law and *shari'a* courts diminished. More generally, law became the exclusive domain of the state and wherever Islamic law retained or regained influence, its scope was determined by the government.[33]

The efforts by Muslim governments to reform the sphere of education and law produced a situation similar to the historical context of the Protestant

Reformation. In Europe prior to the Reformation, political authorities increasingly interfered in ecclesiastical affairs.[34] The growing secularization of education as well as law led in both cases to a process of marginalization of the religious strata of society. However, while the Protestant Reformation was a reaction to the developments occurring within the Roman Catholic Church,[35] in the Middle East and North Africa the religious reformers of the late nineteenth and early twentieth centuries were responding to encroachments by foreign and domestic governments.

The Printing Press

The printing press, invented in the mid-fifteenth century, was central to the success of the Protestant Reformation. Within months of their first appearance, Luther's theses were known throughout Europe. The function of the printing press for the Reformation was not so much one of preservation but rather the transmission of opinions, rapidly and reliably. According to Lindberg, Luther made use of the printing press and dominated the Reformation propaganda to an extent unparalleled even by Lenin and Mao Zedong.[36] The Protestant Reformation preceded the rise of the reading revolution and print-dominated culture that emerged in Western Europe around 1800.[37]

A similar situation existed in the Middle East by the end of the nineteenth century. The Ottomans had adopted the printing press at the beginning of the eighteenth century. In Istanbul, the first official printing house was set up in 1727, joining existing Greek, Hebrew, and Armenian minority presses.[38] Greater Syria had three presses by the middle of that century—in Aleppo (1706), in Shuwayr (1734), and in Beirut (1753). These printing presses, however, did little to alter either the position of the 'ulama or the landscape of Islamic literature because they were not intended to print Muslim religious texts. The presses of Greater Syria produced Christian missionary materials.[39] The main function of the Istanbul press was the publication of Imperial history, dictionaries, and military texts. More importantly, the Ottoman sultan Ahmad III (r. 1703-1730) issued an edict when establishing the printing office in 1727, prohibiting the printing of religious texts.[40] Although the introduction of book printing initially did not diminish the influence of the religious scholars, they must have felt threatened. The official Ottoman printing press was shut down on account of the opposition it aroused, notwithstanding a fatwa from 1727 by the Ottoman Mufti endorsing and praising this new technique.[41] In other parts of the Middle East, it took another century for official printing houses to gain ground. In Egypt, the Bulaq press was established in the 1820s, and it printed overwhelmingly military and technological writings in translation for the Egyptian government.[42]

By the early nineteenth century, the influence of the ban on printing books of religious subjects waned. Religious texts gradually were printed and distributed in the Ottoman Empire. However, the 'ulama still controlled the publication of Islamic literature. It was the *'ulama* who oversaw the guild of booksellers of Istanbul, and religious scholars sat on the board of censors created in 1784.[43] Moreover, they decided which texts, commentaries, and glosses would be produced and were primarily the owners of the manuscripts. In general, up to the 1860s, the materials that were reproduced were mainly secular and the religious books printed were usually traditional Islamic texts.[44] Until the mid-nineteenth century, the printing press had little effect on the *'ulama*'s position in society. Speeches and sermons, given at the mosque as the main meeting place, were still the primary means of addressing large numbers.[45] Control of the flow of information to the people lay in the hands of religious scholars.

The nature of printing Islamic texts changed, however, in the second half of the nineteenth century. Printing, in general, spread. In Damascus, for example, the government set up the first permanent press in 1865.[46] The technique of lithography and a general disregard for the prohibition on printing religious books contributed to the steady rise in Islamic texts published in Istanbul and Bulaq.[47] A general trend in Islamic book printing was that publishers increasingly preferred to reproduce original texts and authors instead of commentaries and glosses.[48] In Egypt a decisive factor for the rise of independent printing presses was the privatization of book production.[49] This resulted in less government interference and state censorship regarding the materials printed.[50]

The print media was not limited to books. The newspaper industry began to flourish in the latter half of the nineteenth century. In Egypt, this seems to have been the result of the ruler's enthusiasm. While the official gazette, *al-Waqa'i' al-Misriyya*, was published beginning in 1828, it was during Isma'il's reign (1863-1879) that the newspaper market boomed. In his time, the first daily Arabic newspapers were founded, including *al-Ahram* (1876), which today continues to be one of the most influential papers of Egypt.[51]

The spread of the printing press varied in the countries of the Middle East and North Africa. For example, Morocco still had few newspapers, or secular schools, prior to World War I.[52] Yet everywhere the increased use of the printing press for publishing religious texts challenged the *'ulama*'s role as guardians and transmitters of knowledge. Printing had serious effects on those scholars involved in the manuscript production. It marginalized an entire industry connected to paper-making as well as the scribes and *'ulama* who proofread manuscripts.[53] Most importantly, once a text was printed and distributed, it was outside the control of the *'ulama*. The printed book was sold to an anonymous public and became part of the emerging public sphere. It was impossible for the *'ulama* to retain influence over the readers' interpretation of the text.[54] Texts and information were available and transmitted through channels other than the *'ulama* and the established institutions of learning. Together with the spread of secular education, printing encouraged the notion that knowledge (*'ilm*) was no longer an attribute specifically reserved for the religious scholars. The intelligentsia became increasingly less synonymous with the *'ulama*.[55]

The new print media made a fast and wide dissemination of ideas possible. Moreover, now that the mainstream *'ulama* had lost control over which religious texts were published, the voices of reform-oriented jurists could be heard throughout the Muslim world. This would not have been possible in the fourteenth century. Earlier scholars who advocated reform measures, like Najm al-Din al-Tufi (d. 1316) or Ibn Taymiyya for that matter, did not have a significant impact on mainstream Muslim thought because the transmission of their thought was dependent on the traditional channels of communicating ideas, mainly within the *madrasa* system.[56]

The reformers of Islamic law were aware of the opportunities that the print media opened up. They skillfully used periodicals and pamphlets to disseminate their opinions to a wide audience. Jamal al-Din al-Afghani and Muhammad 'Abduh printed many of their ideas in the Paris-based journal *al-'Urwa al-Wuthqa*, which they founded in 1884.[57] The magazine was avidly read among the reform-oriented *'ulama* in Damascus.[58] The influential journal *al-Manar*, established by Rida and 'Abduh in 1898, was initially printed in an edition of 1,500; its circulation rose later due to subscriptions from students.[59] Magazines and booklets were not the only channels through which the reformist thought spread. Sometimes it was aided by the traditional way of scholars traveling to study at the centers of learning. The Moroccan scholar Abu Shu'ayb al-Dukkali (1878-1937) came into contact with the thought of 'Abduh and his circle when studying at al-Azhar in Cairo. After his return to Morocco, Dukkali became one of the leading figures in the Moroccan reform movement.[60] In addition, reformist ideas originating in one part of the Arab world were disseminated to other regions through the mail. 'Abduh corresponded with scholars in Morocco where his ideas were well known.[61] Books published in Cairo by the Salafiyya press, which as the name suggests propagated reformist texts, were shipped to Moroccan bookstores and reformist-oriented *'ulama* such as Mawlay al-'Arabi al-'Alawi ensured their distribution.[62]

The choice of texts printed was as important as distribution for the dissemination of reformist ideas. The reform movements selected texts that served their purposes. It was therefore no coincidence that the writings of Ibn Taymiyya, who was heralded as the great reformer of the early fourteenth century (in part because of his rejection of *taqlid*), were selected to be printed in *al-Manar* and other publications. Jamal al-Din al-Qasimi (1866-1914) edited several essays on legal theory by medieval authorities, among them an excerpt of a work by Ibn 'Arabi chosen because he "thought it important to publish the chapter because it would acquaint Ibn 'Arabi's many admirers among conservative ulama with his opinions on legal theory, specifically his critique of emulation, advocacy of *ijtihad*, and adherence to the Zahiri school of jurisprudence."[63] In this collection of essays, printed in Beirut in 1906, Qasimi included a piece by the fourteenth century Hanbali scholar Najm al-Din al-Tufi on the concept of *maslaha* (Qasimi later added to the collection selections by the Andalusian Maliki scholar Shatibi whose whole system of legal theory was built upon the concept of *maslaha*). Tufi's concept of *maslaha* greatly influenced the thought of Rashid Rida on the subject. He reprinted Qasimi's excerpt of Tufi shortly thereafter in his own journal, *al-Manar*. Rida also re-edited in a separate booklet fatwas from *al-Manar* that reflected the main concerns of his reform program.[64] In general, medieval and contemporary texts were published to convey a specific message. Authors whose ideas conformed to those of the reformist movements were naturally preferred over those who were antithetical to the notion of *ijtihad*.

It was not only the reform-oriented jurists who publicized their views in print. *'Ulama* who wanted to preserve the status quo took to the new medium to state their positions. The Damascene scholars opposed to the reformist ideas used the monthly journal *al-Haqa'iq* as their mouthpiece.[65] The press could be used to discredit particular opinions by bringing them into the open. 'Abduh's famous Transvaal fatwa, for instance, was published in 1903 by his enemies in the conservative magazine *al-Zahir*. According to Skøvgaard-Petersen, "the Transvaal fatwa was hotly debated in the Egyptian newspapers, all of which took side [*sic*] in the controversy. The Egyptian debate was followed, not only in the Transvaal, but also in the Indian press, and declarations were published by the *'ulama* of Morocco and Tunisia."[66] The spread of the print media since the latter half of the nineteenth century created a public sphere in the Middle East and North Africa that became the main forum for religious debate.[67]

Reactions by the *'ulama*

The modernization processes described above initiated a profound transformation of the position of the *'ulama* in society and provoked various reactions on their part. Some high *'ulama* of the Ottoman Empire actively supported the changes occurring around them. They helped, for example, in the drafting of legal codes. In Egypt, 'Abduh was among a handful of religious scholars who welcomed the government reforms. Sometimes the reaction depended on the subject matter. The *'ulama* of Aleppo, for instance, supported the authorities in 1850 in calming protests against the compulsory draft policy which enabled them to win draft exemptions for their sons and relatives.[68] Some *'ulama*, however, tried to obstruct the modernizing state policies as much as possible. In 1841, *'ulama* forced the suspension of an Ottoman commercial code derived predominantly from French law. And the Ottoman *Seyhülislam* succeeded in the 1870s in destroying the *Darülfünun*, a modern-type university. The Egyptian *'ulama* were overwhelmingly hostile to the government reforms. The systematic weakening of their position and influence, however, left them too impotent to be a serious threat to the programs. Some of the Syrian *'ulama* who were opposed to the reform policies of the Tanzimat were, ironically, among those entrusted with implementing them. By simply failing to act upon the orders from Istanbul, the Shafi'i mufti and member of the Damascus *majlis* frustrated the realization of the reforms.[69] Other *'ulama* did not seem to be affected or concerned and continued business as usual. The majority of Ottoman and Egyptian *'ulama* did not have close contact with the reforming efforts and remained apart from the modernizing processes.[70] Burke points out that the centralizing measures of the Moroccan government in the nineteenth century had only marginal effects on the *'ulama*. Only in the twentieth century when the reforms threatened their traditional interests did the Moroccan *'ulama* actively oppose the government.[71] Then there were also religious scholars who, while not advocating the same type of reforms as the political authorities, called for reforming Islam and Islamic law. The intellectual concerns of these people, foremost among them figures like Afghani, 'Abduh, Jamal al-Din al-Qasimi, and Rida, concentrated on issues such as establishing Islam's compatibility with reason, returning to the sources of the faith as a means to purify and strengthen Islam, and enhancing the adaptability of Islamic law to the conditions of the time.

An Islamic Legal Reformation

The encounter with European powers and the general notion of decline[72] were crucial factors in provoking calls for a renewal of Islam.[73] Reform was sought through a return to a purified *ur*-Islam and to the spirit of Islam as a way to strengthen Islamic civilization and to counter the onslaught of European domination.[74] In both the Protestant Reformation and the reform of Islamic law in the modern period, reformers turned to the scriptural sources directly and circumvented the interpretation established over the course of the religion's history. Reform-oriented Muslim jurists saw the practice of *ijtihad*, independent legal reasoning on the basis of the sources of the law, as a principal means for reviving Islamic law, increasing its flexibility, and adapting it to society's contemporary needs.[75] Opening the gate of *ijtihad* was believed to be the primary solution for the ills of the current state of Islamic law and Islamic civilization more generally.

Calling for an extensive practice of independent reasoning went hand in hand with questioning the traditional interpretation of Islamic legal theory.[76] The extent to which various figures of the reform movements diverged from previous conceptions of legal methodology has not yet been studied sufficiently to give an accurate account. More research along the lines of Ahmad Dallal and Rudolph Peters[77] about the intellectual bases and developments in reformers' thought is needed. Our lack of knowledge on the reformulation processes limits our ability to present a detailed picture of the approaches to reform Islamic legal theory. Nevertheless, there are some broad features that can be summarized.

The following account on the reform of Islamic law focuses on the changes that occurred in the interpretation of the sources of the law, i.e., the Qur'an, the *sunna*, the concept of consensus (*ijma'*), and legal analogy (*qiyas*). It generalizes and to some extent simplifies complex intellectual processes. The reader ought to keep in mind the plurality of views within reformist thought.[78] The Maliki mufti of Fez, for example, agreed with 'Abduh on the permissibility of Muslims consuming meat slaughtered by Christians (pronounced in the so-called Transvaal fatwa of 1903), yet rejected 'Abduh's view on the issue of intercession of the prophets and saints.[79] Likewise, one ought to realize that the same term did not necessarily mean the same thing for different people. While Rida applied the term *mujtahid*, for instance, mainly to *'ulama*, for Shaltut the qualification for *ijtihad* was self-designation and included the lay population. Their different understanding of the same term had, of course, implications. According to Rida's thought, the decisions of the *'ulama* qualified to pronounce *ijtihad* have to be obeyed in mundane matters, whereas Shaltut held them to be binding only upon the *mujtahid* himself.[80] For the Moroccan reform-oriented jurist 'Allal al-Fasi (1910-1974) the term "*mujtahid*" applied to *'ulama* as well as persons with expertise in mundane matters such as agriculture and commerce.[81]

Rejection of Traditional Authority: The Practice of *Ijtihad*

As previously mentioned, *ijtihad*, loosely translated as independent reasoning, means to exert one's efforts in finding a ruling for a particular case based on the sources of the law. It is the opposite of *taqlid*, following somebody's opinion without knowledge of the bases from which it is derived. *Taqlid* in the legal sphere meant that jurists adhered to the rulings decided by the great authorities of particular schools of law. In practice it was something like ideological discipline within the communist party; one accepted the established views of one's school on previous scholars' rulings without judging them independently in light of the sources of the law. The law as expounded in medieval legal manuals was regarded as the authoritative interpretation and application of the scriptural sources of Islamic law.[82] There is much scholarly debate on how and when the practice of *taqlid* came to be the general rule among Muslim jurists and whether the gate of *ijtihad* was actually ever closed.[83] Historically, the notion of a stagnant and ossified legal practice and theory is untenable.[84] Be that as it may, the reform-oriented jurists of the nineteenth and early twentieth centuries felt that *taqlid* was a reality. Although *ijtihad* and *taqlid* were understood differently by different reformers,[85] *taqlid* was generally perceived as something negative and provoked strong condemnations.

Afghani blamed *taqlid* for the intellectual stagnation of Islam.[86] 'Abduh rejected the doctrine of *taqlid*, asking why previous generations should be more qualified to exercise *ijtihad* when more knowledge was available today. He suggested that scholars' unreflective acquiescence to the rulings of their predecessors was the main cause for Muslims' inability to work for the improvement of their institutions and their society.[87] Rida somewhat vaguely warned that the practice of *taqlid* destroys for Muslims their religion and their world.[88] *Ijtihad*, in contrast, would solve their present-day problems.[89] The Damascene scholar Jamal al-Din al-Qasimi pointed out that the eponyms of the legal schools themselves forbade slavish obedience to their opinions. The practice of *taqlid*, he argued, disrupts the rational discourse because one accepts another man's word as the criterion of truth instead of the divine text. In addition, he maintained that the enforcement of the doctrine of *taqlid* had led not only to rivalries and disunity between the legal schools but also had put hardships on the believers to whom the rulings were applied indiscriminately.[90] The theme of decline continued to be voiced by later reformers as well. The reform-oriented rector of al-Azhar, Mustafa al-Maraghi (1881-1945), attributed the religious, moral, intellectual, and political decline of Islamic peoples to the adherence to *taqlid* and the lack of *ijtihad*.[91] Mahmud Shaltut, under whose rectorship al-Azhar was integrated into the state educational system and its curriculum for the religious sciences modernized, also saw *taqlid* as stifling independent enquiry and reinforcing sectarianism.[92] In short, *taqlid* was associated with intellectual inflexibility, decline, and disunity.

The rejection of *taqlid* and advocacy for *ijtihad*, which was doubtlessly at the heart of the Muslim reformers' message, constitutes the primary similarity between the Protestant Reformation and the reform of Islamic legal theory. In advocating a break from the authority of the schools of law (*taqlid*), reformers rejected—in Weberian terms—a type of traditional authority. By stressing the need to go back to the Qur'an and the *sunna*, they assumed a type of charismatic authority in the sense that they claimed the right to change existing practices. They supported their claim, however, with what Paul Starr calls cultural authority,[93] namely the authority of scriptures and (idealized) practice of the early community. In the Protestant Reformation one finds the same shift. The traditional authority of the Roman Catholic Church was questioned by charismatic figures, such as Luther, Zwingli, Karlstadt, and others, who advocated a return to a cultural authority, the Bible.[94] Who is accorded the right to interpret the cultural authority, be it the Qur'an or the Bible, varies according to reformer. Rashid Rida, as stated above, envisioned the trained experts, the *'ulama*, to practice *ijtihad*. Shaltut appears to be more democratic in his concept of *ijtihad*, leaving larger room for the lay person to exercise her or his interpretation of the sacred texts. Likewise, we find in Protestantism a wide range of views on the extent of lay participation in shaping the doctrine, with Episcopalians on one end of the spectrum and Quakers on the other.

While the Protestant Reformation and the modern reform of Islamic law resemble each other in rejecting traditional authority, one should not forget, however, that it was exactly the lack of a unified authority and the differences and enmities among the schools of laws that prompted the Islamic reformers to advocate overarching principles. In this sense they attempted to catholicize Islamic law.

The rejection of the traditional authority structure by the Protestant and Islamic reformists led in both cases to similar reactions from non-reform-oriented scholars. Just as Luther's "Ninety-Five Theses" were perceived to be a threat to the authority of the Roman Catholic Church, so was the call for the right to practice independent reasoning (*ijtihad*) considered a challenge to the authority of the schools of law. Without a centralized hierarchic body like a church, the reaction by the 'ulama who were committed to the traditional interpretation of Islamic law was perhaps less spectacular than the edict of Worms (1521), the diets of Speyer (1526, 1529), and the official resolution at the Peace of Augsburg (1555).[95] There were, however, incidents showing that the traditional 'ulama attempted to silence what they perceived to be subversive thoughts. In Damascus in 1895/6, a group of reform-oriented 'ulama, including Jamal al-Din al-Qasimi, met regularly to study and discuss texts of premodern scholars who had expressed ideas similar to their own. Opponents to the study circle perceived "the group's practice of gathering to study oral reports and to search for proofs of venerated jurists' decisions . . . to be tantamount to ijtihad."[96] They were able to convince the Ottoman governor that the mujtahid's club, as the group around Qasimi became known, was trying to undermine the Ottoman political authority. An Ottoman investigation presided over by the official Damascene mufti charged members of the group, especially Qasimi, with interpreting the Qur'an and sunna according to their own opinions and rejecting the views of the authoritative imams of the legal schools. Upon realizing that the allegations were purely of a scholarly nature and that the study group posed no political threat, the authorities dismissed the charges.[97] This incident, as politically motivated as it may have been, nevertheless indicates that talking about or practicing ijtihad was perceived as a threat to the established authority of the schools of law. Not having an institutionalized authority structure that could discipline "unorthodox" views, the Damascene 'ulama sought to suppress them through the political authorities.[98] In both the Protestant Reformation and the modern reform of Islamic law the traditional authorities failed.

Returning to the Qur'an and the *Sunna*

One aspect in which the modern reform of Islamic law closely resembled the Protestant Reformation was the desire to purify Islam and restore it to its original strength by returning to the scriptural sources of Qur'an and sunna. Renouncing the recourse to the vast corpus of legal literature on the scriptures, most reformers advocated interpreting the Qur'an and the sunna in light of reason. Reason was considered humans' means to distinguish between truth and falsehood. Believing the revelation to be true, there could be no conflict between reason and the truth received from revelation. As Qasimi pointed out, reason establishes, transmits, and preserves the revelation. Islam, Rashid Rida emphasized, was a religion based on reason. The jurisprudence built on this religion needed to be rational as well.[99]

The desire to reconcile reason with revelation resulted in a general trend of the reformers of the nineteenth and early twentieth centuries to restrict the applicability of the religious texts in deriving law. One way was to delineate narrowly the acceptable scriptural sources. While the authenticity of the Qur'an was not questioned, many reformers wanted to purge the "unauthentic" and "irrational" hadiths from the corpus of the sunna.[100] 'Abduh blamed the acceptance of false *hadiths* and the misinterpretation of *hadiths* for the disunity among Muslims and the spread of non-Islamic customs. In his view, which was followed widely, only those *hadiths* that were transmitted in a widespread fashion (*mutawatir*) ought to be accepted. Solitary reports (*ahad*) were only valid when supported by further legal evidence. These *hadiths* should be judged by the intellect, and those that violated sense perception ought to be rejected.[101] Another way to limit the general applicability of the scriptures was to assign particular statements of the Qur'an and the *sunna* to a specific historical context. 'Abduh, for example, did this with regard to the doctrine of apostasy. The established view among Muslim jurists, based on Prophetic *hadiths*, was that apostates from Islam ought to be killed.[102] 'Abduh contextualized this doctrine by claiming that the *hadiths* requiring the apostate's execution were pronounced in a time of war, thus making the apostate a deserter. As long as the apostate does not attack Islam, no death penalty should be applied.[103]

Further, a distinction was made between scriptural rulings that are binding at all times and those that are adaptable according to circumstances. In general, rulings regulating the relationship between humans and God, i.e., those concerning ritual worship (*'ibadat*) were interpreted to belong to the former type.[104] They were beyond human understanding and ought to be adhered to exactly in the manner prescribed. Within the latter category fell the whole area of *mu'amalat*, interpersonal transactions, including personal status, and political and economic matters. In this mundane sphere, it was argued, God left it for humans to order their affairs.[105] Distinguishing between ritual worship and social transactions was, of course, not novel. Modern reformers differed from earlier legal theorists in their emphasis on the adaptability of rulings concerning social transactions to changing circumstances, and in the way in which these rulings were derived. Consensus (*ijma'*) and legal analogy (*qiyas*), the main procedures in addressing unprecedented cases up to the modern time, were relegated to the sideline.[106] The reformist move to anchor the law in the scriptures required reinterpreting these nontextual, procedural sources of the law.

Reinterpreting Consensus (*Ijma'*)

The reformers bestowed the concept of consensus (*ijma'*) with new meanings. Traditionally, *ijma'* was understood to be a unanimous agreement of the qualified scholars of one generation on a particular issue. The ruling upon which these scholars agreed was considered certain and binding for future generations.[107] The principle of *ijma'* potentially may serve to adapt the law according to social needs, legislate new laws, and provide a measure of unity within the law. In practice, however, it was impossible to establish whether all scholars of one generation actually agreed upon a particular case. Consensus was thus always challengeable on practical grounds. While many jurists upheld this legal fiction when they claimed that on some issue consensus had been reached, the reformers of the nineteenth and twentieth centuries frequently were critical of this concept. Some, like Rashid Rida, restricted *ijma'* to the first generation of Muslims and their practice. Their *ijma'* did not have to be unanimous; Rida considered consensus established as long as nobody was disagreeing with or objecting to the ruling in question.[108] For the contemporary period, Rida envisioned the right to *ijma'* to be transferred to a legislative council made up of those in charge (*ulu al-amr*) whom he identified with the *'ulama*. Their decisions, however, were not considered to be at the level of certainty but changeable according to place and time.[109] Shaltut likewise rejected the traditional interpretation of *ijma'*. Similar to Rida, he thought that true consensus was only possible at the very early time of Islam, when most scholars were residing in the area of Medina. In addition to the practical obstacles in establishing consensus, Shaltut criticized it from a logical point of view. He argued that the subject matter of *ijma'* belongs to the area of *ijtihad*, where differences of opinions were permissible to start with; requiring unanimity over matters of *ijtihad* was thus illogical. He maintained that if consensus could be established at all, then it would have to be by majority decisions that were based on the principle of *maslaha*, and thus changeable.[110] It appears that Shaltut and Rida envisaged the concept of legal consensus in the modern period as "something along the lines of modern decision-making bodies."[111] The rather impersonal concept of consensus of the legal scholars that is binding on all believers received thus a concrete form. Reinterpreting *ijma'* as some type of legislative body under the aegis of a ruler or in a state system, however, also diminishes its status as a source of law for all Muslims since it lacks the authority of unanimity, general bindingness, and the aura of infallibility. Limiting the scope and applicability of the concept of consensus in such a way conforms with the reformist desire to return to the textual sources of the law.

Replacing Legal Analogy (*Qiyas*) with *Maslaha*

One of the most important changes in Islamic legal theory concerned the principle of *maslaha* (literally a source of good, frequently translated as "public interest"). The prominence that the reformers of the late nineteenth and early twentieth centuries gave to this hitherto subsidiary legal principle was a logical consequence of their focus on the scriptures and their insistence that there was no contradiction between revelation and reason. The law, to be rational, had to be revealed for a purpose. The objective of God in revealing the *shari'a* was humankind's well-being (*maslaha*). More specifically, God's laws aim at the preservation of humans' religion, life, intellect, offspring, and property. The theory of the purposes of the law and the concept of *maslaha*, as a means to derive law, had already been formulated and discussed extensively by medieval jurisprudents. While medieval scholars adhered largely to the Ash'ari dogma that the human intellect is unable to grasp God's reasons for laying down rulings (except by the indicants given in scripture) and rejected the principle of causality in God's law, modern reformers were not so shy. Their argument, in a nutshell, went as follows: Since one knows with certainty that God's rulings intend *maslaha* for the believer at all times and in all places, and the manifestation of *maslaha* can be grasped by a person endowed with a sound intellect, rulings may be based on considerations of *maslaha*. The rulings are commensurate with Islamic law even without concrete scriptural evidence. Using *maslaha* as a certain and valid criterion for deriving rulings means that the procedure of legal analogy becomes almost superfluous.

In legal analogy, a jurist seeks to identify a criterion in a Qur'anic or *sunna*ic ruling that can be considered the reason (*'illa*), or *ratio legis*, for laying down this ruling in order to apply the same ruling in other cases that display the same *ratio legis*. The *ratio legis* was mostly understood to be a concrete characteristic pertaining to the case in question. For example, the *ratio legis* of the prohibition of wine is believed to be the intoxicating nature of this substance based on textual indicants and rational considerations (wine's color or that it is liquid are attributes that are deemed irrelevant to its prohibition). This characteristic of intoxication is also found in other alcoholic beverages, such as beer, and thus the prohibition of drinking wine is extended to beer by analogy. Rationalizing the law in terms of *maslaha*, a jurist goes one step further. He does not inquire about the concrete characteristics of the ruling but about its relationship to *maslaha*. Prohibiting the consumption of wine constitutes a *maslaha* by serving to protect the intellect from harm. Whatever harms the intellect can thus be prohibited in congruence to the purpose of the Qur'anic prohibition of wine. While the procedure of legal analogy needs a concrete textual ruling that is extended to situations that display the same characteristics, i.e., *ratio legis*, this is not the case when rulings are based on *maslaha*. Using considerations of *maslaha* allows a jurist to address all those situations to which no *ratio legis* extracted from a textually decided ruling applies. The jurist, thus, does not have to build an analogy based on the sometimes far-fetched existence of the same *ratio legis* in the new situation. Establishing that a ruling entails *maslaha* is sufficient to pronounce it in conformity to the scriptures. For instance, when the Ottoman Constitution was reinstated in 1908, Qasimi endorsed this novel institution by reference to the principle of *maslaha*. He argued that the Constitution provided a way to uphold the general Islamic principles of considering *maslaha* and averting harm from the people. Further, it would allow that laws be changed according to need and ensured that they be based on the principle of safeguarding the public welfare.[112] Qasimi did not refer to a concrete Qur'anic or *sunna*ic statement to pronounce the Ottoman Constitution commensurate with Islamic law. By forgoing the elaborate procedures involved in conducting legal analogy, basing decisions on considerations of *maslaha* proves a less cumbersome method to address new situations.

Further, the concept of *maslaha* may also provide jurists with a means to change or suspend existing laws on the grounds that the ruling no longer fulfills its purpose. For example, in the latter part of the twentieth century the different shares sons and daughters receive in Islamic inheritance law were challenged. It was argued that the Qur'anic injunction was issued at a time when men were the main provider of the family and thus deserved a higher share. Since today women have the opportunity to earn a living and contribute to the family income, this ruling does not serve its purpose any longer. Consequently, the inheritance shares for daughters and sons should be revised and made equal.[113]

How much *maslaha* can be used to adapt the law depends on the way *maslaha* is integrated into legal theory.[114] When it is closely tied to the procedure of legal analogy and instrumentalized as a *ratio legis* in the form of an unattested *maslaha*, a so-called *maslaha mursala*, its scope is limited.[115] Reform-oriented jurists who were more cautious in their reinterpretation of the legal tradition, such as 'Abd al-Wahhab Khallaf (1888-1956), adopted this procedure.[116] When, however, *maslaha* is understood as an independent legal principle, it can be applied to almost any situation that is not textually decided as well as adapt existing laws to changed circumstances. Rida, for example, was a proponent of this latter interpretation of *maslaha*.[117] In general, enlarging the scope of the concept of *maslaha* in deriving law elevates substantive reasoning over formal procedures. While this enhances the law's flexibility and adaptability, it also has the potential to destabilize any uniformity within Islamic law. Since *maslaha* differs not only according to time and place but also by individual assessment, what constitutes a legally valid *maslaha* might largely be determined by subjective factors.

The emphasis that the reformers of Islamic law placed on the concept of *maslaha* represents a shift in epistemology resembling that of Luther's reinterpretation of salvation. The traditional Catholic conception that salvation derives from doing good works left the believer in the realm of uncertainty because it did not answer what is good and what is enough good work. The means of attaining salvation was thus determined with less than certainty. Luther's achievement was to reinterpret the biblical statements concerning this concept in a manner that concluded that salvation itself was certain by the certainty derived from the scriptural texts of God's promise to grant salvation through the act of faith. Salvation now was within the realm of certainty and the believer knew with certainty how to achieve it.[118] The basis of human action was thereby removed from the state of uncertainty or probability to that of certainty. Elevating the concept of *maslaha* to a prominent place in the derivation of laws, the reformers performed a similar epistemological shift. Traditionally the majority of rulings regulating human acts in the mundane sphere (*mu'amalat*) were derived through the procedure of legal analogy. In legal analogy, as stated above, the most important aspect was the identification of the *ratio legis*. This, however, could generally only be done on the level of probability—unless the *ratio legis* was explicitly expressed in the textual sources. There remained then always a measure of uncertainty about the correctness of the *ratio legis*.[119] Declaring, as reformists did, that it is known with certainty that *maslaha* is the purpose of the law, and that it can be used as *ratio legis* to derive rulings, changes the epistemological basis of the *ratio legis* from one of probability to certainty. Deriving rulings based on *maslaha* produces a certainty that the ruling accords with the meaning and spirit of the divine law. In both the Lutheran system of "by grace alone" and the system that uses *maslaha* to validate rulings, the basis for action is certain. To use Lindberg's phrasing, in both systems of thought the argument "if . . . then" (if you do good works, then you will attain salvation; if the *ratio legis* is correct, then the resulting ruling is correct) is replaced by "because . . . therefore" (because God accepts us, therefore we do good works; because *maslaha* is the purpose of the law, therefore a ruling that accords with *maslaha* concurs with the purpose of the law). Admittedly, the theological implications of the change in epistemology were much more profound in Christianity than in Islam. More research on the theological aspects of the shift away from an Ash'ari understanding of Islamic law needs to be conducted.

In sum, the reform of Islamic legal theory, as proposed by many scholars of the late nineteenth and the twentieth centuries, was based primarily on the concept of *ijtihad*. Rejecting the strict adherence to the established doctrines of a particular school of law resulted in profound changes in Islamic legal theory.[120] The practice of *ijtihad* turned the jurists' focus toward the scriptural sources of the law. In order for *ijtihad* not to result in rigid literalism but increase the adaptability of Islamic law, jurists employed two interpretative strategies. First, they limited the applicability of the Qur'an and the *sunna* by delineating which textual statements were acceptable to use as the bases for rulings and by contextualizing textual passages in a manner that made it possible to set aside explicit scriptural rulings. A similar method was applied to the concept of consensus (*ijma'*). It was if not rejected then at least confined to groups that could achieve agreement in a practical manner. Second, a literalist interpretation of the law was avoided by shifting the legal rationality from deductive reasoning to inductive reasoning. The formal procedure of legal analogy was largely replaced by the substantive concept of *maslaha* as a method to derive laws. This shift altered the focus of jurists in the law-finding process from identifying more or less objective characteristics as *ratio legis* of rulings to evaluating whether or not something agreed with the purpose of the law. An individual jurist's subjective assessment of what constitutes *maslaha* plays a greater role in this type of legal reasoning.

The reform of Islamic law of the late nineteenth and early twentieth centuries was primarily based on the reformers' rejection of traditional authority. It led, like the Reformation of Western Christianity to a proliferation of new doctrines that all claimed validity based on the same body of textual material. The challenge to traditional authority by the Protestant and the Islamic reformers would, however, have been of little effect had it not been for two other factors that were present at the time: expansion of education and the rise of the printing press. Despite the fact that the printing press was introduced in the early eighteenth century, its effects on the position of the *'ulama*, on the one hand, and for the movements to reform Islamic law, on the other, were not felt until the latter half of the nineteenth century. Just as Europe prior to the Reformation experienced an expansion of education, so did the Middle East and North Africa as a result of the government reforms of the educational system. The increase in educated Muslims, while not amounting to mass education, nevertheless brought about a critical mass.[121]

The spread of the print media in the latter half of the nineteenth century created a public sphere that became the main forum for religious debate. To some extent, the press replaced the *'ulama* in their function of "teaching, preaching, promoting good and forbidding evil."[122] The plurality of voices in the printed media was reflected by a plurality of interpretations. Ideas in the public sphere were open to public interpretation. Robinson masterly summarizes the effects of printing on the *'ulama*:

> ironically, while print enabled ulama greatly to extend their influence in public affairs, it was also doing serious damage to the roots of their authority. By printing the Islamic classics . . . they undermined their authority; they were no longer necessarily around when the book was read to make up for the absence of the author in the text; . . . their monopoly of the transmission of knowledge was broken. Books . . . could now be consulted by any Ahmad, Mahmud or Muhammad, who could make what they will of them.[123]

The printing press and the expanding educational system supported the emergence of multifarious interpretations of religious texts in the Middle East and North Africa that resembles the impact of the Protestant Reformation on Western Christianity. The intellectual seeds for this Islamic Reformation, however, lie in the insistence of Muslim jurists to possess the right to independently investigate the sources of the law to find solutions for present-day problems. While some might still be looking for an Islamic Luther to post his theses, an Islamic legal Reformation was inaugurated without one in the second half of the nineteenth century.

Notes

1. For varying accounts on the development of the schools of law in the early Islamic period see Norman Calder, *Studies in Early Muslim Jurisprudence* (Oxford: Clarendon Press, 1993), esp. 1-54, 193-226; N. J. Coulson, *A History of Islamic Law* (Edinburgh: Edinburgh University Press, 1964), 21-52; Ignaz Goldziher, *Introduction to Islamic Theology and Law*, tr. Andras and Ruth Hamori (Princeton: Princeton University Press, 1981), 31-66; Wael B. Hallaq, *A History of Islamic Legal Theories* (New York: Cambridge University Press, 1997), 7-21; Christopher Melchert, *The Formation of the Sunni Schools of Law, 9th-10th Centuries C.E.* (Leiden: Brill, 1997), 32-47; Joseph Schacht, *Introduction to Islamic Law* (Oxford: Clarendon Press, 1964), 23-56.

2. Schacht, *Introduction to Islamic Law*, 45-48; Hallaq, *History of Islamic Legal Theories*, 21-35; see also Calder, *Studies in Early Muslim Jurisprudence*, 67-84, 226-42.

3. This point is aptly made by Ahmad Dallal in his comparison of four Islamic reformers of the eighteenth and nineteenth centuries. "The Origins and Objectives of

Islamic Revivalist Thought, 1750-1850," *Journal of the American Oriental Society* 113 (1993): 341-59.

4. Some of the inconsistencies within a scholar's work stem from intellectual maturity. The work of Ghazali is one such example. See his discussion of the principle of *maslaha* in *Shifa al-Ghalil* (Quenching the Thirst), ed. Hamad 'Ubayd al-Kubaysi (Baghdad: Matba'at al-Irshad, 1971), esp. 160-257, and in *al-Mustasfa min 'Ilm al-Usul* (The Prime Selection from Islamic Legal Theory), ed. Hamza ibn Zubayr Hafiz (Jidda: Sharikat al-Madina al-Munawwara, 1993), passim. In other cases, different historical circumstances result in changed views. Rashid Rida's thought, for instance, shows development from a liberal interpretation of Islam to a more traditional one. See Ahmad Dallal, "Appropriating the Past: Twentieth Century Reconstruction of Pre-Modern Islamic Thought," *Islamic Law and Society* 7 (2000): 342; Malcolm Kerr, "Rashid Rida and Islamic Legal Reform: An Ideological Analysis," *Muslim World* 50 (1960): 177-81; Malcolm H. Kerr, *Islamic Reform: The Political and Legal Theories of Muhammad 'Abduh and Rashid Rida* (Berkeley: University of California Press, 1966), 158, 207.

5. See Gudrun Krämer, "Kritik und Selbstkritik: Reformistisches Denken im Islam," in *Der Islam im Aufbruch? Perspektiven der arabischen Welt* (Islam Bursting Forth? Perspectives in the Arab World), ed. Michael Lüders (München: Piper, 1992), 209-10; Rudolph Peters, "*Idjtihad* and *Taqlid* in 18th and 19th Century Islam," *Die Welt des Islams* (The World of Islam) 20 (1980): 144.

6. Dallal, "Appropriating the Past," 333-34; Krämer, "Kritik und Selbstkritik," 210.

7. Peters, "*Idjtihad*," 131.

8. See David Commins, *Islamic Reform: Politics and Social Change in Late Ottoman Syria* (New York: Oxford University Press, 1990), 31; Dallal, "Appropriating the Past," 335; Nikki R. Keddie, *An Islamic Response to Imperialism: Political and Religious Writings of Sayyid Jamal ad-Din "al-Afghani"* (Berkeley: University of California Press, 1983), 41-44; Wolf-Dieter Lemke, *Mahmud Šaltut (1893-1963) und die Reform der Azhar* (Mahumd Shaltut [1893-1963] and the Reform of al-Azhar) (Frankfurt: Peter D. Lang, 1980), 27, 224-25; Mazheruddin Siddiqi, *Modern Reformist Thought in the Muslim World* (Islamabad: Islamic Research Institute, 1982), 2-3, 86.

9. Edmund Burke, III, "The Moroccan Ulama, 1860-1912: An Introduction," in *Scholars, Saints, and Sufis: Muslim Religious Institutions in the Middle East Since 1500*, ed. Nikki R. Keddie (Berkeley: University of California Press, 1972), 116-18; Jamil Abun-Nasr, "The Salafiyya Movement in Morocco: The Religious Bases of the Moroccan Nationalist Movement," *St. Antony's Papers* 16 (1963): 90-91, 95-96, 103-5.

10. See Burke, "Moroccan Ulama," 106-14; Albert Hourani, *Arabic Thought in the Liberal Age 1798-1939* (Cambridge: Cambridge University Press, 1983), 34-66; Moshe Ma'oz, "The 'Ulama and the Process of Modernization in Syria During the Mid-Nineteenth Century," *African and Asian Studies* 7 (1971): 79-81; John Obert Voll, *Islam: Continuity and Change in the Modern World* (Syracuse: Syracuse University Press, 1994), 31-35, 86-87.

11. For an overview of differences among the reform programs see Ira M. Lapidus, *A History of Islamic Societies* (Cambridge: Cambridge University Press, 1988), 557-70.

12. In Morocco, reforms of the state structure that affected the religious scholars similarly to those of the Tanzimat era in the Ottoman Empire did not occur until the twentieth century. See Burke, "Moroccan Ulama," 107-14.

13. See Burke, "Moroccan Ulama," 119; Richard L. Chambers, "The Ottoman Ulema and the Tanzimat," in *Scholars, Saints, and Sufis*, 35-36; Commins, *Islamic*

Reform, 12-13, 19; Daniel Crecelius, "Nonideological Responses of the Egyptian Ulama to Modernization," in *Scholars, Saints, and Sufis,* 180-83, 186; Kerr, "Rashid Rida," 170; Siddiqi, *Modern Reformist Thought,* 1-3.

14. Chambers, "Ottoman Ulema," 36; Afaf Lutfi al-Sayyid Marsot, "The Ulama of Cairo in the Eighteenth and Nineteenth Centuries," in *Scholars, Saints, and Sufis,* 163; Robin Ostle, "The Printing Press and the Renaissance of Modern Arabic Literature," *Culture & History* 16 (1997): 146.

15. Burke, "Moroccan Ulama," 112; Crecelius, "Nonideological Responses," 189, 191-94, 200-2, 204-5; Lemke, *Mahmud Saltut,* passim.

16. Chambers, "Ottoman Ulema," 36, 38; Commins, *Islamic Reform,* 14-16; Crecelius, "Nonideological Responses," 189, 191-94, 200-2, 204-5; Lemke, *Mahmud Saltut,* 20, 24-27, 87-88; Voll, *Continuity and Change,* 87, 94.

17. Crecelius, "Nonideological Responses," 189.

18. Ostle, "Printing Press," 147, quotes Sabry Hafez, *The Genesis of Arabic Narrative Discourse* (London: Saqi Books, 1993), 66, for this number but advises caution regarding its reliability. Crecelius likewise expresses his doubts over the actual knowledge of reading taught at the *kuttab* level. See Crecelius, "Nonideological Responses," 188, n. 48. Even at the end of the twentieth century, as Robinson emphasizes, literacy levels may vary greatly, from 90 percent in Iraq to 14 percent in North Yemen. See Francis Robinson, "Technology and Religious Change: Islam and the Impact of Print," *Modern Asian Studies* 27 (1993): 250.

19. Carter Lindberg, *The European Reformations* (Oxford: Blackwell, 1996), 36, 46.

20. Chambers, "Ottoman Ulema," 35.

21. Burke, "Moroccan Ulama," 107-8.

22. Schacht, *Introduction to Islamic Law,* 101.

23. Burke, "Moroccan Ulama," 118; Chambers, "Ottoman Ulema," 36; Crecelius, "Nonideological Responses," 182; Uriel Heyd, "The Ottoman 'Ulema and Westernization in the Time of Selim III and Mahmud II," in *The Modern Middle East: A Reader,* ed. Albert Hourani (Berkeley: University of California Press, 1993), 52; Marsot, "Ulama of Cairo," 163; Voll, *Continuity and Change,* 87.

24. See Coulson, *History of Islamic Law,* 150-51; Albert Hourani, *A History of the Arab Peoples* (Cambridge: Harvard University Press, 1991), 274.

25. Chambers, "Ottoman Ulema," 43; Commins, *Islamic Reform,* 13.

26. Chambers, "Ottoman Ulema," 41-44.

27. Coulson, *History of Islamic Law,* 152.

28. Commins, *Islamic Reform,* 16; Coulson, *History of Islamic Law,* 151; Crecelius, "Nonideological Responses," 197.

29. Chambers, "Ottoman Ulema," 45.

30. Schacht, *Introduction to Islamic Law,* 92.

31. Chambers, "Ottoman Ulema," 44-45; Coulson, *History of Islamic Law,* 151-52; C. V. Findley, "Medjelle," *Encyclopedia of Islam,* ed. H. A. R. Gibb et al., 2nd ed., vol. 6 (Leiden: Brill, 1954-1971), 971-72; Schacht, *Introduction to Islamic Law,* 92-93.

32. The countries that do not have a codified family law are Saudi Arabia, the United Arab Emirates, Qatar, Bahrain, and Oman.

33. For an account of the reestablishment of Islamic criminal law and how the state limits its application see Rudolph Peters, "The Islamization of Criminal Law: A Comparative Perspective," *Die Welt des Islams* (The World of Islam) 34 (1994): 246-74.

34. Hans J. Hillerbrand, "Reformation," *Encyclopedia of Religion*, ed. Mircea Eliade, vol. 12 (New York: MacMillan Publishing, 1987), 245.

35. Hillerbrand, "Reformation," 253.

36. Lindberg, *European Reformations*, 36-37.

37. Michael Harbsmeier, "Introduction: European Media in the Eyes of 19th Century Muslim Observers," *Culture & History* 16 (1997): 8-9. Eickelman's point that the latter half of the twentieth century with its mass education and mass communication should be looked at as the equivalent to the Protestant Reformation ought, in my view, be revised. See Dale F. Eickelman, "Inside the Islamic Revolution," *Wilson Quarterly* 22 (1998): 82. The Protestant Reformation needed neither *mass* education nor *mass* communication but the existence of enough people who mattered being able to read and communicate with the help of the print media.

38. Harbsmeier, "Introduction: European Media," 12.

39. Ostle, "Printing Press," 145, 149.

40. Reinhard Schulze, "The Birth of Tradition and Modernity in 18th and 19th Century Islamic Culture—the Case of Printing," *Culture & History* 16 (1997): 42. An added consequence of the ban on printing Islamic books was that it emphasized the difference between religious knowledge and other types of knowledge. See Schulze, "Birth of Tradition," 44.

41. Robinson, "Technology and Religious Change," 233; Jakob Skøvgaard-Petersen, "Fatwas in Print," *Culture & History* 16 (1997): 73-74.

42. Ostle, "Printing Press," 145.

43. Schulze, "Birth of Tradition," 42.

44. According to Schulze, the Islamic book production in Istanbul until 1842 was rather low; it comprised no more than 24 percent of the total production. In Egypt, the output of Islamic texts from the Bulaq press was lower still at about 13 percent. Schulze, "Birth of Tradition," 48, 51, 54. See also Skøvgaard-Petersen, "Fatwas in Print," 74.

45. See Commins, *Islamic Reform*, 139; Marsot, "Ulama of Cairo," 153.

46. Commins, *Islamic Reform*, 16.

47. Schulze, "Birth of Tradition," 44-52, provides detailed lists on how many religious texts were printed and on which subject.

48. See Schulze, "Birth of Tradition," 48-49, who attributes this trend, on the one hand, to the change in reading a text. A manuscript is read and studied with its commentaries under the guidance of a teacher. The reader of a printed book could choose not to read the commentary. On the other hand, Schulze suggests that economic factors may have played a role in not printing commentaries with the texts.

49. Skøvgaard-Petersen, "Fatwas in Print," 74; Schulze, "Birth of Tradition," 50, 58.

50. State censorship did, of course, not disappear. The journal *al-Manar*, for example, faced temporary difficulties in its distribution in Syria on account of Ottoman censorship. See J. Jornier, "Al-Manar," *Encyclopedia of Islam*, vol. 6, 360. Books were still subject to official authorization and indices of prohibited books existed in Syria in the early twentieth century. It seems, however, that people knew how to get around these obstacles by having texts printed without their name on the title page or simply in another location. See Commins, *Islamic Reform*, 112-14.

51. While the numbers presented for Egyptian newspapers and periodicals during this period vary, it is clear that they multiplied compared with earlier decades. See Ostle, "Printing Press," 146; Skøvgaard-Petersen, "Fatwas in Print," 76.

52. Burke, "Moroccan Ulama," 95.

53. Commins, *Islamic Reform*, 16-17.

54. Schulze demonstrates how the terminology used in reference to texts was changed by the print medium. Schulze, "Birth of Tradition," 31-49.

55. See Commins, *Islamic Reform*, 16-18, 139-40; Robinson, "Technology and Religious Change," 241, 244; Schulze, "Birth of Tradition," 48; Skøvgaard-Petersen, "Fatwas in Print," 76.

56. The *'ulama*'s control over the dissemination of ideas may have been one of the reasons that Najm al-Din al-Tufi's "unorthodox" interpretation of legal theory fell into oblivion, whereas his more mainstream writings survive in many manuscripts and commentaries. See Felicitas Opwis, "Maslaha: An Intellectual History of a Core Concept in Islamic Legal Theory" (Ph.D. thesis, Yale University, 2001), 194-95.

57. Skøvgaard-Petersen, "Fatwas in Print," 80.

58. Commins, *Islamic Reform*, 31.

59. Jornier, "Al-Manar," 360.

60. Abun-Nasr, "Salafiyya Movement," 97.

61. Abun-Nasr, "Salafiyya Movement," 97-98.

62. Abun-Nasr, "Salafiyya Movement," 98-99.

63. Commins, *Islamic Reform*, 112, 171 n. 33.

64. See Skøvgaard-Petersen, "Fatwas in Print," 84.

65. See Commins, *Islamic Reform*, 118-23.

66. Skøvgaard-Petersen, "Fatwas in Print," 83.

67. Robinson, "Technology and Religious Change," 246; Skøvgaard-Petersen, "Fatwas in Print," 85.

68. Chambers, "Ottoman Ulema," 38-43; Crecelius, "Nonideological Responses," 186-7; Ma'oz, "'Ulama and Modernization," 84; Voll, *Continuity and Change*, 89.

69. Chambers, "Ottoman Ulema," 37, 41; Crecelius, "Nonideological Responses," 181-187; Ma'oz, "'Ulama and Modernization," 82-83.

70. Chambers, "Ottoman Ulema," 46; Crecelius, "Nonideological Responses," 187.

71. Burke, "Moroccan Ulama," 108, 113, 117-23.

72. The notion of the decline of Islamic civilization(s) was widespread among Muslim intellectuals of this period. It became exemplified in a book by the Druse notable Shakib Arslan, *Li-Madha Ta'akhkhara al-Muslimun wa li-Madha Taqaddama Ghayruhum?* (Why are Muslims Backward While Others are Advanced?) (Cairo: Matba'at al-Manar, 1930). See also Yvonne Yazbeck Haddad, *Contemporary Islam and the Challenge of History* (Albany: State University of New York Press, 1982), 13-33.

73. In order to initiate a revival of Islamic civilization Afghani and 'Abduh intended to hold an Islamic convention during the pilgrimage that would delineate the causes and solutions for the decline—though their plan was never implemented. See Haddad, *Contemporary Islam*, 13-14.

74. See Commins, *Islamic Reform*, 69; Dallal, "Appropriating the Past," 335-36; Krämer, "Kritik und Selbstkritik," 210, 214; Siddiqi, *Modern Reformist Thought*, 74, 86.

75. Commins, *Islamic Reform*, 65, 69-73; Krämer, "Kritik und Selbstkritik," 218; Siddiqi, *Modern Reformist Thought*, 1-6, 24-25, 73.

76. See Commins, *Islamic Reform*, 49; Siddiqi, *Modern Reformist Thought*, 45-46, 73, 103.

77. See Dallal, "The Origins and Objectives of Islamic Revivalist Thought"; Dallal, "Appropriating the Past"; and Peters, "*Idjtihad* and *Taqlid* in 18th and 19th Century Islam."

78. The ideas of the reformers of the late nineteenth and early twentieth centuries are very diverse, even if they may claim the same roots. Their systems of thought are too diverse to warrant use of the term "Salafiyya," or fundamentalist, for all of them.

79. Abun-Nasr, "Salafiyya Movement in Morocco," 98.

80. Muhammad Rashid Rida, *Yusr al-Islam wa Usul al-Tashri' al-'Amm* (Islam's Facility and the Sources of General Legislation) (Cairo: Maktabat al-Salam al-'Alamiyya, 1984), 46-48, 159; Kate Zebiri, *Mahmud Shaltut and Islamic Modernism* (Oxford: Clarendon Press), 85.

81. 'Allal al-Fasi, *Maqasid al-Shari'a al-Islamiyya wa Makarimuha* (The Purposes and Noble Traits of Islamic Law) (Casablanca: Maktabat al-Wahda al-'Arabiyya, 1963), 214.

82. Abun-Nasr reports that in Morocco Islamic jurisprudence after the fourteenth century was taught increasingly through summaries only. The *Mukhtasar* (Compendium) of Khalil ibn Ishaq al-Jundi was the leading textbook for Maliki law replacing more detailed works of *fiqh*. Abun-Nasr, "Salafiyya Movement in Morocco," 92-93.

83. See Wael B. Hallaq, "On the Origins of the Controversy about the Existence of Mujtahids and the Gate of Ijtihad," *Studia Islamica* 63 (1986): 129-41; Mohammad Fadel, "The Social Logic of *Taqlid* and the Rise of the *Mukhatasar* [*sic*]," *Islamic Law and Society* 3 (1996): 193-233; Krämer, "Kritik und Selbstkritik," 220-21; Schacht, *Introduction to Islamic Law*, 69-75.

84. The fatwa collection of the fourteenth century scholar Shatibi, for example, demonstrates that jurists accommodated changing times with discarding rulings by previous authorities. See Muhammad Khalid Masud, *Islamic Legal Philosophy: A Study of Abu Ishaq al-Shatibi's Life and Thought* (Delhi: International Islamic Publishers, 1989), 119-40. The author's research on the development of the concept of *maslaha* between the eleventh and fourteenth centuries bears evidence of the vitality of Islamic legal theory. See Opwis, "Maslaha."

85. See, Dallal, "Origins and Objectives," 348-50, 357-59.

86. Keddie, *Islamic Response to Imperialism*, 82.

87. Muhammad 'Abduh, *The Theology of Unity*, tr. Ishaq Musa'ad and Kenneth Cragg (London: George Allen & Unwin, 1966), 38-40, 140-41; Commins, *Islamic Reform*, 32; Siddiqi, *Modern Reformist Thought*, 25, 102-3.

88. Rida, *Yusr al-Islam*, 153.

89. Siddiqi, *Modern Reformist Thought*, 82-83.

90. Commins, *Islamic Reform*, 69-73; 141.

91. Lemke, *Mahmud Saltut*, 68-71.

92. Shaltut saw the mechanism for *taqlid* in the concept of *ijma'* (consensus). For him, the modification of the concept of *ijma'* was connected to the practice of *ijtihad*. See Zebiri, *Mahmud Shaltut*, 85-86.

93. By calling the authority that resides in cultural objects (such as religious texts, scholarly work, or the law) "cultural authority" as opposed to "social authority" (which requires agents), Starr adds to the typology of authority an important aspect missing in Weber's thought. A person advocating reform and gathering followers exercises social authority of the charismatic type, yet the reformer's message might be an appeal to cultural authority. See Paul Starr, *The Social Transformation of American Medicine* (New York: Basic Books, 1982), 13. I thank my husband, Joseph Soares, for pointing out this reference.

94. See Jerry Koch, "Reformation," in *Encyclopedia of Religion and Society*, ed. William H. Swatos, Jr. (Walnut Creek, Calif.: AltaMira Press, 1998), 404-5; Lindberg, *European Reformations*, 12.

95. Hillerbrand, "Reformation," 245-47.

96. Commins, *Islamic Reform*, 51.

97. Commins, *Islamic Reform*, 50-54.

98. For an account of other incidents in which reform-oriented jurists faced opposition from the traditional *'ulama* see Commins, *Islamic Reform*, 55-59, 112-15.

99. Commins, *Islamic Reform*, 54, 67; Siddiqi, *Modern Reformist Thought*, 28-29, 74-75, 83.

100. How to determine, apart from the manner of transmission, whether a *hadith* should be considered authentic or not, was largely left unclear.

101. Commins, *Islamic Reform*, 31; Siddiqi, *Modern Reformist Thought*, 67, 102-3.

102. For different positions on apostasy see Frank Griffel, "Toleration and Exclusion: Shafi'i and Ghazali on the Treatment of Apostates," *Bulletin of the School of Oriental and African Studies* 63 (2001): 339-54.

103. Jornier, "Al-Manar," 361.

104. See 'Abd al-Wahhab Khallaf, *Masadir al-Tashri' al-Islami fima la Nassa fih* (The Origins of Islamic Legislation When there is no Text) (Kuwait: Dar al-Qalam, 6th ed. 1993), 102-3; Subhi Rajab Mahmasani, *Falsafat al-Tashri' fi al-Islam* (The Philosophy of Legislation in Islam) (Beirut: Dar al-'Ilm lil-Malayin, 3rd ed. 1961), 176; Rida, *Yusr al-Islam*, 46, 141-44, 155.

105. Krämer, "Kritik und Selbstkritik," 223-24; Rida, *Yusr al-Islam*, 46-54, 153, 157-60.

106. Rida's writings on the subject of legal analogy (*qiyas*) are somewhat ambiguous. It appears that while not rejecting this procedure altogether he tried to limit its application to those instances where the *ratio legis* is clearly expressed in the Qur'an or *sunna* (Rida, *Yusr al-Islam*, 117, 138-39, 143, 152-53).

107. See Hallaq, *History of Islamic Legal Theory*, 75-81; Bernhard Weiss, *The Search for God's Law: Islamic Jurisprudence in the Writings of Sayf al-Din al-Amidi* (Salt Lake City: University of Utah Press, 1992), Chapter 5: The Ijma', 181-211.

108. Rida, *Yusr al-Islam*, 18, 157.

109. Rida, *Yusr al-Islam*, 46-48, 159.

110. Zebiri, *Mahmud Shaltut*, 84-86.

111. Zebiri, *Mahmud Shaltut*, 86.

112. Commins, *Islamic Reform*, 126-27.

113. Fazlur Rahman, "A Survey of Modernization of Muslim Family Law," *International Journal of Middle East Studies* 2 (1981): 453.

114. For a discussion of different ways medieval jurisprudents integrated the concept of *maslaha* into legal theory and the consequences for expanding and adapting Islamic Law, see Opwis, "Maslaha," esp. 63-70, 340-52.

115. The reformers' emphasis on human ability to understand the rationale behind God's laws led to a tendency of conflating the concept of *ratio legis* (*'illa*) with *maslaha* and God's wisdom (*hikma*). The reformist jurist Subhi Mahmasani (1909-1986) considered only that *ratio legis* sound which displays the legally intended wisdom; though when he illustrated this thought with examples he only mentioned concrete attributes as *rationes legis*. See Mahmasani, *Falsafat al-Tashri'*, 163-64, 168.

116. Khallaf, *Masadir al-Tashri'*, 101-3.

117. Rida, *Yusr al-Islam*, 141-44, 152-53.

118. This analysis of Luther's reinterpretation of salvation is based on Lindberg, *European Reformations*, 62-73.

119. Most of the differences between the schools of law derive from their disagreement over the *ratio legis* of rulings.

120. The rejection of the practice of *taqlid* and of adhering to established school rulings changed the way jurists thought about legal practice. The techniques of *takhayyur* (choosing or selecting an appropriate ruling from among all schools of law) and *talfiq* (amalgamation or combining one or more elements of one school's doctrine with those from another) served to increase the flexibility of Islamic law but also altered its substantive body. For an account of these techniques with extensive examples see Norman Anderson, *Law Reform in the Muslim World* (London: Athlone Press, 1976), 47-58; and Coulson, *History of Islamic Law*, 182-201.

121. The existence of a consumer market for reading materials is indicated by the fact that the official printing press of the Ottoman Empire could not satisfy the demand for books. In addition, printed texts were much cheaper than manuscript copies. See Schulze, "Birth of Tradition," 43-44.

122. Skøvgaard-Petersen, "Fatwas in Print," 85-86.

123. Robinson, "Technology and Religious Change," 245.

3

Islam and Political *Sinn*: The Hermeneutics of Contemporary Islamic Reformists[1]

Michaelle Browers

Since at least the Arab *Nahda* (Renaissance) in the nineteenth century, crises in the Middle East have been accompanied by calls for revival (*nahda*), renewal (*tajdid*), and reform (*islah*). Revivalist and reformist movements have often sought to address the perceived moral, social, and/or political degeneration of the Muslim *umma* (community) through a return to the "fundamentals" of Islam, as well as by claiming the right to *ijtihad* (independent reasoning) in engaging Islam's religious texts. However, as Fazlur Rahman observes, in practice this *ijtihad* has tended to be limited by "the historical belief that the *hadith* genuinely contains the *sunna* of the Prophet combined with the further belief that the *sunna* of the Prophet and the Qur'anic rulings on social behavior have to be more or less *literally* implemented in all ages."[2] Whereas what Rahman refers to as "premodernist reform movements" focused on reforming society, the most recent reformists maintain that it is not sufficient for Muslims to merely revive their traditions in order to achieve that end. In the contemporary Islamic world, "reform" suggests not just a return to the fundamental texts of Islam as a blueprint for mapping the future, but also a substantial rethinking of the "social content" of Islam—a rethinking that causes disruptions with or displaces inherited notions of what constitutes not only Islamic law, but also the broader social values underlying the *umma*.

A number of scholars have commented on this change in Islamic contexts, some going so far as to hail the onset of an "Islamic Reformation"[3] and even to compare particular Islamic thinkers to Reformation figures, such as Martin Luther.[4] The body of literature said to form the basis of this Reformation consists of works by contemporary Muslim intellectuals who have bypassed traditional interpretive authorities and revised orthodox methods of approaching texts and questions in the tradition of Islam. And a number of the reformists who have engaged in such projects have drawn the attention of not only religious authorities, but also academic, legal, and political powers both in the region and globally.

Yet, a number of challenging questions still remain: Does the existence of "reformists" mean that we are witnessing a "Reformation" in Islamic thought? If so, does the comparison between contemporary transformations in Islamic societies and the Protestant Reformations enlighten or obscure our understanding of what is going on in the works of particular Islamic reformists?

It is difficult—and perhaps premature—to assess the extent to which Islamic societies are undergoing something tantamount to an "Islamic Reformation." Such characterizations are best made in hindsight. In addition, there are many historical differences between the two contexts being compared: Islam has no "church" that can form the object of its reformation, nor do most Islamic reformists hearken from the ranks of the traditionally educated Muslim religious scholars (*'ulama*) or appear to be backed by a significant portion of the elite or the masses. As even those who most enthusiastically employ the comparison admit, "in the Muslim world today, there is no one central figure or hierarchy of authority against whom the people are rebelling. There are instead many authorities, and, despite numerous claims to the contrary, no movement or individual speaks for all Muslims."[5] All too commonly, such comparisons also tend to suggest some predetermined end for Islam's "Reformation" or, more problematically, suggest there are only two choices available for the Islamic world: "a state of crisis, dangerously careening to the right" or a "reformation" that leads to "democracy" and good relations with the West.[6]

Despite these hesitations, one aspect of current transformation in Islamic thought has struck me as raising interesting parallels with the Protestant Reformation: the hermeneutical focus of many of the reformers. According to Wilhelm Dilthey, "the most urgent mission of a Lutheran scholar [in the sixteenth century] was to refute the Catholic doctrine of Tradition, which had been just newly formulated." This doctrine asserted "the claim of Tradition to govern the interpretation . . . against the Protestant principle of the Bible's supremacy."[7] Following Dilthey, Hans-Georg Gadamer credits the Reformation—namely, Luther and his view that *Scriptura sui ipsius interpres* (Scripture is its own interpreter)—with the "rediscovery" of the hermeneutical method in the modern period.[8] Gerald Bruns cites Martin Luther's first lectures at the University of Wittenberg as the "symbolic moment of transition between ancient and modern hermeneutics"; Luther's modernism is said to have begun when he asked the students to study not the "notes and commentaries handed down from the Church Fathers," but to "begin the history of interpretation over again, this time to get it right."[9]

Certainly, a number of Islamic reformist thinkers have defined their projects as aimed at the revision of interpretive approaches to the sacred texts in the Islamic tradition—and many have also discovered the political implications of such a "rediscovery." In order to address the question of a presumed emerging

"Islamic Reformation," this chapter explores the ways in which contemporary Muslim intellectuals have employed various interpretive strategies in heeding the call for reform. I approach the object of reform—Islam—in the manner suggested by Talal Asad—as "discursive tradition that includes and relates itself to the founding texts of the Qur'an and the Hadith"[10]—in order to suggest, in the manner of Dilthey, that the most urgent mission of an Islamic reformist thinker in the modern period has been to refute the Islamic doctrine which asserts the claim of Tradition to govern the interpretation.

Islamic Orthodoxies and New Methods of Reform

Two "orthodoxies"[11] of Sunni Islam contribute to the notion that the certain literature from the Islamic heritage (*turath*) should govern all interpretations of the fundamental sources of Islamic doctrine. The first is the notion that the gates of *ijtihad* were declared closed in the thirteenth century—an orthodoxy that contributes to a sense of fixity and finality in the traditional schools of law and basic principles of Islamic doctrine. Calls for "opening the gates" were heard in the nineteenth century, as reformists thinkers such as Sayyid Jamal al-Din al-Afghani, Muhammad 'Abduh, Rashid Rida, Sayyid Ahmad Khan, Muhammad Iqbal, and others began reasserting the need for practicing *ijtihad* in order to vindicate and defend Islam, to adapt it to the new times, to reconcile it with science, and to counter the onslaught of European powers.

However, a second Islamic orthodoxy predates the first and has proven to be in many ways the more trenchant and controversial of the two: the notion of the Qur'an as the uncreated, unmediated word of God.[12] According to Islamic tradition, the Qur'an is to Muslims as Christ is to Christians: not just human but divine. Earlier reformist thinkers have focused on prying opening the "gates of *ijtihad*," but it has taken a new generation of reformist thinkers to begin the process of walking decisively through those gates—and in doing so they have challenged aspects of this second orthodoxy. These Muslim scholars have been characterized by Wael Hallaq as forming a "new phenomenon in Islam": "religious liberalism."[13] In his study of *Islamic Legal Theories*, Hallaq distinguishes between "religious liberalism" and "religious utilitarianism." According to Hallaq, while both trends seek "the reformulation of legal theory in a manner that brings into successful synthesis the basic religious values of Islam, on the one hand, and a substantive law that is suitable to the needs of a modern and changing society, on the other,"[14] they are distinguished by the methods they use to pursue this end. Religious utilitarians—among whom Hallaq places many of the nineteenth century reformists—revise an early and medieval juristic principle of public interest (*maslaha*) as a central component of their interpretive approach. Religious liberals "discard altogether the principles developed by the traditional jurists" in order to develop a new hermeneutic altogether.[15]

It is when the departure from traditional methods of studying the Islamic heritage is seen in conflict with the Islamic orthodoxy regarding the uncreatedness of the Qur'an that the Islamic liberals studied here have been most open to criticism from traditional social forces and suffered such consequences as censorship (in the case of the Syrian professor of civil engineering, Muhammad Shahrour), forced divorce (in the case of the Egyptian professor of Islamic studies and Arabic literature, Nasr Hamid Abu Zayd), and death threats (in the case of the Egyptian professor of philosophy, Hassan Hanafi). It should be apparent to the reader that I wish to draw attention to the presumed *sin*fulness of efforts to offer a reformist *Sinn* (German: sense, meaning, interpretation) of religious texts. Hanafi has expressed skepticism about the possibility of interpreting the Qur'an without political implications.[16] The focus on some of the more controversial reformists reveals the political and theoretical stakes faced both by the interpreters and their detractors, as well as the close relation between hermeneutics and politics. The concluding section of the chapter returns to the question of whether we might view these projects and the response they have generated as a "growing Islamic fundamentalism" or an "emerging Islamic Reformation."

Although it is the focus on constructing a new hermeneutic for approaching religious texts that distinguishes religious liberalism as a trend distinct from religious utilitarianism, as we will see below, the thinkers' particular formulations are also what create divisions within this grouping. Hallaq identifies the "main thrust of the liberalist approach" as "understanding revelation as both text and context."[17] Following Hallaq's lead, I examine the theoretical and political issues involved in Shahrour, Abu Zayd, and Hanafi's textualization and contextualization of the Qur'an before comparing their hermeneutical methods, as such, and the political commitments their approaches reveal.

The Qur'an as Text

The Qur'an is the central cultural text in Islamic societies. Mohammed Arkoun has referred to the Qur'an as a Closed Official Corpus (*le fait coranique*): "*official*" in the sense that it "resulted from a set of decisions taken by 'authorities' recognized by the community"; "*closed*" on account of the fact that it is no longer permissible "to add or subtract a word, to modify a reading in the Corpus now declared authentic."[18] Arkoun identifies two results of the reification of revelation in written, textual form. First, it placed Muslims in a "hermeneutic position; that is to say, they needed to *interpret* the holy texts to derive law, prescriptions, and systems of belief and nonbelief." Second, it "banalized" the Qur'an "by putting it within the reach of everyone, particularly after the invention of paper and then the printing press."[19] Yet, it is precisely the status of the Qur'an as "text" that is questioned in much of contemporary Islamist discourse.[20]

The question of the textuality of the Qur'an has come to be thought of as bearing directly upon another, originally largely semantic, question in Islam: whether the Qur'an is the eternal and uncreated Word of God or whether it is God's Word put into human language and, hence, created. This debate dates back to at least the late eighth century, when those who believed the Qur'an was the uncreated Word of God stood against those who believed the Qur'an was a fiat (*kun*) created in time, like anything that is not God himself. The latter view is most closely associated with the Mu'tazila school, which was instated as the "official state doctrine" by the 'Abbasid caliph al-Ma'mun (813-833), who instituted a *mihna* (inquisition) against opponents of the doctrine. However, a few decades later another 'Abbasid caliph, al-Mutawakkil (847-861), supported by more traditionalist theologians such as Ahmad ibn Hanbal (780-855), revoked the doctrinal position put in place by al-Ma'mun. The ensuing doctrine, which ultimately came to be associated with Abu al-Hasan al-Ash'ari (873-925) and his followers, maintained "that the eternal Qur'an was not so much the physical text in the form of a script, but rather an 'inner speech' (*al-kalam al-nafsi*), an indivisible mental act of God."[21] This view agreed, to some extent, with the Mu'tazila understanding of the material Qur'an rendered in Arabic as created speech. However, whereas the Mu'tazilas maintained that this necessitated the employment of human reason on what is given in the Qur'an, the Ash'aris held that the Qur'an was similar (*tashbih*) to an eternal and uncreated divine speech, and thus must be understood literally, "in its apparent meaning. It is not permissible to understand it in any other way."[22] The Mu'tazila never regained the status they held under al-Ma'mun and, according to one assessment, "by the twelfth century, in part for political reasons that had nothing to do with the intellectual merits of either position, the Ash'arite view had emerged as the orthodoxy in Sunni intellectual circles."[23] This orthodoxy has continued to impede efforts aimed at approaching the Qur'an as a text and as a historical, cultural, and literary phenomenon.

Many of the ideas held by the Mu'tazila have continued to be influential, especially for Islamic reformists. According to the Iranian reformist thinker, Abdolkarim Soroush, "Muhammad Arkoun, Hasan Hanafi, Hamid Naser Abu Zeid [*sic*] and others" are attempting to "revive the *Mu'tazilite* school of thought."[24] However, few reformists have proven willing to associate their reforms with a revival of Mu'tazila ideas.

Of the thinkers discussed here, Abu Zayd places himself most firmly in the Mu'tazila tradition:[25]

I started my academic career provoking the rational trend of Classical Islamic thought as expressed in the Mu'tazila writing as well as in Ibn Rushd and others, but gradually I applied my critical methodology realizing that neither the Mu'tazila nor Ibn Rushd's discourse will sufficiently be able to address our present issues. The question became how to follow up and develop their achievements to address our own problems in the 21st century. The same critical approach should be applied to the modern Islamic reformists, such as Afghani and 'Abdu. So, it would be more appropriate to consider me a critical continuation of the Islamic rationalism, both classical and modern, in the present context.[26]

Most reformists admire the Mu'tazila emphasis on human reason. Yet even in Abu Zayd's thought one detects a certain ambivalence toward the Mu'tazila as intellectual forebears. This is even more apparent in the writings of other liberal reformists. For example, Rahman praises the Mu'tazila theory of rational ethics, yet suggests they were prone to certain excesses and extremes.[27] Arkoun credits the Mu'tazila for contributing to making certain issues "thinkable"—"such as the issue of God's created speech,"[28] while he also deems their focus on human reason as "dogmatic" in its "logocentrism."[29] Shahrour merely mentions the Mu'tazila as one of several competing groups viewing for influence when "the Caliphs and the official Ulema attempted to impose a singular official meaning of Islam which was derived under the influence of circumstantial settings."[30]

Abu Zayd sums up the political-hermeneutical implications of the debate in the contemporary context as follows:

If the Qur'an is not eternal, it is then created in a certain context, and the message it contains has to be understood in that context. This view leaves room for the reinterpretation of religious law, because God's word has to be understood according to the spirit, not according to the letter. The final consequence is that public authorities and/or society are entitled to the prime role in the interpretation and application of the law. If, on the other hand, God's word is eternal, uncreated, and immutable, the idea of reinterpretation within new situations becomes anathema; there is no difference between the letter and the spirit of the divine law, and only theologians are entitled to the prime role in its maintenance and guardianship.[31]

For Abu Zayd, the denial of the textuality of the Qur'an forces strict adherence to a literal, fixed meaning of the text that is accessible only to a religious authority that claims status as the guardian of the Islam. As a result, those who assert the historicity and textuality of the Qur'an have "infringed upon the *'ulama*'s last bastion, thus violating the latter's uncontested authority in their own domain."[32]

Of the thinkers discussed here, Abu Zayd most directly takes on the issue of the createdness of the Qur'an, putting forth the bold view that once revealed to Muhammad, the Qur'an entered human history and became a text like any other text. This claim provided the basis for one of the main charges brought against Abu Zayd in the court case that sought to separate him from his wife on the basis of his alleged apostasy. The plaintiffs in the case quote from Abu Zayd's 1992 book, *Naqd al-Khitab al-Dini* (Criticism of Religious Discourse):

> The text, from the moment it descended to the Prophet, was transformed from being a divine text to a human conception, because it changed from revelation to an utterance. The Prophet's understanding of the text represents the first stages of the transformation to and interaction of the text with a human mind. . . . The Prophet's understanding of the text does not coincide with the reality of the text itself, because this would confuse the stable and the changing, the eternal and the relative, the divine and the human.[33]

The plaintiff asserts that this passage "proves that the defendant denies the divinity of the Qur'an and emphasizes that it is a human text." Yet, this assessment is somewhat misleading. Abu Zayd does not deny the divine origin of the Qur'anic revelation. Nor does he wish to confuse the revelation (*wahy*) Muhammad received, with inspiration, in the sense held by Christians' understanding of the Bible—the former is verbal, whereas the latter is nonverbal.[34] Rather, he maintains that "the state of the original sacred text is a metaphysical one about which we can know nothing except that which the [physical] text itself mentions and which always comes to us via a historically changing humanity."[35] This claim about the inherent unknowability of God would not be contested by many Muslims. However, the hermeneutical implications that Abu Zayd draws from this epistemological claim—that is, the desacralization involved in reading the Qur'an as a literary text—runs counter to the dominant conception of the Qur'an.

Abu Zayd's distinction between a metaphysical "text" and the physical text of God's Revelation is not unlike that made by Muhammad Shahrour, a recently retired civil engineering professor from Syria, who is perhaps most ardent in his call for a return to "the original text of God's revelation to the Prophet."[36] Shahrour distinguishes between "two distinct aspects" of what has become known as the Qur'an. Shahrour applies modern linguistic analysis to distinguish among various words used in the Qur'an:[37]

> The first is prophecy [*nubuwa*], which describes the difference between reality and illusion. The second [is the message, *risala*, and] concerns law and moral behavior. In this sense, the first aspect is objective and thus independent of human acceptance. The second aspect is subjective, depending on human knowledge, as, for example, in the human capacity to know right from wrong.[38]

This distinction is also apparent in the title of Shahrour's first book, in which he outlines his method of studying the Qur'an, *al-Kitab wa al-Qur'an* (The Book and the Qur'an). Shahrour argues that "the Qur'an is not the whole book, but the parts of it that deal with prophecy. The *shari'a* (Islamic law) is the message, which is called 'The Mother of the Book.' The Qur'an and 'The Mother of the Book' [*umm al-kitab*], prophecy and message, were put together and this is *al-kitab* (the book)."[39] While the book (*al-kitab*) does contains *mutashabih* (similar, as in similar to the Qur'an) verses, which are figurative and allegorical, it also contains *muhkam* (prescribed) verses which appear clear to a reader employing good reasoning.[40] These two types of verses correspond to the Qur'an (prophecy) and *Umm al-kitab* (message), respectively. Shahrour also identifies a third type of verse, which he refers to as "*tafsil*" (or *tafsil al-kitab*, explanations of the book).[41] The *tafsil* verses are neither to be accepted as fact nor treated as law, but are provided by God so that we understand how to interpret the book. According to Shahrour, these verses are few and can easily be identified by their direct references to the book (*al-kitab*).

By distinguishing between *mutashabih* and *muhkam* verses, Shahrour is able to further distinguish between the objective and inevitable prophecy, on the one hand, and the message of how one is to live a moral life, in relation to which human beings retain a free will, on the other.[42] The former takes the form of figurative verses that talk about resurrection, heaven, hell, prophecy, and miracles. These cannot be challenged and remain unaffected by human actions, but, he argues, constitute the largest portion of the book. The latter, *muhkam* verses, represent only a very small portion of the book that consists of clear prescriptions and deals with laws regarding things like divorce, inheritance, punishments, charity, and rituals. This distinction allows Shahrour to retain the Muslim creed regarding the divine and eternal nature of the Qur'an, while treating the message as text—that is, as subject to interpretive analysis or *ijtihad* (independent individual judgment).

Hanafi claims to avoid the question of the createdness of the Qur'an through "a declaration of modesty, a recognition of limitations"[43] that prefaces his discussion of hermeneutics. However, like Abu Zayd and Shahrour, Hanafi characterizes religious texts in a way that allows the interpreter to approach the Qur'an using modern methods of textual analysis. Hanafi suggests that the question of the nature of the revelation be put "in brackets": "it does not matter for the interpreter." According to Hanafi, "the Qur'an is considered to be like any other text. It is subject to interpretation as a legal code, a literary work, a philosophical text, a historical document, etc. All texts are subject to the same rules of interpretation. The distinction between the holy and the profane is not related to general hermeneutics, but to religious practice."[44] Thus, Hanafi's "hermeneutics" starts with Revelation as text, for "hermeneutics . . . means the science which describes the passage of revelation from the state of words, to the stage of the world. It is the science of the process of revelation from the latter to reality or from Logos to Praxis, and also the transformation of revelation from the Divine Mind to human life."[45]

However differently stated, the hermeneutical implications of each account are similar in the sense that through asserting the textual character of the Qur'an they affirm the applicability, even necessity, of hermeneutics generally. In Paul Ricoeur's words, they posit a written text that awaits a reading.[46] Further, for each of these thinkers the textual character of the Qur'an allows for the non-coincidence of the author's (God's) creation and the text's meaning. To paraphrase Ricoeur again, the tie between the speaker and discourse, though not abolished, is distended and complicated.

Despite the similarities among the treatments of the Qur'an as text, it is interesting to note that the initial religious-political response to their work has not been comparable. Certainly part of the reason for this lies in the different national contexts in which these writers exist. Shahrour suggests that he escaped persecution of Abu Zayd's type because he "was fortunate to be living in Damascus, Syria."[47] But the fact that both Hanafi and Abu Zayd wrote their works in Egypt and that many of Hanafi's writings predate Abu Zayd's by at least two decades seems to suggest at least two other possible explanations: either the implications of these writings were not fully understood until read closely by the committee of professors who reviewed Abu Zayd's work for promotion or[/and?] the ideas did not or were not deemed to pose so substantial a threat until recently. Neither of these explanations is complete, in and of itself, however, since the question of the createdness of the Qur'an has long been debated in Islamic political thought; and this is not the first time that those asserting the nontraditional view have been persecuted.

In one of the rare cases in which one of these scholars has addressed the thought of either of the other two,[48] Abu Zayd suggests a third possible explanation: that not all interpreters of the Qur'an have been completely forthcoming in their analysis. Abu Zayd has accused his colleagues for intentionally sacrificing "scientific analysis" to "pragmatism." Abu Zayd first cites the case of the nineteenth century Egyptian thinker Muhammad 'Abduh who in the first edition of his treatise *Risalat al-Tawhid* adopted the notion of the non-eternal, created Qur'an, but then "retreated" to the opposite view in the second edition. He then goes on to assert that "such a pragmatic analysis and interpretation is unfortunately the prevailing and commonly practised not only in the so called *Islamist* political discourse but also in the so called *enlightenment* discourse." In regard to the latter he singles out Hanafi and Shahrour, as well as Mahmud Muhammad Taha (a Sudanese mystic who was executed in 1985) for "pragmatically" avoiding the question of the createdness of the Qur'an.[49] Yet, in May 1997 Hanafi was attacked by the Front of al-Azhar *'ulama* for, among other things, his approach to interpreting the religious heritage. Interestingly, at least one of Hanafi's critics cited him with not only "denying the [teachings] of the holy Qur'an," but also with having "brought up the likes of another *murtad* [apostate], Nasr Abu Zaid."[50] So too, Shahrour clearly states in at least one work that "the Qur'an, as a word, is created."[51] Ultimately, the similar hermeneutical implications of their textualization of the Qur'an prove more significant than any differences that exist at the level of articulating that textualization. At the same time, there *are* a number of important differences among Hanafi, Abu Zayd, and Shahrour in regard to how they contextualize the text.

Revelation as Context

Shahrour calls upon Muslims to read the text *"as if Muhammad had passed away yesterday."*[52] Shahrour intends this appeal to affirm the timelessness of the Qur'an. Yet it also asserts that contemporary readers should reject the intermediary role traditionally played by the legacy of scholarship on the Qur'an in order to undertake a direct re-reading of the text, "freed from all historic additions that were added arbitrarily by authoritarian or sultanic governors."[53] In regard to the rulings of the Islamic jurisprudence (*fiqh*) in particular, Shahrour argues that the lack of agreement among the jurists and the stamp of the society in which these rulings were made render them an inappropriate basis for contemporary Islamic society.[54]

Shahrour also reduces the claim of other traditional points of reference to guiding the interpretation. For example, while Shahrour acknowledges the exemplary life of the Prophet Muhammad, he maintains that Muhammad only provides a model for contemporary Muslims in the sense that he lived according to God's message, "not in the sense that we must make the same choices that he made. The life of the Prophet is the first historical variant of how the rules of Islam can be applied to a tribal society of the time. But it is the first variant, not the only one or the last one."[55] This means that not only the *sunna* (the traditions and sayings {*hadith*} of the Prophet), but also the first community of believers, held up by most Muslims as the ideal community, remain tangential to a contemporary reading of the Qur'an. One should emulate the Prophet Muhammad and his contemporaries as interpreters, but not in their interpretation: just as they "read" the received revelation in the light of their intellectual capacities and worldviews, so should contemporary Muslims read the text in light of theirs. In addition, Shahrour believes that the advancement of knowledge puts each generation of Muslims in a better situation to understand the Qur'an than their predecessors—both generally and in terms of understanding it for their own purposes.

Shahrour understands Islam as embodying "the capacity to evolve through legislation and morality."[56] He takes this to mean that the interpreter need not pay heed to the context of the Revelation's initial reception and compilation; rather, the text evolves over time with each subsequent interaction with a community of interpreters. The most important context for interpreting the Qur'an is, in his view, the current political and intellectual context of an existing *umma*, and the only limits on interpretation within that context are provided by the language of the text itself and the requirements of the modern age to which the text must speak.

In contrast, at least part of Abu Zayd's project focuses largely on a critical-historical analysis of precisely these contexts Shahrour bypasses. He defines his project as "develop[ing] a hermeneutics of the Qur'an based on its specificities as text"[57] and asserts the necessity of analyzing and interpreting the Qur'an (and the "authentic" traditions of the Prophet Muhammad) "within the contextual background in which they were originated."[58] Since God, the sender of the message that was codified in the Qur'an "cannot be the object of scientific study," Abu Zayd argues that "the scientific introduction to the analysis of the Qur'anic text should be through its contextual reality and culture." Thus, Abu Zayd approaches the meaning of the text by looking at the "socio-political conditions which embraced the actions of those who were addressed by the text, and which embraced the first receiver of the text [the Prophet Muhammad]" and the "culture" of the initial reception, which he defines as "the world of concepts which are embodied in the [Arabic] language [of the time]."[59]

Abu Zayd also identifies another "side" relevant to the Qur'an's emergence of the text: "the other side of it is that the Qur'an has become a producer of a new culture."[60] The first "side," the original context, according to Abu Zayd, reveals the "meaning" (ma'na) of the text, "which is fixed because of its historicity." Yet, the second "side," reveals the "significance" (maghza) of the text, "which is changeable."[61] A study of both contextual facets is necessary for an understanding of the "true message of the Qur'an." Abu Zayd asserts that the (contemporary) significance must be "firmly related and rationally connected to the meaning" through a process of "decoding" the Qur'an and its interpretations throughout history with the aim of "extract[ing] the 'historical' and 'temporal,' which carry no significance in the present context." Thus, for example, when in regard to women's inheritance, the text specifies that women should inherit half of that of men, we must take into consideration that this was written at a time when women were unjustly not allowed to inherit.[62] The orientation of the text—its significance—points to advancing women's just inheritance. Since women are now equal, Abu Zayd argues, they should inherit equally today. Abu Zayd believes this process of determining the text's significance is necessary in order to understand the ways in which the Qur'an has served ideological and political purposes in the past and in order to expose and resist its manipulation by such powers in the present. "The position of women expressed in the Qur'an, in general, is relatively and historically speaking progressive. It could be easily reinterpreted according to what it reveals by its historical and contextual significance in order to unfold its implication and, therefore, to foster the basic principle of equality inherit in the concept of justice."[63]

Hanafi also incorporates a critical-historical dimension into his example. Like Abu Zayd, Hanafi is critical of most expressions and forms of Islam throughout its history. At the same time, Hanafi is concerned with affirming

Islam's universalism. Like Shahrour, Hanafi claims that not only is the question of how the text came about unimportant, but the entire prehistory of a given text is irrelevant to the interpreter. According to Hanafi, when approached in the proper manner, the Qur'an can provide the basis for a universal consciousness. The issue for Hanafi is not "how," but "why" and "what for." He agrees with Abu Zayd that "the text is only a vehicle for human interests and even passions" and that "the conflict of interpretation is essentially a socio-political conflict, not a theoretical one." But Hanafi further maintains that "each interpretation expresses the socio-political commitment of the interpreter"; and he views this as not only unavoidable, but consciously seeks to put that fact to particular use in his own work.[64]

It is not only in Hanafi's writings that we find some measure of correspondence between the type of approach employed and the desired political-hermeneutical aim of those who employ it. Though less explicit, the relationship between interpretative approach and political inclinations of each, and the differences among them, is apparent in the thought of all three thinkers.

Divergent Approaches, Competing Political Projects

As mentioned above, Shahrour employs a linguistic approach to delineate various meanings of the words found in the Qur'an. It is on this basis that Shahrour distinguishes between that which is "divinely sanctioned (*halal*) and the divinely prohibited (*haram*) and the humanly forbidden (*mamnu'*)," maintaining that "the basic tenet of Islam is that everything not specifically prohibited is permitted."[65] Further, he claims that "the only authority for divine prohibitions (*tahrim*) is God"; that is, neither the Prophet Muhammad or any other human being may "make lawful the divinely forbidden or forbid the divinely sanctioned." However, an existing Islamic community is free to allow or disallow based on God's message.

In order to understand how Muslims are to be guided in their regulation of that which falls outside of the realm of the divinely forbidden, Shahrour applies what he has learned from engineering and the sciences to cast light on his linguistic analysis. Examining the Qur'anic verses containing the words "curvature" (*hanifiyya*) and "straightness" (*istiqama*), Shahrour argues that the two are not so much intended as opposites, but as two paths coexisting in an important relation to each other. *Istiqama* means following a straight path, whereas *hanafiyya* means deviating from a straight path. Shahrour locates curvature in the material world where the laws of physics confirm that all things in nature move, not in straight lines, but in curves, like the orbit of planets. Since straightness is not a quality of the natural world, it can only be divinely ordained. Human beings exist within this curvature, yet they look to God to guide them along "the right path" (Qur'an 1:5).[66]

Shahrour identifies the straightness that God provides for human beings as they move about in their curvature through his "Theory of God's Limits." Human legislation is permitted in the space between the limits (*hudud*) that the "Book" sets for all human actions (and natural phenomena). Shahrour distinguishes at least six different types of limits.[67] For example, Shahrour maintains that the various punishments specified in the Qur'an represent the upper limit setting the maximum penalty for a given offense, not some prescribed absolute penalty. So too, the Book sets a number of minimum penalties for various crimes. Within these limits human societies are not only free, but obligated, to develop and adapt their legislation according to the conventions and sociopolitical circumstances of their society. Thus, Shahrour's approach involves a form of the hermeneutical circle that relies upon dialogical interaction between citizens in a particular context within the limits set by the linguistic structure of the text of the Qur'an.

As such, Shahrour sees his theory of God's Limits as revealing the modern meaning of what he views as a core Qur'anic principle: *shura* (consultation). Consultation is what is called for to work out the legislative questions for a modern polity within the limits set by God; and the outcome of that process of consultation will need to be relative to the particular curves—the particular social, economic, and political circumstances—of each political community. Shahrour's own political convictions are clearly revealed as he concludes that "in our time, genuine *shura* means genuine pluralism of points of view, *and* democracy."[68]

Abu Zayd advocates a literary approach to exegesis (*al-minhaj al-'adabi lil-tafsir*), one that involves both linguistic analysis and a rationalist hermeneutics that ultimately results in his privileging a metaphorical interpretation over a more literalist one. In regard to the former, Abu Zayd focuses on the historical reality of the texts of revelation (the Qur'an and *hadith*), for example, arguing that these texts were not given all at once in a complete form, but were formed over a span of time,[69] and focusing on whom the message addresses, for example, the people of Mecca or Medina, or believers, nonbelievers or humanity as a whole.[70] This allows the reader to understand the way in which, for example, prohibitions against certain types of drinks (such as wine) or foods (such as pork) took place gradually.

However, Abu Zayd's approach is not limited to historicizing the texts and recovering the original meaning (*dalalatuhu al-asliyya*) of specific commandments by placing them in the context of their formation. Much of Abu Zayd's analysis is also aimed at the significance of the Qur'an for the present, as indicated by the example of women's just inheritance equal to men, discussed in the previous section. According to Abu Zayd, "there is misunderstanding of so many Qur'anic concepts caused by the de-contextualization of these verses."[71] Understood in context, Abu Zayd finds support in the Qur'an for a concept of economic, social, and political forms of justice in many ways in keeping with

European notions of welfare liberalism. For example, Abu Zayd maintains the necessity of justice for atheists and polytheists based on the concept of *fitra*, nature or, more precisely here, the original healthy constitution of the nature of humans as created by God. As Abu Zayd interprets it, *fitra* is the divine law inherent in every human soul, a "self-inherent eternal contract" that is based on a form of individual responsibility. Each individual must recognize that contract by "being sincere and 'just' to his inherent nature. Unsaved souls are those who have not been able to do 'justice' to them selves; they fail to recognize their own inner *fitra*, so, it is their own responsibility."[72] Determination of those "saved" and "unsaved" is a matter not of one's particular faith or of one's standing within the community, but of "absolute Divine Justice" and "the absolute responsibility of every human for his eternal destination."[73]

The concept of *fitra* goes some way toward mitigating a literal reading of the Qur'anic passages that might be read to suggest external human enforcement of right belief, such as 2:191, which states that polytheists should be slain whenever they are found. But Abu Zayd adds that this passage must also be understood in the context of "the behavior of the prophet," which reveals that "the early Muslims did not consider that those verses convey an obligatory religious duty" and offers "substantial proof against the literal understanding."[74]

So too, an understanding of both historical context and textual (Qur'anic) evidence reveals that the aim of *zakat* (alms) and the criticism of *riba* (usury) are interconnected "as a basic ground for attaining socio-economic justice."[75] Abu Zayd points out that *zakat* is incumbent upon all Muslims as one of the basic pillars of Islam and cites numerous passages that call for Meccans to "recognize that in their wealth and possession there is 'certain right' for the needy and the unprivileged."[76] It is the context of this call for the establishment of a more just distribution of wealth that Abu Zayd argues the condemnation of *riba* must be understood, as those charity-givers who help the needy are contrasted with those practitioners of usury who would exploit them. The many Islamic banks that have been established throughout the world have "ignored the nature and circumstances within which usury was forbidden; they also ignored totally its purpose." As a result, these banks deal no more in justice than banking systems based on interest and have become "a false issue of Islamization void of the central Qur'anic concept of justice."[77]

The examples regarding polytheists and usury suggest another facet of Abu Zayd's contextualization of the Qur'an: a critical analysis of the way in which contemporary Islamists intentionally use a selective interpretation of religious texts. For example, in his *Critique of Religious Discourse* (*Naqd al-khitab al-dini*), Abu Zayd places the discourse of official Islam (embodied in those religious figures who are prominent on television and in newspapers and other official channels) and the banned "extremists" on the same political level by maintaining that they all use the accusation of *takfir* (unbelief) as a political tool against their opponents and as a means of censoring any form of knowledge of religion that is not derived from the *'ulama* or "recognized religious sources."[78] In addition to what he views as the ideological manipulation of Islamic religious texts in the form of such institutions as the Islamic investment companies (a scandal in which Egyptian investors lost their life savings), Abu Zayd criticizes such projects as the "Islamicization of knowledge," an attempt to Islamicize such fields as economics, medicine, and literature which, he argues, contributes to censorship and other forms of oppression and corruption. Only by clarifying the contemporary context and the practical-political goals that motivate contemporary interpreters can one distinguish the ideological content of those interpretations from the original meaning and develop a more "objective" (*mawdu'i*) and "scientific" (*'ilmi*) understanding of the text's significance. One must historically recontextualize the message in order to differentiate between the text's historical and universal aspects.

Charles Hirschkind rightly points out a tension in Abu Zayd's work between his "negative judgment on the utility of past history" and his "call for Muslims to continue to interrogate the Qur'an." In other words, if past examples cannot guide us in confronting present problems, what significance can the text hold for the present? However, Hirschkind focuses too much on Abu Zayd's historicization of the text at its origin, neglecting the other side of hermeneutical inquiry that Abu Zayd identifies: significance that reaches into the present.[79] Abu Zayd's point is not to render religious texts meaningless for the present (something he maintains orthodox Islam does by privileging past interpretations over new ones), but to bridge that historical horizon through an allegorical or metaphorical interpretation of the text that privileges the spirit over its letter, that reads it more like poetry than a guide to political action. While arguably Abu Zayd may not have resolved the tension Hirschkind identifies, he does point to an ongoing dialectic that addresses this tension.

In contrast to Abu Zayd's attempt to situate religious texts according to their historical reception, Hanafi criticizes a "word-for-word" or "longitudinal" approach to the Qur'an; that is, interpretations that view the Qur'an as a series of distinct verses to be understood sequentially. The problem with such a view is that it breaks up the discussion of major themes and it "lacks a coherent ideology or global worldview that links particular aspects of the theme in a global view."[80] Instead he calls for a "thematic method" for interpreting the Qur'an. This method has several rules including: 1) the interpreter must be committed to reform; 2) he or she must address the text as one seeking a solution to a problem; 3) the verses relevant to the interpreter's interest are compiled according to themes. Thereafter the interpreter proceeds by 4) classifying the linguistic forms in order to analyze the text's content; 5) building the theme as an ideal structure from the linguistic forms; 6) diagnosing the factual reality of the current social reality; 7) comparing the ideal set out by the text and the reality presented by the social context; and 8) undertaking action to overcome the distance between the ideal world and the real world.[81]

Hanafi characterizes his method of thematic interpretation as "phenomenological." What he means by this is that all meanings exist in relation to particular, concrete, historical existence. As such, he places human beings and their needs at the center of his interpretation in order to reconstruct "Islamic culture at the level of consciousness in order to discover subjectivity. Instead of being theocentric, it becomes anthropocentric. [It] provides the method for analyzing lived experiences and describing the process of linguistic pseudo-morphology."[82] Hanafi's interpretation of Islamic texts aims at what he himself has characterized as an Islamic equivalent to Latin America's liberation theology.[83] In response to those who lay emphasis on Islam as "submission," Hanafi maintains that the term *aslama* yields "a double act of negation and affirmation" as it asserts a surrendering to God but rejects the yielding to any other power and states his intention as reasserting

> the other aspect of Islam, intentionally hidden, namely the rejection, the opposition, and the revolt, taking into consideration the actual needs of the Muslim Masses. . . . The ambiguity of the word Islam is consequently a reflection of the dual socio-political structure of society: Islam as both submission to the political power and the upper classes, and as revolt by the ruled majority and the poor classes.[84]

Hanafi seeks to contribute to a revolutionary religious consciousness aimed at facing modern conditions of inequality, poverty, underdevelopment, domination, westernization, and alienation. His interpretation of Qur'anic passages asserts the necessity of "the implementation of social justice and the foundation of an egalitarian society," one based on public ownership of such things as "agriculture, industry, [and] mining" since verse 59:7 dictates: "What God has bestowed on His Apostle (and taken away) from the people of the townships— belongs to God, to this Apostle and to kindred and orphans, the needy and the wayfarers."[85] Hanafi's Islamic society is also one in which the "application of the Law is an individual and societal commitment," and in fulfilling that commitment, "the scholars of the law" play a central role as the "guardians of the city": "They are the educators of the people and the conscience of the rulers. They can denounce the tyrants and mobilize the masses. Their words are substantiated by their deeds. Their ideas correspond to their feelings. The revolution of Transcendence [what Hanafi calls God] is a revolution of Thought, of knowledge and of Science."[86]

Although both Abu Zayd's and Hanafi's political-hermeneutical projects aim at "objectively" re-reading the tradition as it "really happened" and at exposing the ideological and political circumstances that led to particular articulations of that tradition, the two are very much at odds in another sense. While Abu Zayd focuses on breaking free of the selective re-reading of past interpretations in the present, he is also concerned with setting forth *methodological limits* of certainty and interpretive scope for religious texts, due to the profound influence they wield over political and social life. In other words, Abu Zayd would *not* leave Islamic texts open to interpretation by all according to their social, political and/or ideological needs, but continues to temper even his "metaphorical" or "allegorical" interpretation with an understanding of historically embedded meanings (hence the tension discussed above). In this sense, Abu Zayd mitigates (but, again, does not eliminate) the extent to which religious texts can inform and generate present action.

Hanafi, on the other hand, holds that there is no single interpretation, nor is any one interpretation right or wrong. Rather, in Hanafi's view, "the validity of an interpretation lies in its power."[87] By "power" Hanafi means not only explanatory power (which Abu Zayd also seems to seek), but also a form of political power relevant to the present. This is seen in a dialectical method commonly used by Hanafi to resolve conflicting interpretations in the religious heritage, aptly summed up by Esposito and Voll: "the line of argument starts from a description of an apparent clash or contradiction between two positions or concepts. Hanafi then posits a third alternative that resolves the contradictions and does so in a way that creates an imperative for human action."[88] The "power" of this interpretation lies not only in its resolution of the conflict, but also for the way in which it provides a basis for social action that addresses the needs of contemporary life. In fact, Hanafi's method manifests itself as a form of the hermeneutical circle that emphasizes the relationship between the interpretation of the Qur'an and political action guided by a particular understanding of social justice. Hanafi baldly announces that "interpretation is an ideological weapon"[89] and puts forth his own "thematic interpretation" as a means of finding a scriptural basis for sociopolitical activism.

An Islamic Reformation?

A direct return to the text that privileges the individual reasoning of the interpreter to the history of interpretations involves a bypassing or break with religious authorities, past, and present. Further, the increasingly textual quality of Islam—that is, the focus on (re)reading religious texts as a method of religious reform, as well as the increased literacy and expanded media forms[90]— seems to opened the doors of *ijtihad* fairly wide by contributing toward an increase in both the plurality of hermeneutical strategies, as well as the possibility of an increase in the number of members of the Islamic *umma* (community) permitted to exercise their individual reasoning in engaging with and revising the religious tradition they have inherited. The plurality of hermeneutical approaches further seems to foster a plurality of approaches to social and political reform in Islamic societies. Each of these reforms is significant and suggests compelling similarities with the Reformation in Europe.

Yet, the hermeneutical point of similarity between Reformations might define the limits of the comparison; and, further, it might suggest more questions about the general received view of the European Reformation (which tends to be seen as unified and leading toward a secular modernism) than answers it might provide about the character of particular Islamic reformists. Too often comparisons between East and West obscure these writers' intentions by presuming that Islamic thought is following a historical trajectory parallel to or the same as that of the West (in either case, the assumption is that Islamic civilization must "catch up"). This is seen in a number of scholars' attempts to assess the extent to which various Islamic liberals have "succeeded" in putting forth secular visions of Islam. In fact, only Abu Zayd has claimed to be doing so and then only in his most recent writings, after his legal troubles in Egypt.[91]

In the cases of Shahrour and Hanafi, I think it is more accurate to describe their efforts as aimed at reformulating Islamic jurisprudence and at reconstructing a universal Islamist consciousness, respectively, not at separating religion from the political realm (legally or ideologically). Both Shahrour and Hanafi have criticized Arab secularist projects. According to Hanafi, reform undertaken "in the name of secular ideologies of modernization . . . will have always partial successes and several setbacks, one step forward and two steps backward, as modern history of Muslim societies would tell."[92] According to Shahrour,

> since religion has an important normative role in the Middle East societies, it is impossible to ignore it. Liberals tried to do so, and they failed in their attempt to transport Western political formula to the Arab/Muslim states. Marxists wanted to impose a secularization, to deconstruct religion, and also failed. Anyhow, there could be secularism in the Arab or Islamic states, but it would not solve anything. The Middle East problem is not secularism, but democracy. The secular state has been there for seventy years, it was imposed upon society and it did not work.[93]

Shahrour further suggests that whereas those who hold on to past readings of the Qur'an risk rendering the text irrelevant, his reading will provide the proof of the continued relevance of Islam: "Those who genuinely fear the consequences of departing from traditional interpretations of Islam have lesser faith than those who are more confident in the viability of Islam in the modern world."[94] This is a sentiment expressed above by Abu Zayd as well. Further, a commitment to the Islamic notion of *tawhid* (unity of God, humanity, the universe) asserted by all three of the thinkers (though the extent to which this remains true in Abu Zayd's case in light of his recent championing of secularism and the extent to which this notion is understood differently by each of the thinkers remain to be studied) suggests that the intended outcome of these reformist projects is unlike the process of modernization articulated by Habermas as a process of increasing separation of value spheres and corresponding worlds.

It is also possible that the points of comparison Abu Zayd suggests—with classical Islamic thinkers and movements, such as the Mu'tazila, the Ash'ara, Ibn Rushd, and Ibn Tufayl, as well as with earlier modern Islamist reformists, such as Jamal al-Din al-Afghani, Sayyid Ahmad Khan, or Muhammad 'Abduh—could prove to be more enlightening as to what this current debate will amount to. As Hirschkind rightly notes, "the last few hundred years have seen an ongoing attempt to adapt the conceptual resources of Islam in order to accommodate, understand, and achieve practical mastery over a reality that is organized increasingly by discourses whose historical locus and most formidable bases of power lie in the West."[95] Whether the hermeneutics of Abu Zayd, Hanafi, and Shahrour represent only the latest manifestation of that ongoing project or depart from it in some significant respect remains to be seen. What is clear is that the possibilities are multiple and the outcome is not entirely in the hands of the reformists, but must vie with competing visions of Islam. And as history has shown time and again, often what comes as a result of a thought or action does so above the intentions of the actor or doer. As Max Weber noted: "the cultural consequences of the [Protestant] Reformation were to a great extent . . . unforeseen and even unwished-for results of the labors of the reformers. They were often far removed from or even in contradiction to all that they themselves thought to attain."[96] Whether the political-hermeneutical projects of contemporary reformists give birth to a Reformation, and the outcome of such a Reformation should it truly take root, remains to be seen.

Notes

1. An earlier version of this paper was presented at the 2001 American Political Science Association Annual Meeting in San Francisco.

2. Fazlur Rahman, "Revival and Reform in Islam," in *The Cambridge History of Islam*, ed. P. M. Holt, Ann Katharine Swynford Lambton and Bernard Lewis (Cambridge, England: Cambridge University Press, 1970), 640, his emphasis.

3. Abdullahi Ahmed an-Na'im, *Toward an Islamic Reformation: Civil Liberties, Human Rights, and International Law* (Syracuse: Syracuse University Press, 1996); Robin Wright, "Two Visions of Reformation," *Journal of Democracy* 7 (1996): 64-75; Saqir Abu Fakhr, "Trends in Arab Thought (Interview with Sadek Jalal al-Azm)," *Journal of Palestine Studies* 27 (1998): 70.

4. See Dale F. Eickelman, "Inside the Islamic Reformation," *The Wilson Quarterly* 22 (1998): 80-89. Paul Donnelly, "Tariq Ramadan: The Muslim Martin Luther?" *Salon.com*, February 15, 2002, www.salon.com/people/feature/2002/02/15/ramadan/ index_np.html (30 March 2003).

5. Eickelman, "Inside the Islamic Reformation," 89.

6. "Is the Muslim world in a state of crisis, dangerously careening to the right, or is it undergoing a 'reformation'? This is the most important question of our era concerning the interaction between Islam and the West and all the consequences that flow from it."

Toby E. Huff, "Rethinking Islam and Fundamentalism (Review Essay)," *Sociological Forum* 10 (1995): 501.

7. Wilhelm Dilthey, "The Rise of Hermeneutics," in *The Hermeneutic Tradition: From Ast to Ricoeur*, ed. Gayle L. Ormiston and Alan D. Schrift (Albany: State University of New York Press, 1990), 107-8.

8. Hans-Georg Gadamer, *Truth and Method* (New York: Continuum, 1993), 173-75.

9. Gerald L. Bruns, *Hermeneutics Ancient and Modern* (New Haven: Yale University Press, 1992), 139, 140.

10. Talal Asad, *The Idea of an Anthropology of Islam* (Washington, D.C.: Center for Contemporary Arab Studies, Georgetown University, 1986), 14.

11. Many scholars oppose the application of the term "orthodoxy" to Islam. While one cannot speak of "Islamic orthodoxy" according to the paradigm of the medieval Christian regime, if one follows Asad in understanding orthodoxy as "a (re)ordering of knowledge" that "seeks to construct a relation of discursive dominance" in governing what forms "correct" Islamic practice, it is possible to identify an orthodox discourse since at least the twelfth century. See Asad, *Genealogies of Religion*, 210-11. Certainly, many contemporary reformists perceive "the rise of a Sunni orthodoxy in Islam as a body of doctrine and practice [that] owes itself largely to earlier sectarian developments." See Rahman, *Revival and Reform in Islam*, 30-68. For a discussion of medieval Muslim heresiographers who gave rise to this discourse, see Alexander Knysh, "Orthodoxy and Heresy in Medieval Islam: An Essay in Reassessment," *Muslim World* 83 (1993): 48–67. According to the most renowned Islamic heresiographer, al-Shahrastani (1086-1153), "Ash'ari's views and methods were adopted by the Orthodox." See Muhammad al-Shahrastani, *Muslim Sects and Divisions: The Section on Muslim Sects in "Kitab al-milal wa 'l-nihal,"* tr. A. K. Kazi and J. G. Flynn (London: Kegan Paul International, 1984), 78.

12. A third orthodoxy—that Muslims are required to uphold the *sunna* of the Prophet as a complement to the Qur'an—is also undertaken by Shahrour's reformist project, but could not be dealt with here at length. See my "Shahrour's Reformation: Toward a Democratic, Pluralist, and Islamic Public Sphere," *Historical Reflections/Réflexions Historiques* (forthcoming 2004).

13. Wael B. Hallaq, *A History of Islamic Legal Theories: An Introduction to Sunni Usul al-Fiqh* (New York: Cambridge University Press, 1997), 214.

14. Hallaq, *A History of Islamic Legal Theories*, 214.

15. Hallaq identifies Muhammad Sa'id 'Ashmawi, Fazlur Rahman, and Muhammad Shahrour as "religious liberals." Hallaq includes among the "religious utilitarians" such figures as Rashid Rida, 'Abd al-Wahhab Khallaf, 'Allal al-Fasi, and Hasan Turabi.

16. Hassan Hanafi, "Method of Thematic Interpretation of the Qur'an," in *The Qu'ran as Text*, ed. Stefan Wild (Leiden: E. J. Brill, 1996), 195-211.

17. Hallaq, *A History of Islamic Legal Theories*, 231.

18. Mohammed Arkoun, *Rethinking Islam* (Boulder, Colo.: Westview Press, 1994), 33.

19. Arkoun, *Rethinking Islam*, 33, his emphasis.

20. Abu Zayd reports that a professor at al-Azhar protested against the very use of the term *"nass"* (text) in reference to the Qur'an. "His argument was that: 'In all the history of Islam, no one has used in reference to the Qur'an words other than those God himself used in the Qur'an. None of the *'ulama* has ever dealt with the Qur'an as a text,

may God forgive this, because it is an orientalist European (not Islamic or Arabic) way of dealing with the Qur'an.'" See Nasr Hamid Abu Zaid, "Divine Attributes in the Qur'an: Some Poetic Aspects," in *Islam and Modernity: Muslim Intellectuals Respond*, ed. John Cooper, Ronald L. Nettler, and Mohamed Mahmoud (London: I. B. Tauris, 1998), 192.

21. Ebrahim Moosa, "Introduction," in Fazlur Rahman, *Revival and Reform in Islam: A Study of Islamic Fundamentalism* (Oxford: Oneworld, 2000), 12.

22. *Abu'l-Hasan 'Ali ibn Isma'il al-Ash'ari's al-Ibanah 'an Usul ad-Diyanah* (The Elucidation of Islam's Foundation), tr. Walter Conrad Klein (New Haven, Conn.: American Oriental Society, 1940), 57.

23. Sohail H. Hashmi, "Islamic Ethics in International Society," in *Islamic Political Ethics: Civil Society, Pluralism, and Conflict*, ed. Sohail H. Hashmi (Princeton: Princeton University Press, 2002), 151.

24. Abdolkarim Soroush, "Keynote Address," Center for the Study of Islam and Democracy 2nd Annual Conference, Georgetown University (April 7, 2001), at www.islam-democracy.org/SoroushAddress.shtml (15 May 2003). Soroush claims that "[these reformists'] goal is to show that rationality per se is acceptable in the Islamic milieu, even when not based on religion. They strive to demonstrate that there are values that need not be derived from religion."

25. Soroush claims that it was "the Mu'tazilite ideas" of Abu Zayd's work that "ran afoul of the *Ash'arite* sensibilities of the Egyptian religious establishment." Soroush, "Keynote Address."

26. "Chess Interview: The Egyptian thinker and Qur'an researcher Professor Nasr Abu Zayd," January 28, 2003, www.anis-online.de/pages/_orient-online/Nasr-Abu-Zayd.htm (30 March 2003).

27. Rahman, *Revival and Reform in Islam*, 60-62.

28. Mohammed Arkoun, *The Unthought in Contemporary Islamic Thought* (London: Saqi Books, 2002), 13.

29. Mohammed Arkoun, *Essais sur la Pensée Islamique* (Paris: Maisonneuve et Larose, 1984), ch. 5.

30. Muhammad Shahrour, "The Case against Modernity," *ISLAM21* 5 (August 1996), www.islam21.net/pages/keyissues/key1-4.htm (30 March 2003).

31. Abu Zaid, "Divine Attributes in the Qur'an," 198.

32. Ami Ayalon, *Egypt's Quest for Cultural Orientation* (Tel Aviv: The Moshe Dayan Center for Middle Eastern and African Studies, 1999). Abu Zaid also advances a semantic argument about the changing meaning of *nass* (text) to account for the opposition to the notion of the textuality of the Qur'an on the part of many contemporary Muslim scholars. See, for example, Abu Zaid, "Divine Attributes in the Qur'an," 192-93.

33. Nasr Hamid Abu Zayd, *Naqd al-Khitab al-Dini (Critique of Religious Discourse)* (Cairo: Sina lil-Nashr, 1992), 93-94. From the excerpts of the verdict of the court of appeals, published on the Legal Research and Resource Center for Human Rights in Cairo's website, www.geocities.com/lrrc.geo/Zaid/appeals.htm (30 March 2003), with my minor corrections of their translation of Abu Zayd's work.

34. Abu Zaid clarifies the distinction in "Chess Interview."

35. Abu Zaid, *Naqd al-Khitab al-Dini*, 93.

36. Mohammad Shahrour, "The Divine Text and Pluralism in Muslim Societies," *Muslim Politics Report of the Council on Foreign Relations* 14 (July-August 1997): 3.

37. Shahrour has studied modern linguistics with the Syrian linguist, Ja'far Dik al-Bab, who wrote the preface and contributed a concluding section on "Asrar al-lisan al-'arabi" (Secrets of the Arabic Language) to Muhammad Shahrour, *al-Kitab wa al-Qur'an: Qira'a Mu'asira (The Book and the Qur'an: A Contemporary Reading)* (Damascus: al-Ahli lil-Taba'a wa al-Nashr wa al-Tawzi', 1990), 19-27, 741-819.

38. Shahrour, "The Divine Text," 4.

39. Muhammad Shahrour, "Reading the Religious Text—A New Approach," *Islam21* 21 (December 1999): 2-3.

40. Shahrour, *al-Kitab wa al-Qur'an*, 103-11.

41. Shahrour, *al-Kitab wa al-Qur'an*, 113-21.

42. Shahrour, *al-Kitab wa al-Qur'an*, 112-13.

43. Hanafi, "Method of Thematic Interpretation of the Qur'an," 202.

44. Hanafi, "Method of Thematic Interpretation of the Qur'an," 202.

45. Hasan Hanafi, *Religious Dialogue and Revolution: Essays on Judaism, Christianity, and Islam* (Cairo: Anglo-Egyptian Bookshop, 1977), 1.

46. Paul Ricoeur, "The Model of the Text: Meaningful Action Considered as a Text," in *Understanding and Social Inquiry*, ed. Fred R. Dallmayr and Thomas A. McCarthy (South Bend: University of Notre Dame Press, 1977). Hanafi studied with Ricoeur while in Paris.

47. Shahrour, "The Divine Text," 8.

48. It is unfortunate that none of these thinkers has engaged the others' works. Further, of the three, only Abu Zayd has undertaken a systematic response to his critics. See, for example, Nasr Hamid Abu Zayd, *al-Tafkir fi Zaman al-Takfir: Didda al-Jahl wa al-Zayf wa al-Khurafah (Thinking in the Age of Declaring Unbelievers: Against the Ignorance, Falsity and Superstition)* (Cairo: Sina lil-Nashr, 1995) and the interviews and documents compiled in Burhan Khalil Zurayq, ed., *Nasr Hamid Abu Zayd bayn al-Takfir wa al-Tanwir: Hiwar, Shahadat, Watha'iq (Abu Zayd Between Unbelief and Enlightenment: Interviews, Testimonies and Documents)* (Cairo: Markaz al-Mahrusah, 1996). Shahrour maintains that he had to choose between spending his time responding to his many critics or continuing to develop his ideas further, and he chose the latter option. See Shahrour, "The Divine Text," 8. His second book does contain a short discussion of some of the critical responses to his first book. Muhammad Shahrour, *Dirasat Islamiyyat Mu'asira fi al-Dawla wa al-Mujtama' (Contemporary Islamic Studies on State and Society)* (Damascus: al-Ahli lil-Taba'a wa al-Nashr wa al-Tawzi', 1994), 15-46.

49. Nasr Hamid Abu Zaid, "Islam and Human Rights" (Cairo: Egypt, Legal Research and Resource Center, 1998), geocities.com/~lrrc/Zaid/zaidhr.htm (30 March 2003).

50. Richard Engel, "Apostate Ruling Endangers Professor," *Middle East Times*, 11 May 1997, metimes.com/issue19/eg/03apostate.htm (25 May 2003).

51. "All beings in the universe are words of God, because his words have no language. The word 'sun' for God is the sun itself. The world 'sun' in English is shams in Arabic, but for God 'sun' is the sun itself. So, the Qur'an, as a word, is created, because if it is not created, it means that God is an Arab." Shahrour, "Reading the Religious Text," 2-3.

52. Muhammad Shahrour, *al-Kitab wa al-Qur'an*, 41; Shahrour, *Dirasat Islamiyyat Mu'asira*, 23; Shahrour, "The Divine Text," 7.

53. Shahrour, "The Divine Text," 7.

54. Muhammad Shahrour, "Islam and the 1995 Beijing World Conference on Women," in *Liberal Islam: A Source Book*, ed. Charles Kurzman (New York: Oxford University Press, 1998), 141. "Since the interpretation of the legislative verses and their application is a human activity, it is fallible and can only be relatively right. What is valid for one era may be irrelevant to another in spite of the fact that the sanctity of the legislative verses is eternal. For this reason, no human interpretation or practice ought to be accepted without discussion as it carries relative historical characteristics and will vary from one period to another, and differ from one society to another." Muhammad Shahrour, "Proposal for an Islamic Covenant," *Islam21* (May 2000), www.islam21.net/pages/charter/may-1.htm (30 March 2003).

55. Shahrour, "The Divine Text," 8.

56. Shahrour, "Islam and the 1995 Beijing World Conference on Women," 141-42.

57. Abu Zayd, "Chess Interview."

58. Abu Zaid, "Divine Attributes in the Qur'an," 200.

59. Abu Zaid, "Divine Attributes in the Qur'an," 199.

60. Abu Zaid, "Divine Attributes in the Qur'an," 199.

61. Abu Zaid, "Divine Attributes in the Qur'an."

62. Nasr Abu Zayd, *Mar'ah fi Khitab al-Azmah* (Women in the Discourse of Crisis) (Cairo: Dar al-Nusus, 1994).

63. Nasr Abu Zayd, "The Qur'anic Concept of Justice," *polylog. Forum for Intercultural Philosophizing* 2 (2001): 18.

64. Hanafi, *Religious Dialogue and Revolution*, 202.

65. Shahrour, "Islam and the 1995 Beijing World Conference on Women," 141.

66. Shahrour, *al-Kitab wa al-Qur'an*, 439.

67. Shahrour, *al-Kitab wa al-Qur'an*, 453-64. Shahrour's account of how he formulated his theory of God's Limits is telling of his method of combining modern science and linguistics in an analysis of the Qur'an:

> One day an idea occurred to me when I was lecturing at the university of civil engineering. I was talking about how to make compaction roads. We have what we call a proctor test, in which we sample and test soil used in fills in embankments. In this test, we exclude and interpolate. We have x and y. A hyperbole. We have a basic risk. We plot a curve and put a line on the top of it. This line is the upper limit. Then I thought of the concept of "God's limits" (*hudud illah*). I returned here to the office and opened the Qur'an. Just as in mathematics we have five ways of representing limits, I found five cases in which the notion of God's limits occurred. What they have in common is the idea that God has not set down the exact rules of conduct, but only the limits within which societies can create their own rules and laws. I have written about ideas of integrity (*al-istiqama*) and universal moral or ethical codes. The ideas was a first only a footnote in my last chapter, but I saw that it applied to my main argument, so I corrected everything that I wrote about *hudud illah* in the book in order to be consistent. Then I considered my argument to be sound.

Dale F. Eickelman, "Islamic Religious Commentary and Lesson Circles: Is There a Copernican Revolution," in *Commentaries = Kommentare: Aporemat* 4, ed. Glenn W. Most (Göttingen, Germany: Vandenhoeck & Ruprecht, 1999), 143.

68. Shahrour, "The Divine Text," 8.

69. Nasr Hamid Abu Zayd, *Mafhum al-Nass: Dirasah fi 'Ulum al-Qur'an (The Concept of the Text: A Study of the Sciences of the Qur'an)* (Cairo: al-Hayat al-Misriyyat al-'Amma lil-Kitab, 1990), 25-26.

70. Abu Zayd, *Mafhum al-nass*, 70.

71. Abu Zayd, "The Qur'anic Concept of Justice," 22.

72. Abu Zayd, "The Qur'anic Concept of Justice," 11.

73. Abu Zayd, "The Qur'anic Concept of Justice," 13.

74. Abu Zayd, "The Qur'anic Concept of Justice," 22-23.

75. Abu Zayd, "The Qur'anic Concept of Justice," 32.

76. Abu Zayd, "The Qur'anic Concept of Justice," 30.

77. Abu Zayd, "The Qur'anic Concept of Justice," 33.

78. Abu Zayd, *Naqd al-Khitab al-Dini*.

79. Charles Hirschkind, "Heresy or Hermeneutics?: The Case of Nasr Hamid Abu Zayd," *The American Journal of Islamic Social Sciences* 12 (1995): 468-69.

80. Hanafi, "Method of Thematic Interpretation of the Qur'an," 196. This essay is also found in Hassan Hanafi, *Islam in the Modern World: Vol. I—Religion, Ideology and Development* (Cairo: Anglo-Egyptian Bookshop, 1995), 407-28.

81. Hanafi, "Method of Thematic Interpretation of the Qur'an," 203-5.

82. Hassan Hanafi, *al-Din wa al-Thawra fi Misr: 1952-1981 (Religion and Revolution in Egypt)* (Cairo: Maktabat Madbuli, 1988), 231.

83. For a summary of Hanafi's understanding of his own role in the founding of "a social phenomenology applied to the Muslim world," see Hassan Hanafi, "Phenomenology and Islamic Philosophy," in *Phenomenology World-Wide: Foundations, Expanding Dynamisms, Life-Engagements—A Guide for Research and Study*, ed. Anna-Teresa Tymieniecka (Boston: Kluwer Academic Publishers, 2002), 318-21.

84. Hassan Hanafi, "Islam and Revolution," in *The Philosophical Quest: A Cross-Cultural Reader*, ed. Gail M. Presbey, Karsten J. Struhl, and Richard E. Olsen (Columbus, Ohio: McGraw-Hill, 2000), 184.

85. Hanafi, "Islam and Revolution," 186-87 and fn. 13.

86. Hanafi, "Islam and Revolution," 189.

87. Hanafi, "Method of Thematic Interpretation of the Qur'an," 210.

88. John L. Esposito and John Obert Voll, *Makers of Contemporary Islam* (Oxford: Oxford University Press, 2001), 85.

89. Hanafi, "Method of Thematic Interpretation of the Qur'an," 203.

90. See the contributions to *New Media in the Muslim World: The Emerging Public Sphere*, ed. Dale F. Eickelman and Jon W. Anderson (Bloomington: Indiana University Press, 1999).

91. For example, Shahrour argues that "a religious state was created in Iran and it is the strongest state in the Middle East, because it emerged from religion and appealed to the culture of the people among whom it appeared." See Shahrour, "Proposal for an Islamic Covenant." This and other passages suggest that Clark is mistaken in viewing Shahrour as "stating the secular case for Islam." See Peter Clark, "The Shahrour Phenomenon: A Liberal Islamic Voice from Syria," *Islam and Christian-Muslim Relations* 7 (1996): 337-41.

92. Hanafi, "Islam and Revolution," 190.

93. Shahrour, "Proposal for an Islamic Covenant."

94. Shahrour, "Reading the Religious Text," 2-3.

95. Hirschkind, "Heresy or Hermeneutics," 465.

96. Max Weber, *The Protestant Ethic and the Spirit of Capitalism* (London: Routledge, 1992), 48.

4

Critics Within: Islamic Scholars' Protests against the Islamic State in Iran[1]

Charles Kurzman

Unlike Catholic Christianity, there is no established church in Islam. This endlessly repeated statement may be true in many senses. But in at least one sense it is misleading. Virtually since the emergence of a specialized class of Muslim religious scholars (*'ulama*), Muslim rulers have selected among them, establishing a hierarchy of one sort or another, enforcing the edicts of some and repressing others. This system was institutionalized in the Ottoman office of the *Seyh-ül-Islam*, the chief religious authority of the empire, who was appointed and dismissed at the discretion of the sultan. Since the break-up of the Ottoman Empire, Muslim-majority countries have continued the practice under various rubrics. Each of these countries has its official religious authorities, and almost every country also has religious scholars in opposition who deride the official authorities as puppets of the regime.

These official authorities are not full-fledged churches in the Catholic Christian sense, embodying the message of God. They have no equivalent of the papal claim to infallibility. And they do not, generally, direct state administration in the way that the pope used to do.

That is, until the coming of the Islamic Republic of Iran. It is a common complaint among Iranians that the revolution of 1979 turned Shi'i religious scholars into an established church in many senses of the term. The constitution of the Islamic Republic guarantees *'ulama* various leadership positions in the state. It grants the *vali-ye faqih*, or jurist-ruler, ultimate authority in state affairs, which reach inevitably into religious affairs as well. And, though it is not written in the constitution, the *vali-ye faqih* and his followers have sought to cast themselves as the sole legitimate interpreters of the true faith. This turn of events has arguably turned many Iranians against the *'ulama*. The usual run of

79

grievances with the state now serves as fodder for anticlericalism, exacerbated by the clerics' mismanagement of various sectors of the state.

Perhaps more surprising is the emergence of protest against the Islamic state within the community of Islamic scholars, on Islamic grounds. These critiques cover numerous substantive issues. When presented with the equivalent of cease-and-desist orders from the state's clerical leaders, the critics then faced a fundamental issue of established churches: whether the supreme religious authority has the right to squelch debate among qualified religious scholars. Statements to the negative have landed the critics in jail.

On this issue, oppositional clerics in Iran are engaged in a classic Reformation project. Martin Luther, too, began with substantive critique of the Christian Church, namely abuses in the sale of indulgences. He was naïve enough to send his famous "Ninety-Five Theses" to a nearby archbishop, and an explanation of the theses to the pope himself, in hopes that the Church would see fit to reform itself. Top religious officials took Luther's position as an attack on the authority of the pope, and responded that religious scholars such as Luther were heretics if they criticized the policies of the Church. Only then did Luther press the argument that the pope was fallible and that scholarly debate could not be curtailed.[2] In Luther's words, "The pope [wrongly claims that he] has the power to interpret and to teach Holy Scripture according to his will and allows no one to interpret it otherwise than he wants."[3]

Luther and many of his fellow Reformists were academics; so too are many Shi'i 'ulama. For both groups, the question of authority involved a clash of institutional norms: the established church's norm of hierarchy versus the scholarly norm of permanent debate. For both groups, the critique of religious authority raised the specter of relativism, which they countered with another, conflicting scholarly norm of expertise.

Seminary Norms of Debate

The norms of authority and interpretive originality strain against one another in the seminaries of Shi'i Islam, the predominant form of Islam in Iran. Authority is institutionalized through the office of marja'iyat (literally "model-hood"), by which a leading religious scholar is held to be a model for his (never her) followers. This scholar, called marja'-e taqlid (or marja', for short), is simultaneously a "source of imitation" for his followers, a collector of tithes, an administrator of seminaries and other philanthropic enterprises, and a seminary instructor—a combination of scholarly and administrative authority that can be used to silence critics within the seminary community. The peak of marja'iyat, prior to the founding of the Islamic Republic in 1979, was achieved in the 1950s by Ayatollah Hossein Borujerdi, whose scholarly eminence was so outstanding that he was recognized as the sole marja' of his era. Imam—then known as

Ayatollah—Ruhollah Khomeini held political and theological opinions at variance with Borujerdi. Khomeini, far more critical of the Iranian monarchy than Borujerdi, believed that religious scholars should be more politically engaged than Borujerdi deemed appropriate. Borujerdi, as *marja'*, had the authority to keep Khomeini from writing and teaching his heterodox opinions, and actually placed Khomeini under virtual house arrest. "There was no coming and going in the *imam*'s house," a supporter recalled. "His relations with everyone were cut off."[4] After Borujerdi's death in the early 1960s, there was some discussion among Islamic reformers about the drawbacks of centralized religious authority.[5] But Khomeini drew the opposite conclusion from his experience of Borujerdi's authority, arguing that centralized authority is useful and justified, if in the right hands.

The head of state of the Islamic Republic of Iran, the jurist-ruler, is in essence a *marja'* whose scholarly and administrative authority was extended from the seminary to the state. According to Khomeini's proposal for an Islamic state, expounded in exile in 1970, the jurist-ruler "will possess the same authority as the Most Noble Messenger (upon whom be peace and blessings) in the administration of society, and it will be the duty of all people to obey him."[6] This analogy to the Prophet Muhammad was not written into the Constitution of the Islamic Republic of Iran, but the constitution nonetheless claims for the jurist-ruler unspecified powers with regard to "leadership of the affairs and guidance of the people," plus certain specific administrative responsibilities.[7] In practice, during Khomeini's tenure in this office, from 1979 until his death in 1989, the jurist-ruler's proclamation on any subject was generally acknowledged to be the final word of debate.[8] Indeed, Khomeini's followers considered his judgment so authoritative that even his unofficial statements, including passing remarks recalled by his family and associates, were compiled in several volumes after his death so that the devout might seek guidance from his words[9]—a practice that harkens back to the millennium-old compilations of statements and deeds (*hadith*) of the Prophet Muhammad and (in Shi'i Islam) his divinely guided descendants, the twelve imams.

The second norm of interpretive originality has coexisted with the norm of *marja'iyat* in Shi'i seminaries since late eighteenth century, when Usuli scholars won out over their Akhbari rivals. Usulis held that Shi'is must not rely on the ancients for their religious guidance, but must seek out contemporary authorities—a position that generated both the institution of *marja'iyat* and a model of interpretive change, as each generation of seminarians was encouraged to establish distinct interpretations.[10] Anthropologist Michael Fischer, doing fieldwork in Qom in the mid-1970s, noted that "all teaching is on a dialectic principle of argument and counterargument in which students are encouraged to participate insofar as they have the preparation to do so." In advanced classes, "One calls upon these standard sources [basic works taught in earlier classes] as well as all other sources one can command: the opinions of various scholars, the etymology of technical terms, the context of Qur'anic and hadith injunctions, the validity of the sources, and one's own ingenuity."[11] Roy Mottahedeh's account of the life of a religious scholar in the seminaries of Qom and Najaf includes many such instances. "We'll come to that point tomorrow," the instructor would say when a student's critique stumped him.[12] In a conversation in Tehran in 1999, three advanced seminary students from Qom confirmed for me that debate such as this remains the ideal in seminary settings, though some instructors are more open to criticism than others. Indeed, as in Western academic settings, the rewards of promotion and respect are in principle granted to young scholars who are especially creative and original. These students are encouraged to continue their studies, receive teaching positions and administrative duties, and earn their license (*ijaza*) to engage in interpretation (*ijtihad*). No doubt there are limits to the arguments that may be presented and the extent that authorities may be critiqued, but the seminary system is designed to cultivate—among advanced practitioners, at least—the same culture of critical discourse sometimes associated with Western universities.[13]

The openness of debate is reflected, for example, in periodicals such as *Seminary Circle* (*Howzeh*) and *Critique and Perspective* (*Naqd va Nazar*), published at the seminaries of Qom. Since the late 1980s, *Seminary Circle* has published articles critical of seminary practices, for example, their emphasis on obscure issues of ritual purity, failure to address modern problems, and atrophying of *ijtihad*.[14] *Critique and Perspective*, founded in 1994, has published discussions of religious pluralism; articles on or by Søren Kierkegaard, John Rawls, and other Western philosophers; and a paper by Nasr Hamid Abu Zayd, the Egyptian scholar who had recently been declared an apostate by the Egyptian Supreme Court, at the behest of Islamists who objected to his approach to Qur'anic studies.[15] In addition, *Critique and Perspective* published a debate and responses on "The Role of Time and Place in the Process of *Ijtihad*," introducing potentially relativistic themes from studies in the sociology of religion.[16]

The openness of seminary discourse has also been reflected in a scholarly debate in 1997 over the position of the jurist-ruler. Ata'ollah Mohajerani, the reformist minister of culture and Islamic guidance, contrasted the openness and courtesy of the seminary milieu with the bitter acrimony of newspaper politics:

> Dr. Mehdi Ha'eri Yazdi, the son of the late Shaykh 'Abdolkarim Ha'eri, the founding member of the Qom Theology School, has written a book about criticism of *velayat-e faqih*. One can approach this book and this view in two ways. One approach is a journalistic approach, with slandering and accusations from the top to the bottom of editorials. The other approach is the one that has been adopted by the publication of the Islamic governing body of the secretariat of the school, in charge of which is Ayatollah [Ebrahim] Amini. That is to say that Mr. Mehdi Ha'eri writes an article [in this periodical] and Ayatollah ['Abdollah] Javadi-Amoli replies. The publication itself is the publication of the Secretariat of the Experts, that is, the Assembly of Experts, which is the most important foundation for protecting the

cause of *velayat-e faqih*. This publication, too, refers to both sides
with praise, and the publication announces that this is a method that
we have used with experts.[17]

Mohajerani was later forced to resign by hard-liners in the Iranian parliament
who were less sympathetic to open debate.

The two seminary norms, authority and originality, are in conflict over the
question of closure: Does scholarly authority include the right to end a debate?
Do qualified scholars have the right to continue debate? Even Khomeini, with
his extensive popularity—the Constitution self-referentially notes that it received
"a majority of 98.2% of those who had the right to vote"[18]—never fully achieved
scholarly obedience. The most famous case in point involved Ayatollah Kazem
Shari'atmadari, who was widely considered to be Khomeini's senior in terms of
religious scholarship. Shari'atmadari consented only grudgingly to Khomeini's
revolutionary movement against the monarchy, stating openly that he preferred a
constitutional monarchy, as stipulated in Iran's 1906 constitution, to an Islamic
republic.[19] After the monarchy fell, Shari'atmadari lent his support to a political
movement based in Azerbaijan, his home province, which challenged the
ascendancy of Khomeini's followers in the new republic. In response,
Khomeini's seminary allies set out to discredit Shari'atmadari, including as part
of their campaign the publication of a book entitled *Shari'atmadari in the Court
of History*, which recounted what it called a lifetime of collaboration with the
monarchy.[20] Soon thereafter, Khomeini in essence defrocked Shari'atmadari and
had him held under house arrest until his death in 1985. Other clerical critics of
the regime, including some who had been active in organizing the revolution,
were silenced in various ways or retired from political life.[21]

Khomeini's hand-picked successor, Ayatollah 'Ali Khamene'i, lacking his
predecessor's prestige, has had greater difficulties in attempting to squelch
seminary debate. His scholarly standing was insufficient to assume the role of
marja', a constitutional qualification for the jurist-ruler, so parliament revised
the constitution in the month after Khomeini's death, removing this stipulation so
that Khamene'i could legally serve as jurist-ruler.[22] A decade later, scholarly
debate was proving to be such a threat to the regime that an intelligence officer
warned a foreign reporter to "stop interviewing clerics in Qom."[23] Rather than
appeal to the "Court of History" to silence this debate, Khamene'i relied instead
on a new institution, the Special Clergy Court, which Khomeini had established
in 1987 to deal with crimes by religious scholars.[24] Almost all of the figures to
be discussed in the next section were brought before this court and found guilty.

The Critics' Case against Closure

The five high-profile cases reviewed in this chapter share a common strand:
Each of these religious scholars ran afoul of the authorities on some substantive

political issue, was pressured to shut up in deference to the ruling interpretation, and subsequently adopted a more radical position rejecting the jurist-ruler's right to insist on interpretive closure.

These scholars' positions were not originally subversive of the political order, but were intended rather to strengthen it by elaborating what they considered proper Islamic reforms. These reforms—allowing the contest of political parties, in Montazeri's work, for example, or granting further rights to Iranian women, in Sa'idzadeh's work—would save the Islamic Republic from becoming sterile, unpopular, and ineffective. The Islamic reasoning for these positions involved the same sacred sources and scholarly forms of exegesis as other scholars used in proposing policies that Khomeini and Khamene'i had endorsed. In keeping with seminary discourse, their conclusions took the form "Islam says . . . ," where the ellipsis refers to an act that they argued was either required or allowed. This form of reasoning corresponds to the tropes I have called the "liberal *shari'a*" and the "silent *shari'a*": the former argues that *shari'a* (revealed law) requires Muslims to adopt liberal positions; the latter argues that *shari'a* allows Muslims to devise their own solutions to certain sorts of issues on which revelation in silent.[25]

Facing silencing by closure, these scholars shifted to a different form of reasoning, one far more radical in its implications. They may have chosen to emphasize the continuity of their thought, but their new form of argumentation rejects the form, "Islam says . . . ," in favor of the form, "X says that Islam says . . . ," where X is a fallible human being whose understanding of Islam may be contested by other fallible human beings. This form corresponds to what I have called the "interpreted *shari'a*," which holds that interpretation of divine revelation is a human project and thus eternally plural.[26] In Iran, this form of argumentation has been associated for a decade with the work of philosopher Abdolkarim Soroush, who also came to this position after confrontations with closure—being fired from his university position, refused air-time on radio and television, and roughed up by paramilitary units. Soroush says he "recognized religious knowledge as human and treated it as a humanly gained wisdom. The implication of this thesis is that the disciplines of the *Hawzeh* [seminaries] are as prone to criticism and skepticism (by the experts, of course) as are the rest of the sciences."[27] Soroush is not among these "experts," however, despite his tremendous erudition and familiarity with seminary scholarship, because he lacks an advanced seminary degree. Perhaps for this reason, or because he is a political "hot potato," the scholars considered here do not, to my knowledge, cite Soroush favorably, though there are reports that Soroush's work is quite popular among seminarians.[28]

Fall 1997: Hossein-'Ali Montazeri

For a decade, Ayatollah Hossein-'Ali Montazeri was Khomeini's hand-picked successor as jurist-ruler. A long-time follower of Khomeini, he was one of the initial proponents of including the position in the constitution.[29] In the mid-1980s, however, he began to disagree with his mentor, Khomeini—specifically over the execution of a relative of Montazeri's, and more generally over the direction in which the Islamic Republic was being taken. In private letters that became public several years later, Montazeri complained to Khomeini that the security police were "far worse" than under the monarchy.[30] "The time has passed," Montazeri said, "when we can declare people infidel, when we can excommunicate them or when we can level various accusations at them because they declare some truths. One cannot turn back the clock. The revolution released certain forces from bondage."[31] Montazeri's scholarly work continued to support the position of *vali-ye faqih*, the jurist-ruler, but urged that the office be subject to popular election and limited to general direction rather than detailed supervision of the government.[32] Months before his death in 1989, Khomeini asked for Montazeri's resignation as successor, and replaced him with Khamene'i. Under Khamene'i's leadership, Montazeri continued his public complaints, leading to a brief arrest in 1993. In November 1997, after the presidential elections that brought a new set of faces into the government on a reform platform, Montazeri gave a lecture in Qom that urged the jurist-ruler and his allies to leave the reformists alone:

> If two or three people sit and make all the decisions for the country, it will not progress in the contemporary world. "Republic" means "government of the people." Of course I should mention: In the same way that people must have political parties, they must have organizations, at the time of elections they should be awake, they should choose people intelligently, insightfully, and independently. Along with all this the "rulership of the jurist" is also mentioned in our Constitution. But its meaning is not jurist-ruler as jack of all trades—that would make the "republic" meaningless. The jurist-ruler, with the conditions and responsibilities that are specified for him in the Constitution, his main responsibility—what is most important—is to supervise the affairs of society so that the policies of society do not deviate from the standards of Islam and truth. "Jurist" refers to this.

> In the communist government of the Soviet Union, when they wanted to run the government on the basis of Marxism and Communism, they put in power a party ideologue who could implement the political, cultural, and economic plans for the country on the basis of the doctrines of Communism. Well, this is only natural. However, while we want our country to be run on the basis of Islam and religious law, it is also a republic. All people must participate, there must be political parties, there must be organizations. . . .

They [the jurist-ruler and his allies] have no right to set aside someone who is competent. Someone who is competent from a religious perspective, and also knowledgeable in political, cultural, and economic matters, who is not sycophantic, who is independent— who is like the late Modarres, who single-handedly stood up to the entire government of Reza Khan. . . .

You [Khamene'i] are not of the rank and stature of a *marja'*. . . . The Shi'i *marja'iyat* was an independent spiritual authority. Do not try to break the independence of the *marja'iyat* and turn the seminary circles into government employees. That is harmful to the future of Islam and Shi'ism. Whatever your supporters may claim, you give no evidence of filling the scholarly position of Imam [Khomeini], may God have mercy upon him. Do not allow the sanctity and spirituality of the seminary to become mixed up with the political work of [government] agencies.[33]

In addition to challenging Khamene'i's credentials and accusing him of a hostile takeover of the seminaries, Montazeri managed in the course of a brief speech to liken the jurist-ruler to a Communist dictator and to Reza Khan, founder of the Pahlavi dynasty that the Islamic Republic overthrew. The basis of the comparison was the jurist-ruler's involvement in the governance of the country, abrogating the contributions of popular and scholarly leaders. The phrase, "They have no right to set aside someone who is competent," refers primarily to newly elected parliamentary representatives whom the jurist-ruler and his allies wished to remove from office—but we may guess that the reference is also to Montazeri himself, who was set aside by Khomeini.

Supporters of Khamene'i ransacked Montazeri's seminary the following week. Khamene'i threatened to have him executed for treason, but settled for house arrest.[34] The following year, three of Montazeri's followers, middle-ranking religious scholars (given the title of *hojjat al-Islam*) Hadi Hashemi, Mohammad Hasan Movahedi-Savoji, and Esma'il Zamani, were also arrested in a move to stifle support for Montazeri's critiques.[35]

Summer 1998: Mohsen Sa'idzadeh

Hojjat al-Islam Mohen Sa'idzadeh was arrested in late June 1998, a month after writing a newspaper article comparing proposed legislation, barring male doctors from treating female patients, with Taliban policies in Afghanistan.[36] Several weeks earlier, he had written a magazine article criticizing a new press law that made it a crime to publish material "producing conflict between women and men through the defense of [women's] rights outside of religious and civil law." A law that sought to criminalize "conflict," Sa'idzadeh wrote, would in effect criminalize all religious debate on women's rights: "Since debate by definition involves conflict, who can prove that [people defending women's rights] are observing Islamic and legal limits?" Moreover, the law's reference to arguments "outside of religious and civil law" was completely ambiguous, Sa'idzadeh argued: "What exactly are the religious and legal limits that the designers of the law have in mind?"[37] Sa'idzadeh's defense of the rights of women, dating back to articles published in the early 1990s,[38] had led him to question the enforcement of limits in Islamic debate.

Sa'idzadeh appears to have come to this conclusion by 1995, when concluded that there was a crucial principle in Islam of "separation between givens and interpretations," according to which a "distinction must be made between data and their interpretations. In other words . . . : religion is distinct from its interpretations."[39] In an interview with anthropologist Ziba Mir-Hosseini, Sa'idzadeh argued that his analysis of gender relations in Islam reflected the true religion, while other religious scholars—centuries of them—had engaged only in "interpretation." Under persistent questioning, he admitted that his own work also involved interpretation.[40] The crucial issue, he then argued, was the permissibility of different interpretations in debate:

> There's a need for expert knowledge; thus Islam needs qualified interpreters, the Jurists, and the 'ulama [religious scholars]. But the question is whether this knowledge should be in the hands of one group or not. I say that the door of research is open to all, and their findings can be followed provided they are based on correct methods. In other words, knowledge of religious texts isn't confined to one group.[41]

Mir-Hosseini glosses the reference to "one group" as "clerics." If this is correct, Sa'idzadeh was saying that he wished to allow non-clerics to engage in jurisprudential debates. From the context, however, it seems equally likely that Sa'idzadeh intended the term "one group" to refer to one *segment* of the clerics, his theological opponents, who sought to monopolize debate. Elsewhere in the interview, Sa'idzadeh noted that he was forced to practice *taqiyeh*—the separation of beliefs from actions—because, despite his clerical standing and his use of standard seminary modes of argumentation, it was dangerous for him to express his opinions. "I do *taqiyeh* because I'm afraid of consequences. For instance, I think that men and women can shake hands, but in Iran you'd never see me shaking hands with any women."[42] Fear did not stop Sa'idzadeh from objecting in print to his opponents' monopolization of theological debate, however, for which objections he was jailed.

Spring 1999: Mohsen Kadivar

During the revolution of 1978-1979, Hojjat al-Islam Mohsen Kadivar was an eighteen year-old seminary student whose "heart beat for the revolution."[43] Twenty years later, as a mid-level cleric and reformist newspaper publisher, Kadivar was somewhat disappointed with the revolution's accomplishments. In an interview with the newspaper *Khordad* (*June*), Kadivar assessed the revolution's first two decades and found it significantly lacking in the realm of freedom, especially freedom to criticize the government:[44] "In the seminaries, we don't have absolute obedience at all in our social relations. So when we see that some of the official spokesmen mention absolute obedience and such like as religious values, this can only be understood as a continuation of authoritarian relations and thinking among the leadership of the country."[45] Kadivar's comparison of the Islamic Republic with the monarchy—a comment no doubt intended to shock, like Montazeri's more pointed comments along the same lines—followed from the comparison of seminary norms with political practice in the Islamic Republic. In the seminary, Kadivar could write a book about Shiʻi political thought that discussed Khomeini's theory of *vali-ye faqih* and implicitly criticized it by concluding: "Our political thought is based on the simple point that 'Different theories on a point are possible' and 'Any theory may be wrong.'"[46] Such a challenge was permitted in seminary debate, phrased in academic terms, but not in the newspapers, phrased as political provocation.

The week after the interview was published, Kadivar was summoned before the Special Clergy Court. His long defense statement, published as a book within weeks of its delivery, challenged the indictment head-on. Kadivar began his defense by calling the Special Clergy Court unconstitutional, since the jurist-ruler had no right to establish a court outside of the constitutionally established legal system.[47] He then turned to answer, in painstaking detail, the charge of "propaganda activity against the regime of the Islamic Republic." He denied that his studied opinion constituted "propaganda," and he denied that his calls for reform of the regime could be called "against" it:

> If among the believers and supporters of the Islamic Revolution and the Islamic Republic there may be found two or more analyses or readings of the regime of the Islamic Republic, which differ from one another in many principles of governing society, the scientific critique of the adherents of one reading against the other reading cannot be counted as propaganda activity against the order of the Islamic Republic, because 1) scientific and scholarly critique is not propaganda activity, 2) this activity is against a specific analysis and reading of the regime of the Islamic Republic, and not against the regime of the Islamic Republic, and 3) this scientific and analytical critique seeks to reform the deviationist retractions and mistaken analyses of the regime of the Islamic Republic, and the critic himself is actively attentive to the constitution of the Islamic Republic of

Iran. . . . Must all religious scholars think just like the authorities of the Special Clergy Court? Is having different perspectives with the esteemed prosecutor unbecoming to a religious scholar?[48]

Kadivar was found guilty and sentenced to 18 months in prison, but was unrepentant upon his release: "I stand by what I said then—word for word."[49]

Fall 1999: 'Abdollah Nuri

Perhaps the most popular religious scholar to argue against interpretive closure is Ayatollah 'Abdollah Nuri, who was convicted in November 1999 of allowing his newspaper to report the opinions of liberal oppositionists. Nuri was a key strategist in Khatami's presidential campaign and was appointed minister of the interior in 1997; he was impeached by parliament the following year, but Khatami immediately appointed him as a vice-president. At the same time, he ran an outspokenly reformist newspaper. His defense statement—most of which he was not allowed to present to the court—was published as a book within weeks of his conviction, and the initial press run of 10,000 copies was sold in a single day.[50] The book is entitled *The Hemlock of Reform*, and constitutes an extended indictment of the Iranian regime, on theological, philosophical, and constitutional grounds, which the text summarizes in seventeen points:

1. No fallible human can claim to be the only one in possession of the truth.
2. Religious knowledge is relative, and various and diverse readings of religion are entirely possible.
3. Piety, without reluctance and compulsion, will bring to pass the sublime realization of the essence of religion, that is, faith and religious experience.
4. There is no red line limiting the debate of perspectives and political problems, except that which is expressly specified and designated by the Constitution. No official is immune to criticism and questioning.
5. Iran belongs to all Iranians, and securing citizens' fundamental rights is their divine and legal right. Dialogue among all social forces is imperative and necessary.
6. Within the framework of religious law, [civil] law, and morality, diverse ways of life are imaginable and possible. Nobody can or should, in the name of religious law, impose his way of life on others and consider it definitive.
7. Cultural rights are among the fundamental rights of citizens. Cultured persons have a variety of views and tastes. A univocal monopoly of culture is neither possible nor desirable.
8. Cultural circles are completely independent of politics. Cultured persons and their viewpoints can not be opposed on the basis of

political affiliations and tastes.

9. The legal order of society and the relations between citizens and government are based on the people's right to rule.

10. The establishment of security and stability in society is not possible or practical without the recognition of the rights of the opposition.

11. No single group should consider the country as its own. Efforts should be made to convert even radical oppositionists into legal oppositionists.

12. The standards and criteria for debates over society and politics are the security and interests of the nation, not the security and interests of any particular group.

13. Abrogation of freedom is the sign of a government's weakness, not its strength.

14. The increase and deepening of respectful emotional ties among citizens, and the spread of solidarity and familiarity between the government and the people, are requisites for the stability and survival of society and government.

15. A spirit of freshness, joy, and liveliness is the secret to the health, survival, and flourishing of society.

16. Flattery and sycophancy will lead to the deterioration of humanitarian values and the destruction of the foundations of the regime. In view of this, propagation and reverence of such things as "critique and protest," which tend to promote the legitimacy and strength of the political regime, are of urgent necessity. Based on this premise, it is the government's duty to banish the sycophants and praise the critics, not vice versa.

17. Detente with all the states and nations of the world, based on national interests and the civilizational dialogue, is essential in all fields.[51]

Nuri was convicted and sentenced to five years in prison, plus additional years' banishment from journalistic and political activity. Several senior religious scholars expressed displeasure with the verdict: Ayatollah 'Abdolkarim Musavi-Ardabili called Nuri's father to express his sympathy, and Ayatollah Jalaluddin Taheri—Khamene'i's representative and the official Friday prayer leader in Isfahan—told Nuri supporters he felt the sentence was "unjust."[52]

Fall 2000: Hasan Yusefi-Eshkevari

The severity of sentences in each of the above cases escalated from house arrest for Montazeri to six months in prison for Sa'idzadeh, eighteen months for Kadivar, and five years for Nuri. The latest scholar to undergo a high-profile trial in the Special Clergy Court, Hojjat al-Islam Hasan Yusefi-Eshkevari, was originally sentenced to death.[53] But even the Special Clergy Court's prosecutor-general, Gholam-Hossein Mohseni-Ezhe'i, held a press conference to criticize the ruling.[54] On appeal, the sentence was reduced to defrocking and two years in prison, with five additional years tacked on later.[55]

Eshkevari was convicted not just of insulting the regime and its leader, as the others had been, but also of apostasy and war against Islam. Yet the statements for which Eshkevari was convicted seem hardly more critical than those of other scholars tried in the Special Clergy Court. Eshkevari's indictment referred specifically to lectures he gave in April 2000 in Berlin, Germany, at a conference on current trends in Iran. The conference was regarded by many in Iran, even many reformists, as scandalous, because it brought together the opposition in exile and the opposition inside Iran, exposing the latter to accusations of collusion with foreign enemies. It was doubly scandalous for the appearance of leftist protestors, especially a woman who bared her breasts in protest against Iranian laws requiring women to wear *hejab* (modest garb). These protestors and many of the oppositionists in exile criticized Eshkevari and others for working with the Iranian regime, rather than trying to overthrow it. At the same time, conservatives in Iran accused them of trying to overthrow the regime.

Eshkevari's first speech at the conference called for the democratization of Iran, and suggested that this transition was imminent: "The historical lifetime of the supporters of despotism has reached an end in Iran."[56] His second speech at the conference spelled out the Islamic basis for his position, and included this attack on interpretive closure:

> *Ijtihad* in the sense of novel thinking and the reconstruction of religious thought, in its bases and branches, [may be called] the motor of the deepening and grounding of Islamic thought and culture. *Ijtihad* also makes possible the critique of tradition, as well as the critique of modernity and the reformists, and it makes feasible the independent design of an Islamic renaissance and the carrying forward of reforms. Without *ijtihad*, no piety is possible in the contemporary era, and there is no use or utility in science and technology and the products of human experience. Of course, *ijtihad* does not mean only jurisprudential *ijtihad*. . . . For example, under present circumstances, the laws of retribution and some of the rights of women need to undergo a fundamental review through *ijtihad*. Of course, this sort of *ijtihad* depends first of all on the reconstruction of the bases and methods of traditional religion and education.[57]

This was not a novel argument for Eshkevari. In 1999, for example, he told a newspaper reporter:

So far as the theoretical discussion is concerned, no limitations
should exist about religion. Especially since in the principles of
religion, emulation is unlawful and forbidden, and the principles of
religion should be linked with exegesis. In the principles of religion,
no one emulates another [scholar]. And it is not acceptable that some
specialist individuals should exist, so that the people could follow
them. In addition, those who claim that only religious specialists have
permission to express their opinion in the field of religion, do not
permit them to publish a treatise or discuss this matter themselves.
. . .

Not all Muslims and Islamic authorities have the same idea about the
concepts of Islam. Monotheism, resurrection, and prophecy are the
foundation of Islam. But there are doubts about which interpretation
is considered contrary to the concepts. Ayatollah [Mohammad Taqi]
Mesbah-Yazdi [a leading conservative] has a particular interpretation
of religion, and so does the Press Court, so that when a teacher
propounds a religious question, they decide to imprison him.
Therefore, there should be liberty at least in interpretation.[58]

Eshkevari's arrest warrant was issued two weeks after the Berlin conference,
and one day after a Tehran newspaper attacked him as a "pseudo-clerical"
proponent of "American-style Islam," in contrast to "the true, pure
Muhammadan Islam, whose greatest savior was Imam Khomeini":

Don't the seminaries and clerics have a responsibility to stand up to
the insults of a bunch of pseudo-clerical shysters and nobodies? To
maintain a sound and healthy body, one must cut out and amputate
infected and putrefied organs. The disgrace of a pseudo-clergyman
[Yusefi-Eshkevari] at the Berlin conference was so shameful that it
pained every noble heart. No clergyman, regardless of his personal
inclination or political preference, would consider such a person
worthy to wear these sacred robes.[59]

But various senior seminarians resented the state's efforts at amputation,
especially after Eshkevari's conviction. Ayatollah Mohammad Sadeghi-Tehrani
defended Eshkevari in a radio interview, saying that Eshkevari's judgments, even
if they differed from the jurist-ruler's, were part of the "scientific" enterprise of
religious scholarship, and could not be considered apostasy.[60] Ayatollah 'Ali-
Akbar Mohtashami, an opponent of Eshkevari's views,[61] wrote that the charges
of apostasy and *muharib*—one who engages in war against Islam—should not be
applied to scholarly disagreements: "The *'ulama* [religious scholars] believe that
muharib is someone who has resorted to arms and is going to destroy the
Muslims, not someone who expresses a different view. Yusefi-Eshkevari might
have made mistakes in his political and cultural stances, but he is a Muslim."[62]
Hojjat al-Islam Mehdi Karrubi, then-speaker of the Iranian parliament, called the

verdict "unacceptable": "Although I do not agree with his views on *hejab* [modest garb], I consider him a Muslim [and not an apostate]."[63] Ayatollah Mohammad 'Ali Gerami told a group of students that he and several other senior scholars had expressed their view that "this was not a case of apostasy and corruption."[64]

There may be a material as well as a normative aspect to these scholars' support for critics of the jurist-ruler: according to a recent press report, Khamene'i sent a representative to the Qom seminaries, proposing to channel religious tithes through the jurist-ruler's office, taking these funds out of the hands of other senior seminarians who have traditionally collected and distributed this money. All but one of the seminarians reportedly rejected the proposal.[65]

Resisting Relativism

Conservatives have branded the critics as relativists. A group of conservative seminary scholars in Qom issued an open letter to Nuri's seminary supporters, accusing them of consorting with people who argued that "right and wrong are relative" and that "even the *imam*s and the prophets were not absolute."[66] Ayatollah Mesbah-Yazdi argued, "The culture of tolerance and indulgence means the disarming of society of its defense mechanism."[67] The *Kayhan* (*Globe*) newspaper—a mouthpiece for the far-right in Iran—drew the epistemological conclusion in an editorial several weeks after Nuri's conviction, entitled "Truth is Unknowable, Do Not Seek It!":

> [Nuri] writes: 'The main message of that article is that truth is not evident, and each of us must accept the possibility of slipping, and making mistakes.' This argument reminds us more than anything of the translated [that is, inauthentic] and foreign concept of 'religious pluralism.' In this concept, a famous story is used, where an elephant is placed in front of some blind men, and each offers a definition of the elephant based on his incomplete senses. Not only was none of their definitions complete, but at the end the collected definition of the blind people did not arrive at the true meaning of the elephant. Therefore, saying that the truth is not evident, or our understanding can slip, starts out a path whose tools and results are the relativity of religious righteousness, multiplicity [of views], and thus perturbation and doubt about the beliefs and definite fundamentals of Islam. By accepting that the truth is not evident, not only does this promise of Mr. Nuri's come into doubt and question, but his previous thoughts come into question as well, and therefore his whole life, and the question of whether or not he holds rational and reasonable thoughts become questionable.[68]

This accusation of relativism is familiar to any observer of the sociology of knowledge in the West, with which Nuri and other critics' arguments share a considerable likeness. If knowledge is fallible, then so is the contention that knowledge is fallible. If knowledge is socially constructed, then on what grounds are we to accept the argument that knowledge is socially constructed, or any other argument? The epistemology of critique would seem to call itself into question. The sociology of knowledge has devised several responses to this dilemma:

> Position #1: to argue that knowledge, though fallible, is ever-progressing, in ways that we can measure;
> Position #2: to hold that knowledge, though fallible, can be justified by necessity;
> Position #3: to embrace relativism, admit one's own fallibility, and reduce "knowledge" to "belief."[69]

The Iranian clerical critics have not, to my knowledge, faced up to this epistemological challenge. Montazeri, for example, seems confident that he has access to higher truths than the religious scholars who disagree with him. "Although some senior officials believe that the *vali-ye faqih* [jurist-ruler] is appointed by the infallible imams, I have disputed this theory in detail," he wrote in a faxed interview while under house arrest. "It is certain that the legitimacy of this post is acquired by popular election."[70] This certainty is an indication of position #1, suggesting that he supports the traditional seminary hierarchy of religious interpretation and does not feel the need to justify this hierarchy. Sa'idzadeh, forced to address the issue in his interview with Mir-Hosseini, stumbled between position #3 and position #1: "I too am interpreting," he said, but "I believe my understanding is valid; I'm a realist; they're in the wrong."[71] I have not seen Nuri or Yusefi-Eshkevari's positions on this subject. I have seen, however, an extensive discussion of relativism by Mohsen Kadivar.

Kadivar's position emerged in a debate, published in three installments in a Tehran newspaper, with the philosopher Abdolkarim Soroush.[72] Kadivar began the debate by spelling out three possible responses to the evident fact of religious plurality in the world:

> First interpretation: Some religious believers consider only their own way the exclusive way for human guidance. They do not consider other ways proper or as the ideal.

> Second interpretation: Some others, even though they consider their own way to be the way to reach the ideal, do not reject all other religions and paths. They establish a relationship between other religions and their own and somehow are "inclusive" in their own religious beliefs in regards to other religions and sects, in the sense that every religion, sect, or doctrine has some truth, is not absolutely

false, and is rewarding in proportion to how much truth it has, but complete truth is only found in one religion.

Third interpretation: One group regards this "actual plurality" as "true plurality" and have tried somehow to speak of different and authentic experiences of religion, and even in numerous sacred affairs to speak of direct paths and not a direct path, numerous truths and not a single truth. This interpretation constitutes religious pluralism.

As he made clear later in the debate, Kadivar favored the second interpretation—a mixture of what I've called position #1 and position #2. Faiths other than one's own—and, through an analogy he makes later in the discussion, divergent religious interpretations within one's own faith tradition—are to be tolerated as the product of God's having sent different prophets to different peoples (position #2), but are to be rejected as incomplete because some prophecies are more final than others (position #1).

Soroush denied that his position corresponded to Kadivar's characterization of religious pluralism: "actually, we are not trying to provide the criteria of truth and falsehood. We are not engaged in a theological discussion." Soroush argued that he merely took believers of various faiths at their word, "because we are not subject to divine inspiration, and we do not want to rely on internal evidence and experiences in this connection. Hence, if someone has a reason [for his faith], and his reason is acceptable, we accept what he says." (Unlike this translation by the Foreign Broadcast Information Service, the Persian original did not use gendered pronouns.)

Kadivar questioned this blanket acceptance of faith claims: "should we believe that every religion or every claim (even though likely false) which has given reason as its claim is on the same level as the reasons of other religions (even though those religions are right)?" He continued by rejecting Soroush's attempt to remove his inquiry from the field of theology:

> Religious pluralism is incompatible with faith and certainty. Saying that the issue of pluralism is not related to the issue of truth and falsehood does not solve any problem, because, on the basis of religious pluralism, we cannot consider one religion to be true and another false. The impossibility of separating truth from falsehood is the logical requirement of religious pluralism. The implied basis of religious pluralism is absolute relativity in the area of knowledge.

We need a criterion to distinguish correct religious interpretations from incorrect ones, Kadivar argued, or we will lose our certainty and our faith. Fortunately, divine revelation has given such criteria:

> My question is, why are you negligent of "divine wisdom"? Does not "divine wisdom" . . . offer general directives in regards to correcting

human understanding of the supreme and the sacred, which is called
religion? This is the claim of divine religions, that God has provided
us with such general guidance through His prophets.

Soroush politely suggested that Kadivar's understanding of "divine wisdom"
was just as vulnerable as the understanding of people in other religions. If
Kadivar wished to argue that others were misled by the circumstances of their
birth, or by the inability of their intellect, to comprehend and accept the true
religion, then such challenges could be made against him too: "no matter what
opinion we give about plurality, it will come back to us, because we ourselves
are facing plurality. We cannot separate ourselves from others." Soroush, having
the last word in the debate, concluded by challenging Kadivar to spell out the
criterion of "divine wisdom" that would settle all disputes and show clearly
which religious interpretations were more correct than others: "Moreover, I am
still waiting to see what your criterion is that will eliminate plurality and all the
differences."

This final challenge is analogous to Paul Feyerabend's challenge to Imre
Lakatos in their debates in the philosophy of science: what possible criteria can
be spelled out that haven't been violated in one or another classic piece of
scholarship, including your own?[73] Lakatos's response was to hypothesize
plausible criteria and test them with historical research on the actual practice of
productive scientists.

The clerical critics in Iran, by contrast, seem to resist the relativist
implications of their position by stressing their conformity to the tacit standards
of seminary scholarship. Rather than make these standards explicit, they use
them as a shield, in two ways. First, at the theoretical level, the shield serves as a
boundary of expert knowledge preventing outsiders such as Soroush from
challenging their arguments. Second, at the political level, the shield may be
intended to protect them from the Special Clergy Court, by emphasizing their
affiliation with an undifferentiated community of religious scholars. Both aspects
bring us back to seminary norms. On one hand, seminary norms privilege the
authority of experts, and on the other, seminary norms privilege the right of
experts to disagree. Clerical critics in Iran, forced by the country's clerical rulers
into a potentially radical opposition to interpretive closure, are trying to criticize
the authority of the jurist-ruler without undermining their own authority as
experts.

The Christian Reformation faced a similar dilemma in its first centuries.
Protestant Christianity later came to be known for democratizing religious
authority, emphasizing the right of all believers to engage with divinity directly,
without clerical intermediaries. Yet in its early years, and still in some
denominations today, many Protestant theologians have resisted the relativistic
implications of spiritual democratization. Their claim of expertise often includes
an insistence that their interpretation of the faith is the one true path, and other
interpretations are to be condemned. The religious radicals who rejected papal

authority, including Luther, could themselves be authoritarian.[74]

In Iran, as in Reformation-era Europe, epistemological debates have political implications. Because the Islamic republic stakes its legitimacy on the scholarly authority of its jurist-ruler, the regime takes such debates quite seriously. Through the Special Clergy Court, the regime has tried to clamp down on relativism, calling it a violation of the country's constitutional order. Through the media, the regime's supporters have tried to undermine relativism, calling it self-defeating. The dissident seminarians, too, have distanced themselves from relativism, calling themselves legitimate religious authorities. It is unclear how the dissidents will reconcile the two seminary norms of open debate and scholarly authority, or what political ramifications might follow from such a reconciliation. It is already clear, though, that the dissidents are creating an unprecedentedly rich documentary record of Islamic critiques of the Islamic state.

Notes

1. Earlier versions of this chapter were presented to the American Council for the Study of Islamic Societies, Villanova, Pennsylvania, April 29, 2000, and published in the *International Journal of Politics, Culture, and Society* 15, no. 2 (Winter 2001): 341-59. I thank the participants at that conference, as well as Sükrü Hanioglu, Shayee Khanaka, Margaret Phillips, and Mahmoud Sadri, for their assistance in the preparation of this chapter.

2. For a brief review of this episode, see Carter Lindberg, *The European Reformations* (Oxford, England: Blackwell Publishers, 1996): 76-87.

3. Martin Luther, "Why the Books of the Pope and his Disciples Were Burned by Doctor Martin Luther" (1520), in *Luther's Works*, vol. 31, ed. Harold J. Grimm (Philadelphia: Muhlenberg Press, 1957), 392.

4. 'Ali Davani, "Khaterat-e Hojjat al-Islam Aqa-ye 'Ali Davani" (Memoirs of Hojjat al-Islam Mr. 'Ali Davani), *Yad* (*Memory*) 8 (1987): 49.

5. Mohammad Hossein Tabataba'i et al., *Bahsi Dar-bareh-ye Marja'iyat va Ruhaniyat* (*A Discussion of Religious Leadership and Religious Scholars*) (Tehran: Sherkat-e Sehami-ye Enteshar, 1962); A. K. S. Lambton, "A Reconsideration of the Position of *Marja' al-Taqlid* and the Religious Institution," *Studia Islamica* 20, (1964): 115-35; Shahrough Akhavi, *Religion and Politics in Contemporary Iran: Clergy-State Relations in the Pahlavi Period* (Albany: State University of New York Press, 1980), 117-29.

6. Ruhollah Khomeini, "Islamic Government" (1970), in *Islam and Revolution*, translated by Hamid Algar (Berkeley, CA: Mizan Press, 1981), 62.

7. *Constitution of the Islamic Republic of Iran* (Tehran: Islamic Propagation Organization, 1979), Articles 5, 110.

8. Asghar Schirazi, *The Constitution of Iran: Politics and the State in the Islamic Republic*, translated by John O'Kane (London: I. B. Tauris, 1997), 63-73.

9. Gholam-'Ali Raja'i, *Bar-dasht'hayi az Sireh-ye Emam Khomeini* (*Selections from the Life of Imam Khomeini*), 3 vols. (Tehran: Mo'aseseh-ye Chap va Nashr-e 'Oruj,

1997-1998).

10. Juan Cole, "Shi'i Clerics in Iraq and Iran, 1722-1780: The Akhbari-Usuli Conflict Reconsidered," *Iranian Studies* 18, no. 1 (1985): 3-34; Said Amir Arjomand, *The Turban for the Crown: The Islamic Revolution in Iran* (New York: Oxford University Press, 1988), 13-15.

11. Michael M. J. Fischer, *Iran: From Religious Dispute to Revolution* (Cambridge: Harvard University Press, 1980), 63, 66.

12. Roy Mottahedeh, *The Mantle of the Prophet: Religion and Politics in Iran* (New York: Simon and Schuster, 1985), 196.

13. Alvin W. Gouldner, *The Future of Intellectuals and the Rise of the New Class* (New York: Seabury Press, 1979).

14. Schirazi, *The Constitution of Iran*, 258-65.

15. *Naqd va Nazar* (*Critique and Perspective*), edited by Mohammad-Mahdi Faqihi (Qom, Iran: Daftar-e Tablighat-e Eslami, 1994-). Articles referred to in the text: vol. 2, nos. 3-4 (Summer-Fall 1996): 330-36 (religious pluralism); vol. 1, nos. 3-4 (Summer-Fall 1995): 62-81 (Kierkegaard); vol. 3, nos. 2-3 (Spring-Summer 1997): 80-93 (Rawls); vol. 3, no. 4 (Fall 1997): 376-433 (Abu Zayd).

16. *Naqd va Nazar* 1, no. 5 (Winter 1996): 10-79; vol. 2, no. 2 (Spring 1996): 297-332; vol. 2, nos. 3-4 (Summer-Fall 1996): 313-29.

17. "Vision of the Islamic Republic of Iran, Network 2" (20 August 1997), translated by the British Broadcast Corporation (BBC) Worldwide Monitoring.

18. *Constitution* (1979), Article 1.

19. *Los Angeles Times* (9 December 1978): 12.

20. Hamid Ruhani (Ziyarati), *Shari'at-Madari dar Dadgah-e Tarikh* (*Shari'at-Madari in the Court of History*) (Qom, Iran: Daftar-e Entesharat-e Eslami, 1982).

21. Ziba Mir-Hosseini, *Islam and Gender: The Religious Debate in Contemporary Iran* (Princeton: Princeton University Press, 1999), 144; Dariush Zahedi, *The Iranian Revolution Then and Now* (Boulder, CO: Westview Press, 2000), 80-81.

22. *Constitution of the Islamic Republic of Iran* (1989), Article 107. See the International Constitutional Law web site (ICL Document Status: 1992), www.oefre.unibe.ch/law/icl/ir00000_.html (accessed March 29, 2003).

23. *The Washington Post* (4 March 2001): B4.

24. Schirazi, *The Constitution of Iran*, 154.

25. Charles Kurzman, "Liberal Islam in its Islamic Context," in Charles Kurzman, editor, *Liberal Islam: A Sourcebook* (New York: Oxford University Press, 1998), 14-16. I use the term "liberal," with extensive caveats, to refer to the broad tradition of thought that includes a concern with democracy, rights, equality, and progress. The authors discussed in the present paper might be categorized as "liberal" in this sense, though they probably would not adopt the identity themselves. I will not insist on the term.

26. Kurzman, "Liberal Islam in its Islamic Context," 16-18.

27. Abdolkarim Soroush, *Reason, Freedom, and Democracy in Islam*, translated by Mahmoud Sadri and Ahmad Sadri (New York: Oxford University Press, 2000), 176.

28. Mir-Hosseini, *Islam and Gender*, 253; Zahedi, *The Iranian Revolution*, 84.

29. Schirazi, *The Constitution of Iran*, 37-38.

30. Shaul Bakhash, *The Reign of the Ayatollahs*, revised edition (New York: Basic Books, 1990), 282.

31. *Los Angeles Times* (1 February 1989): 1.

32. Shahrough Akhavi, "Contending Discourses in Shi'a Law on the Doctrine of

Wilayat al-Faqih," *Iranian Studies* 29 (1996): 253-59; Chibli Mallat, *The Renewal of Islamic Law: Muhammad Baqer as-Sadr, Najaf and the Shi'i International* (Cambridge, England: Cambridge University Press, 1993), 92-95.

33. Hossein-'Ali Montazeri, *Bakhshi az Khaterat* (*Selections from the Memoirs*) (Tehran: www.montazeri.org, 2000), 779-80, 783.

34. *Newsday* (New York) (9 December 1997).

35. Iran Press Service (6 July and 3 September 1998).

36. *Jame'e* (*Society*) (28 May 1998); Iran Press Service (6 and 29 July 1998).

37. Mohsen Sa'idzadeh, "Bandi Digar: Defa' az Hoquq-e Zanan Mamnu'!" (Another Subsection: Defense of the Rights of Women Banned!), *Zanan* (*Women*) 42, (1998): 6-7. "Bandi" refers to a subsection of the press law, but also means "a rope."

38. Ziba Mir-Hosseini, "Stretching the Limits: A Feminist Reading of the *Shari'a* in Post-Khomeini Iran," in Mai Yamani, editor, *Feminism and Islam* (Berkshire, England: Ithaca Press, 1996), 284-320.

39. Mir-Hosseini, *Islam and Gender*, 256.

40. Mir-Hosseini, *Islam and Gender*, 253.

41. Mir-Hosseini, *Islam and Gender*, 257-58.

42. Mir-Hosseini, *Islam and Gender*, 267.

43. Mohsen Kadivar, *Baha-ye Azadi: Defa'iyat-e Mohsen Kadivar dar Dadgah-e Vizheh-ye Ruhaniyat* (*The Price of Freedom: Mohsen Kadivar's Defense Statement in the Special Clergy Court*), ed. Zahra Rudi, third printing (Tehran: Nashr-e Ney, 1999), 148.

44. Kadivar, *Baha-ye Azadi*, 155.

45. Kadivar, *Baha-ye Azadi*, 158.

46. Mohsen Kadivar, *Nazariyeh'ha-ye Dowlat dar Feqh-e Shi'a* (*Theories of the State in Shi'i Jurisprudence*), fourth printing (Tehran: Nashr-e Ney, 1998), 33.

47. Kadivar, *Baha-ye Azadi*, 49-57.

48. Kadivar, *Baha-ye Azadi*, 101, 104.

49. *New York Times* (18 September 2000): 3.

50. I happened to be in Tehran that day and could not find a copy to purchase.

51. 'Abdollah Nuri, *Shukran-e Eslah: Defa'iyat-e 'Abdollah Nuri be Peyvast-e Ra'ye Dadgah-e Vizheh-ye Ruhaniyat* (*The Hemlock of Reform: 'Abdollah Nuri's Defense Statement Together with the Opinion of the Special Clergy Court*), third printing (Tehran: Entesharat-e Tarh-e No, 1999), 253-55.

52. *Hamshahri* (*Compatriot*) (2 December 1999).

53. Islamic Republic News Agency (16 October 2000).

54. Voice of the Islamic Republic of Iran (22 October 2000), translated in BBC Summary of World Broadcasts.

55. Islamic Republic News Agency (2 November 2002).

56. *Iran-Emrooz* (*Iran Today*) (8 April 2000). Audio files, transcripts, and related material from the Berlin conference were available in fall-winter 2000-2001 at http://members.nbci.com/_XMCM/asghar1/berlin_direc.html.

57. *Iran-Emrooz* (9 April 2000).

58. *Iran* (*Iran*) (18 October 1999): 5, translated by the Foreign Broadcast Information Service, Near East and South Asia, FBIS-NES-1999-1211.

59. *Jomhuri-ye Eslami* (*Islamic Republic*) (24 April 2000): 15, translated in FBIS-NES-2000-0523.

60. BBC Persian Service (19 October 2000).

61. *Bayan* (*Statement*) (20 April 2000): 1.

62. *'Asr-e Ma (Our Era)* (21 October 2000): 1, translated by BBC Worldwide Monitoring.

63. Islamic Republic News Agency (22 October 2000).

64. *Hayat-e No (New Life)* (29 January 2001): 4, translated by BBC Worldwide Monitoring.

65. *International Herald Tribune* (21 December 2000): 1.

66. *Abrar (The Good)* (14 December 1999): 3, translated in FBIS-NES-1999-1227.

67. *Resalat (Prophecy)* (16 May 2000): 6, translated in FBIS-NES-2000-0614.

68. *Kayhan (The Globe)* (9 December 1999): 14, translated in FBIS-NES-2000-0111.

69. Charles Kurzman, "Epistemology and the Sociology of Knowledge," *Philosophy of the Social Sciences* 24 (1994): 267-90.

70. *Mideast Mirror* (26 January 2000).

71. Mir-Hosseini, *Islam and Gender*, 253-54.

72. *Salam (Peace)* (1, 8, and 15 January 1998), translated in FBIS-NES-98-099.

73. Paul Feyerabend, *Against Method* (London: Verso, 1975), 196; Matteo Motterlini, *For and Against Method* (Chicago: University of Chicago Press, 1999), 4.

74. Joseph Lecler, *Toleration and the Reformation*, translated by T. L. Westow (New York: Association Press, 1960), 2 vols.; Ole Peter Grell and Bob Scribner, eds., *Tolerance and Intolerance in the European Reformation* (Cambridge: Cambridge University Press, 1996).

5

The Politics of Historical Revisionism: New Re-Readings of the Early Islamic Period

Salwa Ismail

This chapter examines a number of recent Arabic-language works dealing with the founding period of Islam; in particular, with the life of Muhammad, the society of Mecca, and the Medinan community. The primary focus is on the works of two Egyptian authors, Mahmud Sayyid al-Qimni and Khalil 'Abd al-Karim.[1] Their works form part of a wider dialogic and discursive field in which various positions on the nature of Islam as a religion, its role in society and politics, and the status of the Islamic heritage are articulated. This field has a history. However, identifying the points of its emergence and what constitutes its center and periphery is not only subject to debate but is necessarily influenced by the research problematic of a given inquiry, its subject and terms of framing. One such problematic is that of "reform." In conventional accounts of intellectual trends that emerged in Muslim countries in the early modern period, certain figures are pivotal. Muhammad ibn 'Abd al-Wahhab, for instance, is viewed as representing a reform movement of purification, religious discipline, and so on. However, the conservatism of the ethics propagated by Wahhabi religious thinking appears today to place this movement outside the frame of reform (and of Reformation).

In current scholarly debates, the Reformation analogy is used to draw parallels between the thought and objectives of contemporary Muslim thinkers such as Abdolkarim Soroush, Muhammad Shahrour, Nasr Hamid Abu Zayd, on one hand, and those of the Protestant Reformation thinkers, primarily Luther, on the other. This construction merits closer scrutiny which is beyond the scope of this chapter. However, I will briefly elaborate on several issues that render the Reformation analogy problematic.

One common objection affirming the inappropriateness of the analogy points to the structural dissimilarities in the formal edifice of both religions. In one, there is a central authority, the Church, which was historically dominant and which structured the lives of the believers. The other is lacking such an encompassing authority. Rather, Islamic religious authority is decentralized. The structural argument must also be placed in the wider historical context of the changes forming the subject of examination and comparison in both Christian and Muslim societies. In this respect, the analogy posits a stage-like view of change that claims to draw upon the particular experience of the Christian West. However, both sides of the analogy are suspect: it seems to imply that pre-Reformation Europe was as totally dominated by religious authority as the stereotype of contemporary Islam.[2] Further, it reproduces a unilinear view of development and progress found in progressivist views of history and the meta-narrative of historical development that we find in oversimplified terms in modernization theory. Accordingly, Islam is presumed to be undergoing, lacking, or in need of a Reformation akin to the Christian experience. This seems to presuppose that Islam is in its Middle Ages and needs a Reformation before proceeding to the age of Enlightenment and then perhaps moving on to secular modernity.

If we follow the stagist perspective suggested by the Reformation analogy, we lose sight of the fact that, historically, the interaction between Islamic religious traditions and the social meant that in many respects these traditions were secularized. For instance, Islamic laws incorporated local customs in adapting to social reality. As such, Islamic traditions, like other religious traditions, were shaped by the social world. In other words, the idea that Islam was fixed at a particular moment in time, whether the founding age or the medieval period, fails to take into account the dynamics of change that shape the interaction between religion and the social. Further, it is important to take account of the processes of secularization that were initiated in many Muslim countries in the twentieth century and that have contributed to the entrenchment of secular modes of organization. This is not to suggest that Islamic societies are "Early Modern" any more than they are "pre-Reformation," but to call into question the anachronistic comparison altogether. In short, the varying trajectories of Muslim societies cannot be summed up under an Islam that totalizes the lives of its adherents, nor is an understanding of those trajectories furthered by comparison with a totalizing notion of Europe in the sixteenth century.

In order to understand the reformations that are under way in Islamic societies, as well as their significance, the imperative is to contextualize the ongoing debates in Arab and Islamic thought. To do so, one must pay particular attention to the dialogic dimension of the discourses on the Islamic heritage and the role of Islam in politics and society. This is necessary in order to gain an understanding of the stakes involved. At the turn of the twentieth century, Muslim thinkers leading the modern reform movement entered into dialogue with their own societies and with the West. Their problematic centered on the need for Muslim awakening in response to Western material progress. Thinkers like Muhammad 'Abduh and Rashid Rida interrogated the heritage on questions of the bases of the collective good of the *umma* (Muslim community). At the close of the twentieth century, there is no doubt that some of the questions persist, but new currents, ideas, and practices have to be contended with. Again, we find Muslim thinkers interrogating the heritage, some with a view to authenticating reason and rationality, others, with the clear objective of instituting a historical perspective on the heritage.[3] This objective is formulated and defined in dialogue with the Islamists but also with the Islamic establishment's reading of the early Islamic history.

Islamists have produced an idealized narrative of early history which is then deployed in contest over meaning and claims to truth. In many respects, their narrative does not diverge from that of Official Islam, but dislocates positions of authority and opens up spaces for challenging political and religious authorities. However, in activating certain premises as foundational for the political community as, for instance, the idea of the Text as the ultimate source of authority, and by setting the example of the Companions as a frame of reference, the Islamists have brought into focus the need to revisit the foundational period to address the status of revelation, the model society, and the process of producing orthodoxy.

In this dialogic field, then, 'Abd al-Karim and Qimni's rereadings of the early Islamic period seek to provide a corrective to the contemporary Islamists' idealized and mythologized image of the original Islamic community. Basing themselves on classical historical sources, Qimni and 'Abd al-Karim reconstruct the socioeconomic, political, and intellectual context of the rise of Islam. The central objective of their works is to institute an historical perspective on Muhammad's message and the community/state he founded. In their writings, divinity and Revelation take a back seat to historicity. As discussed below, this focus suggests some similarities with European scholars' use of historical research techniques in the wake of the Enlightenment in order to reevaluate the nature of the Gospels as historical documents. However, it has little in common with historical studies during the Reformation. These latter either remained uninterested in history for its own sake or, if interested in presenting the historically most accurate account of Jesus and the apostolic era, did so with the aim of affirming confessional identity.[4]

This chapter argues that the writings of 'Abd al-Karim and Qimni represent a politics of contestation and subversion of the claims to power and authority of Islamic "orthodoxy." These writings assert a historical perspective on the religious heritage with the ultimate aim of abolishing the founding period as a social and political ideal. This argument will be elaborated through the following methodological and analytical undertakings:

1. outlining the central themes of these writings, and investigating the intellectual and political environment in which the works operate and with which they are engaged;

2. assessing the novelty of the authors' enterprise by situating their writings in relation to the celebratory and laudatory historical accounts found in earlier works of the modern period by authors such as 'Abbas Mahmud al-'Aqqad,

Muhammad Husayn Haykal, Taha Husayn (post *Fi al-Shi'r al-Jahili*), and Tawfiq al-Hakim;

3. locating the authors' own claims to "truth" and "authenticity" as indicated by their documentary sources, namely their use of "al-Azhar approved sources";

4. analyzing the reception of their works by the religious establishment and by Arab and Muslim intellectuals (both authors are on an al-Azhar ban list, both have been subject to police interrogation; their works have been confiscated, then released and reprinted; at the same, the authors have been subject to attacks by some Islamist ideologues, but, generally, they have been ignored);

5. assessing the challenge that these works represent to official Islam and evaluating their likely impact on militant Islamism.

The chapter is divided into four sections. The first consists of a background discussion on the tradition of writings about Muhammad and the early Islamic period. It focuses, in particular, on a body of works that emerged in the modern era, namely the Muhammad biographies penned by Egyptian authors in the 1930s and 1940s. These works serve as an important early twentieth-century counterpoint to the revisionist writings under study. The two sets of writings share a general subject matter, but are sharply divergent in approach, objectives, and orientation. The second section highlights the main themes in the revisionist works and gives the basic outline of 'Abd al-Karim's and Qimni's arguments. Following this, section three proceeds to an examination of these writings in terms of the aims and implications of the revisionist project in the present sociopolitical context. The discussion revolves around a fundamental question: why have these authors embarked on this particular project? Section four focuses on the politics of reception. Its main aim is to gauge responses to the revisionist enterprise at various levels of Egyptian society and polity: within the religious establishment, the "intelligentsia," the mass media, and among the Islamist activists. The chapter concludes with a brief assessment of the implications the revisionist writings have for the constitution of Muslim identities.

Defensive Histories or Rationalist Exposés: Biographies of the Prophet in the Early Modern Period

Before proceeding to my exposé and analysis of the revisionist writings on the early period of Islam, it is important to investigate briefly how this period is dealt with in other works of the modern era. The most relevant literature in this regard is the biographical texts of the 1930s and 1940s dealing with the life of Muhammad and the founding moment of Islam. These texts dealt with the same historical period as the works of the contemporary authors examined here. However, the biographers chose to deal with personalities, focusing either solely on Muhammad, as in the case of Tawfiq al-Hakim, or on Muhammad and the

Companions.[5] In this respect, the early biographers' construction of that period serves as a counterpoint for the significantly unconventional accounts we find with the revisionists. In general terms, the biographers produced laudatory histories of Muhammad and the believers, constructing Muhammad as the example for humanity and validating the idea of the foundational period as a model. In contrast, as we shall see, the revisionists provide a critical account of the founding period. The image of Muhammad that emerges in their writings is quite "unorthodox" if judged in reference to the standards of existing biographies written by Muslims. This will be elaborated on below.

It is important to locate the modern biographers and the contemporary revisionists in their contexts. This will help in understanding the variation in the orientation of their writings and in the frames of reference which guide them. Let us begin with the early modern biographers. The position of the biographies, part of what is known as the *Islamiyyat*, in Egyptian intellectual history is subject to much controversy. Students of the subject have highlighted certain reasons for the emergence of this literature, chief among which, are the need to respond to missionary activities, the desire to produce a modernist account of religion, and the need to engage with a new public.[6] In her study of the *udaba*, Zahia Ragheb Dajani situates the biography literature which dealt with the life of Muhammad and the Companions in the context of the challenge posed by missionaries and western scholars.[7] Critiques of Islamic values and of Islam's teachings prompted this defensive posturing. A tradition of western biographical works on Muhammad, dating to the Middle Ages, expressed doubts as to his status as prophet.[8] Thus, the modern biographers aimed at responding to the negative image of Islam and Muhammad constructed in the western accounts.[9] According to Dajani, these negative portrayals of Muhammad prompted many intellectuals to deal with his biography.[10]

In a similar manner to Dajani, E. S. Sabanegh notes that the aim of the 1930s biographical writings was to counter the orientalist attack on Islam and particularly its critical and sometimes negative view of Muhammad. This objective was declared by all of the early-modern-period Muhammad biography writers.[11] As such, the approach, to some extent, is defensive, and, according to Sabanegh, apologetic.

It may be argued that this defensive literature occupies a similar position to that assumed in the exchanges between earlier Muslim reformers such as al-Afghani and 'Abduh and Western thinkers. Both Muslim reformers engaged in exchanges with Western thinkers in defense of Islam as a religion and civilization.[12] This defense was an important component of the *Nahda* (renaissance) project. However, the biographers were writing more than three decades after these exchanges had taken place. During the intervening period, a liberal trend had begun to flourish. Egypt's intellectual life was undergoing rapid transformations. New institutions of secular learning such as Cairo University were established.[13] Political parties espousing liberal ideas had been active on the political scene for some time and a new basis for participation had developed. So, how can we explain the recourse to a genre of writing which is based on religious history and why was it felt that there was the need for defensive posturing? The answer lies in the coincidence of several factors: the rise of a new political movement, namely the Muslim Brothers, basing itself on religio-political principles; continued British occupation; the beginning of polarisation of national politics between Wafdists and liberal constitutionalists; and various episodes expressing factionalism in the 1920s and 1930s as exemplified by growing dissension in the Wafd and the rise of the Sa'adist group.[14]

These conditions, along with consciousness of Western attacks by orientalists[15] and missionaries on core elements of the religion (that is, on its founder and the principles he represented), propelled the eminent literary writers to undertake the task of defense and of authenticating their claims to civilization by producing a rationalist and humanist foundation. Haykal and Taha Husayn were associated with the Liberal Constitutionalists.[16] Their works were written against the background of the campaign for the restoration of democracy and the 1923 Constitution.[17] Charles D. Smith argues that they aimed to placate the emerging religious trend while proceeding with their modernist project. On the other hand, Israel Gershoni and James P. Jankowski argue that in the 1930s and 1940s, the Islamic heritage became central to national life. They contend that it constituted the basis for an alternative nationalist concept, in their terms, a supranational ideology where emphasis was placed on an Islamic entity.[18] This discursive context accounts for the need to enter into dialogue with a broader reading public, in particular, the rising social force of new *effendiyya* (the title given to urban educated middle-class Egyptians in the early twentieth century).[19] The complexity of the context and the multiplicity of interlocutors with whom the literature was engaged are factors that influence the level of reading and interpretation.

The biographers proceeded by establishing Muhammad's prophethood in terms of preparations and attestations of his mission and so on. This part of the narrative is meant to dispel any doubt about the status of Muhammad as a Prophet. In their defensive endeavor, the biographies focused on those episodes in the life of Muhammad which were the subject of orientalist criticisms and attacks.[20] For instance, Haykal's *Hayat Muhammad* and al-'Aqqad's *Abqariyyat Muhammad* paid attention to such episodes as Muhammad's marriage to Zaynab Bint Jahsh (the wife of his adopted son) and his relationship with women in general, his decision to exile the Jewish tribe of the Banu Nadir, his orders against Banu Qunayqa' and Banu Qurayza, and his engagement in various raids and wars. The examination of these subjects was motivated by the desire to counter orientalist charges of lasciviousness and cruelty made against Muhammad. On the issue of war and violence, Haykal justifies the Prophet's actions within a normative framework that is seen as compatible with western principles: Muhammad's action was undertaken in the name of brotherhood, a higher value.[21]

One important characteristic of these biographical writings is their claims to being scientific. There are a number of points to signal about these claims. As noted, these authors belonged to the liberal modernist trend that emerged in the encounter with the West. In some sense, they represent a continuation of the line of Muhammad 'Abduh. They wanted, like 'Abduh, to prove that there was nothing in Islam that was inherently incompatible with science. The importance of the scientific approach is evidenced in the view held by the Grand Shaykh of al-Azhar about Haykal's methodological principles. According to Shaykh Mustafa al-Maraghi, Haykal subjected all of his research sources and documents to the workings of reason, and made no a priori assumptions.[22] It should be noted that the classical *sira* texts constituted the main sources for these biographies. Thus Ibn Ishaq's *Sira* of Muhammad as presented by Ibn Hisham was one of the primary sources used. Other key texts include those of al-Waqidi, Ibn Sa'd, and al-Tabari. The writings also drew on certain orientalist sources which were seen as fair and trustworthy.

The issue of the relation between faith and science arises in the biographies when dealing, for instance, with some of the events that were recorded in the *sira* and that stood outside the boundaries of science (e.g., miracles). The authors either distanced themselves from these accounts or took a neutral position.[23] Thus, in dealing with episodes which represent attestations and confirmations of Muhammad's prophethood and his perfection, Haykal cast aside stories found in the *sira* such as the monk Bahira's prediction of Muhammad's prophethood and the opening of Muhammad's chest by an angel.

Where, then, did they stand on the issue of Revelation? The authors' affirmation of the divinity of the message was expressed in the conventional view that the Qur'an itself is a miracle, a "rational miracle," in Haykal's terms. It does not seem that the biographers addressed the question of the applicability or relevance, for modern times, of the message as revealed in the Qur'an. Instead, their focus was on the exemplarity of the life of Muhammad. The overall image of Muhammad places an emphasis on his humanity but also on his perfection. In Haykal's and al-'Aqqad's works, idealized images extend to the *Sahaba* (the Companions). The search for edifying models and terms for grounding modern values in the heritage, as argued by Smith, was pursued with the purpose of providing bases for social cohesion and progress.[24] In this pursuit, the early biographers were constrained by the need to accommodate the religious sentiment of the expanding educated public and as such avoided tackling the question of the status of Revelation.

Revisionist Historiography: Counternarratives

Following the period of *Islamiyyat*, few biographical works were written. They were influenced by the receptivity to socialist ideas at the time, one notable example being Sharqawi's *Muhammad Rasul al-Hurriyya* (Muhammad, Prophet of Freedom). Added to this was the unconventional fictional portrayal of Muhammad in *Awalad Haritna* by Naguib Mahfouz. The subject of Muhammad's life and his mission reemerged in the early 1990s in the writings of a number of Egyptian authors. These are not biographical writings per se, but works presented as critical readings of the founding period of Islam. My focus here is on two authors who are identified with this trend, namely Khalil 'Abd al-Karim and Sayyid Mahmud al-Qimni. 'Abd al-Karim and Qimni are both engaged in the same project: that of placing the rise of Islam in its historical context, and situating its emergence in relation to the social, economic, political and cultural conditions of sixth and seventh century Arabia. In fact, each authored a book bearing a similar title and dealing in a parallel manner with that period. 'Abd al-Karim's *Quraysh min al-Qabila ila Dawla Markaziyya* puts forward the thesis that Muhammad's message was an expression of the societal contradictions of that period, and also the culmination of a process which began a century earlier, namely the unification of Quraysh and its rise to dominance in Arabia. The privileged position occupied by Quraysh allowed it to be the main power in the formation of a new state. Qimni's *al-Hizb al-Hashimi wa Ta'sis al-Dawla al-Islamiyya* develops a similar argument. However, in his narrative, the Hashimite faction of Quraysh, rather than the whole of Quraysh, is the force behind the establishment of the new state.

In methodological terms, both authors aim to historicize the founding period. That is, they aim to bring it out of the transcendental mould in which it has been cast in traditional narratives. In what follows, I will give a brief outline of the main texts under consideration, and then proceed to an analysis of the revisionist project of which the texts are an important component.

'Abd al-Karim's *Quraysh* in Outline

In the introduction to *Quraysh*, Khalil 'Abd al-Karim states that his purpose is to rid the writings on the early period of Islamic history from mythologies and metaphysics which cloud reason. The line of narrative of *Quraysh* proceeds in a systematic fashion to establish the conclusion that the social, economic, political, intellectual, and spiritual context of sixth and seventh century Arabia was ripe for the development of a religion. The main thesis is that Muhammad established the state of Quraysh as a central state in control of all of Arabia, thereby realizing the dream of his great-great-grandfather, Qusay ibn Kilab—a dream which was shared by Kilab's grandson Hashim and great-grandson 'Abd al-Mutalib.

To support his central propositions, 'Abd al-Karim examines the socio-historical and cultural factors which prepared the ground for the rise of Islam. It is within a framework of power plays and competing interests that he explains Qurayshite leaders' own desires for power and for a state to promote their tribe's interests. Qusay, Hashim and 'Abd al-Mutalib are not just Muhammad's ancestors but the figures who laid the foundations upon which he built his state. The individual aspirations of Muhammad's ancestors were given shape by the political, economic, cultural, and religious context. The existence of certain political institutions such as *hilf al-fudul* (pact of the virtuous) and *hukumat al-mala* (council of clans) in pre-Islamic Mecca indicates a stirring for the establishment of a state.[25] The elders of the tribe recognized the importance of uniting the different Quraysh clans, and sought various means to achieve unity.

The family tale meshes with the historical developments of the time. 'Abd al-Karim identifies the regional and political conditions that were favorable to the rise of a new regional power based in Arabia. The weakening of Sassanids and the Byzantines empires made it possible for other contestants to appear on the scene. Regional conditions contributed to changes in the economic position of Mecca, such as the expansion of trade, thus precipitating the Quraysh dream of controlling trade routes and the entire trade sector. In 'Abd al-Karim's account, Meccan trade grew as a result of Hashim bin 'Abd Manaf's efforts in securing trade routes to the Levant after negotiations with the Byzantine ruler and in concert with the Arab tribes inhabiting the areas traversed by the caravans.[26] As a result, Quraysh acquired greater wealth, and private property developed and expanded.[27]

The economic success of Quraysh brought about transformations in social relations, which necessitated a rearrangement of the political order. This dimension of the account bears similarities to Montgomery Watt's narrative structured around the idea that changing social relations and the weakening of tribal values brought turmoil to the society and required some form of redress.[28] At the same time, the spiritual climate was appropriate for the development of a more puritanical and egalitarian form of organization. The *hanif* group represents the spiritual striving of the time. The hypothesis is that this group influenced Muhammad. As support for this thesis, 'Abd al-Karim, in a similar line to Qimni, presents 'Abd al-Mutalib (Muhammad's grandfather) as a *hanif*.[29] The practices of the *hanif* differed from those of the wider society. They were ascetics who abstained from drink and other worldly pleasures. Other sources of influence include the Jews of Yathrib (Medina) and other areas of the Hijaz, as well as Christians. The Arabs became familiar with both Christianity and Judaism as a result of their commercial travels (the winter and summer caravans).[30] Moreover, the idea of a messenger and the expectation that a prophet was about to appear were common at the time.[31] 'Abd al-Karim contends that Islam is an Arab religion appealing to the character of the Arabs.

Qimni's *al-Hizb al-Hashimi* in Outline

As noted above, the narrative line of *Quraysh* proceeds in a manner very similar to that of Qimni's *al-Hizb al-Hashimi*. In *al-Hizb*, we find an outline of the social and economic foundations of the rise of Islam. The intellectual and spiritual developments of the period are closely linked to the struggle over trade routes and the conflicts between the Hashimite and Ummaya factions of the Quraysh tribe. Commerce and trade routes were central factors in the social and political transformations which laid the ground for the emergence of the religion. Qimni presents a materialist reading of these developments, in some respects echoing the thesis advanced by Watt. At the origin was the development of Mecca and Yathrib as transit stations on the caravan routes and the competition which ensued between them. The expansion of the Meccan commercial role had the effect of upsetting the social balance and unsettling the egalitarian norms. Wealth disparities contributed to the emergence of strong personalities with leadership aims and expansionist aspirations.

Within a perspective of clan and tribal struggles, the idea of establishing a state became a frame for the perpetuation of group dominance. Qimni contends that this state was planned as a Hashimite state. As such, it was the Hashimites who recognized the need for an ideology that would allow them to attain dominance. Given the spiritual conditions of the time, the idea of a new religion and of a prophet coming out of Hashim appealed to the founders of the state. From this perspective, 'Abd al-Mutalib prepared for this religion, propagating the notion of an awaited prophet and recounting dreams and predictions that validated the claim that a messenger was about to appear.[32] As for the revealed message, it was inspired by the cultural conditions and the intellectual developments of the time.[33] Qimni advances the Hanifite thesis, but also demonstrates that the message was prefigured in poetry from the period.

Sexuality, Morality, and Social Relations in the Model Society

At this stage it is important to look briefly at two other works by 'Abd al-Karim, one dealing with sexuality in the Medinan society and the other with Muhammad and the Companions. The first book entitled *Mujtama' Yathrib* (The Society of Yathrib) focuses on the social mores of Medina, particularly interaction between the sexes. The early Muslims appear to have been concerned with worldly matters and with the pleasures of the flesh, contrary to the image of puritanism and asceticism advanced by many contemporary Muslims, and particularly Islamists, who seek to model their conduct after al-Salaf al-Salih, the Muslims of the early period. Rather than being perfect individuals, the members of the society of Medina at the time of Muhammad and the four Rightly Guided Caliphs were human beings who erred. It is important to point out that 'Abd al-Karim's account aims at undermining these images of perfection. Again, he mobilizes examples and documented evidence from that period to provide an unconventional reconstruction.

In *Shadw al-Rababa bi ahwal Mujtama' al-Sahaba: Muhammad wa al-Sahaba* (The Fiddle's Chants on the Society of the Companions: Muhammad and the Companions), the reader is presented with an account of Muhammad's relations with the Companions. In it, he appears as a strategist concerned with amassing supporters, using cunning and flattery when necessary. 'Abd al-Karim's idea of Muhammad's humanity differs significantly from that of the early modern biographers. For the latter, it is the perfect humanity. For the former, it is the humanity of a political leader with a message and a project. 'Abd al-Karim dwells on Muhammad's strategy of renaming his followers. He sees this as a means of disconnecting them from their pre-Islamic roots, separating them from their families and binding them to the new religion. He also highlights Muhammad's usage of flattering names to privilege his Companions and his announcement of a promised paradise to ten of his Companions, all of whom happened to be from Quraysh. It emerges that Muhammad favored Quraysh, although his main support came from the Medinans. This orientation of the narrative is again unconventional.

'Abd al-Karim's reconstruction of Muhammad's relations with the *Sahaba* represents an archeological study of power practices. Thus, attention is given to the methods employed by the Prophet to bring about a psychological break between *Jahiliyya* and the new society. In the process, his political astuteness is demonstrated. Further, weaknesses in the character of the *Sahaba* are stressed, as is the notion that *Jahiliyya* values survived after the advent of Islam. The idea here is that the *Jahiliyya*/Islam divide is exaggerated—a thesis paralleling that of Taha Hussayn in *Fi al-Shi'r al-Jahili* (On Pre-Islamic Poetry).[34] If this idea is to serve as a premise, a number of conclusions follow. The model society is not so distinct from the one that preceded it and the opposition between *Jahiliyya* and Islam is not so stark. A related proposition follows from a question: if Muhammad's companions, during and after his lifetime, did not undergo the transformation presented in conventional accounts, how could such a transformation be expected of modern-day Muslims who are fifteen centuries removed from the ideal society? The need to pose this question arises from the place occupied by the *Sahaba* in the Islamic imaginary. The *Sahaba* had been elevated to a status which put them beyond reproach. Moreover, by the Islamic medieval period, there developed juristic opinions on what was to be termed "*Sab al-Rasul wa Sab al-Sahaba*" (Insulting the Prophet and the Companions). According to the medieval rulings, *Sab al-Sahaba* amounts to an act of blasphemy.[35]

Revisionist History in Context

After this brief outline of the revisionist historiography of 'Abd al-Karim and Qimni, we should proceed to explore the purpose of these writings, the novelty of the enterprise and the effect it is likely to have in the sociopolitical context with which it is engaged. The context of writing is marked by the interruption of the secular nationalist discourse and the rise of Islamist movements which seek to alter the nature of the polity. Their objective of establishing the Islamic state is justified in reference to early Islamic history and by the deployment of religious texts. The Islamist challenge elicited responses from official Islam, and from the secular intellectuals who sought to deny Islamists monopoly over religious history and knowledge. The complexity of the discursive field can be discerned by taking into account the various Islamist articulations. In addition to the militant and oppositional Islamist discourse, a variety of interlocutors have come to claim the position of moderate, enlightened, and liberal Islam.

One question that arises in reference to the revisionists—and was posed with regard to the early modern biographers—deals with the why of their project. Indeed, neither of the authors is an historian of the early period of Islam. 'Abd al-Karim's career is difficult to pigeonhole. He is a former activist with the Muslim Brotherhood, a present-day member of the Progressive Unionist Party. He is a political commentator, a leftist activist, a lawyer by vocation and a writer. However, he is not an historian. Al-Qimni is a researcher by training and has worked mainly in the area of ancient Semitic studies. This biographical note is not meant to disqualify either author. Rather, it is intended to highlight the point that the writings are not purely scholarly exercises in rereading and rewriting the founding period of Islam. Rather, these authors, much like Sa'id al-'Ashmawi and the late Faraj Fuda, have chosen historical narrative as a weapon in battle.[36] Their texts are deployed in a combat with their Islamist opponents of conservative and militant shadings.[37] Khalil 'Abd al-Karim situates his writings within the enlightenment group project associated with the Dar Sina publishing house. This group includes Qimni, Abu Zayd, 'Ashmawi, and Fuda. For 'Abd al-Karim, the writings by authors in this group are dialogic in nature and aim at combating the "obscurantist" trends which he identifies most significantly with another group of writers conventionally viewed as *mustanirun* (enlightened), including Muhammad Imara, Fahmi Huwaydi, Tareq al-Bishri, and Muhammad Salim al-'Awa. 'Ashmawi and Fuda dealt with the period of the Caliphate, focusing on the Rightly Guided Caliphs and Ummayad and Abbasid rule. In their writings, they argue that the Caliphate was not an Islamic institution and that it failed to realize Islamic values. Fuda, in fact, operated on the same ground as his Islamist opponents—focusing his contest on questions of morality, presenting a position of "my Islam versus your Islam" and concluding that the Islam of today's rulers is better than that of the Caliphs.[38]

The revisionists, meanwhile, have returned to a period of history that precedes the Rightly Guided Caliphs and the dynasties which succeeded them. They zero in on the society of Muhammad in Mecca and Medina. This revisiting of the period from a critical perspective is a novel undertaking in the contemporary period. As the cases of 'Ashmawi and Fuda demonstrate, secular liberal critics of the Islamists focused their counternarratives on the periods which, to some extent, are open to reevaluation and contestation. The founding period, however, constitutes an area of investigation which has been "off-limits."

The revisionist project can be better crystallized in comparison with the early modern biographers. While the latter conceived of their writings as part of a process of authenticating values and norms and of providing a model from their heritage, the contemporary revisionists are questioning the model as presented by the Islamists. The early modern biographers were defending Muhammad and the religion against certain charges made mainly by orientalists. Hence they focused on the episodes of Muhammad's life and career which were used by orientalists to disparage his name and image (his relations with women, his conduct in battle, his manner of dealing with the Jewish tribes of Arabia). It is safe to say that such a defensive posture is absent from the revisionist writings and, as a result, many of these episodes are not dealt with. However, because their objective is to reassess the idealized image found in conventional accounts and espoused by the militants, they delve into the issues of morality, and, for 'Abd al-Karim in particular, the issue of sexuality becomes central. On this account, 'Abd al-Karim's reading of Muhammad's marriage to Zaynab Bint Jahsh is not meant as a justification or a defense of Muhammad's morality. Instead, consistent with his materialist perspective, the episode is explained in reference to the social structure and the prevailing mores of the time: Bint Jahsh married Zayd, the freed slave and adopted son of Muhammad, even though his social status was below her own; she aspired to reverse this situation and did so through marriage to Muhammad. In 'Abd al-Karim's account, therefore, the incident reads as the expression of the sociopolitical and economic relations which structured marriage and sexuality in seventh-century Arabia.

As indicated, morality occupies a key place in contemporary Islamist politics. It is around moral issues that the Islamists call on the founding period as a model. The question which should be raised here is whether 'Abd al-Karim and Qimni operate on the same moral grounds as their opponents. In other words, are they critical of the early period because it does not live up to standards of morality they espouse; standards that underlie their writings and that are parallel to those of the Islamists? In addressing this question, it should be noted that both authors situate the actions of Muhammad and the Companions in their sociohistorical context, showing how they were shaped by power relations and were part of power struggles. If they have an implied normative assessment, it is not one that is puritanical and based on ideas of moral and sexual propriety. Instead, the normative values which appear to guide their unexplicitly stated assessment have more to do with justice, fairness, equality, and liberty. On these counts, they are critical of the founding period. For instance, 'Abd al-Karim notes the inegalitarian system of booty distribution as well as the preferential treatment which Mohammad reserved for the Hashim clan and Quraysh tribe. 'Abd al-Karim stresses the exclusivist claims made by the Qurayshite Companions that were used to establish their tribal dominance, and, which had as their correlate, practices of discrimination against the Ansar (the Medinan supporters). These acts are seen as political strategies and power practices, yet they were justified in the name of the religion. It thus emerges that "the Companions did not form the Golden Society and their period was not golden."[39]

At the heart of their revisionist endeavor is a radical historicization of the founding period. This involves a reopening of the authoritative books, a return to the heritage and an archeological reconstruction of the social and political history of the time. Both 'Abd al-Karim and Qimni use classical sources in their historical accounts. 'Abd al-Karim draws extensively on a number of classics in the sciences of interpretation: the works of Tabari, Qurtubi, al-Suyuti, Ibn Kathir, and al-Fayruz Abadi; in *Sira* he uses Ibn Hisham, Ibn Sa'd, Ibn Kathir, al-Waqidi, al-Tabari, etc.[40] The choice of these sources is also tactical. According to 'Abd al-Karim, these are "al-Azhar approved sources." This represents a line of defense, allowing the authors to argue that the information they call upon to highlight certain aspects of the Meccan society and of the Medinan community is drawn from trusted sources. The authors, as such, do not question the reliability of their sources, as it is part of their offensive to turn their opponents' weapons against themselves. If al-Azhar finds fault in the material, then it must reevaluate the heritage books, an undertaking which is precisely what the revisionists want to see accomplished.

A further question that arises is whether the revisionists are solely interested in providing a corrective to the mythologized image of the founding period or whether there is some other purpose to their writings? There is no doubt that their accounts constitute a radical break with the conventional writings by Muslims on the period. However, in their emphasis on the materialist foundations of the religion, they are working within an existing tradition which had its earlier expressions in the works of both Muslim authors, such as Bandali al-Jawzi, and Western writers, notably Maxime Rodinson.[41] We may add that many of their theses and propositions recapture arguments and interpretations found in modern Western historical studies of the period.[42] As noted, there are strands in the revisionists' explanations of the rise of Islam that echo Montgomery Watt's social transformation thesis. Recent studies concerning the importance of Meccan trade routes have precipitated new controversies as well as a revival of classical scholarship.[43] Furthermore, the idea that Islam is an Arab religion grounded in the tribal structure of the period has been put forward by Patricia Crone.[44] 'Abd al-Karim and Crone concur on another point and that is the Abrahamic tradition in which Islam should be placed. 'Abd al-Karim devoted a section of *Quraysh* to the spiritual influences on Islam of other religions, including Judaism. This is not meant to imply that the revisionists have appropriated or rehashed Western scholarship.[45] Rather, the point is to draw out the distinction between the knowledge content of the revisionist writings, on the one hand, and the methodological and conceptual principles they have adopted in these writings, on the other.

'Abd al-Karim and Qimni's radical historicization of the early Islamic period follows many of the suggestions made by Muhammad Arkoun in both *Rethinking Islam Today* and *Tarikhiyyat al-Fikr al-'Arabi al-Islami*.[46] Arkoun's project of establishing a science of applied Islamology (*science Islamologique)* proposes methodological principles and conceptual categories which should guide the study of Islamic history and particularly the development of Islamic reason. Integral to this project is a rereading of the founding period, in Arkoun's terms *al-'Asr al-Tadshini*.[47] Priority, here, is given to the Qur'an and the Medinan experience, the generation of the Companions, the struggle for the Caliphate/Imamate, Tradition and Orthodoxy (these occupy the top four places on his list of privileged areas of research).[48]

In Arkoun's project, the interaction between the Qur'an, Muhammad's experience, and the materiality of the society should constitute the subjects of investigation.[49] This undertaking aims to recover the historicity of the Text, as can be shown, for example, in the distinction between Meccan and Medinan Qur'anic verses. According to this approach, the meanings and interpretations of the text must be understood in relation to the lived context at the time of Revelation.[50] Arkoun clearly aims at identifying the meanings that were later projected onto the Text and which invested in subsequent readings the idea of the transcendence of meaning. In the same vein, he proposes a retracing of the process which resulted in the mystification of the personalities of the Companions. He points to Abu Hajr al-Asqalini's writings as having contributed to the production of the Companions as transcendental individuals. Arkoun suggests that the historian pay attention to the role of myths in *Sira* production and in "consolidating the "real" or "true" foundational information that constitutes the Islamic heritage."[51]

'Abd al-Karim and Qimni did not undertake precisely to study the history and development of the myths that enter into the production of the exemplary life of Muhammad and the Companions. Rather, they undertook an archeological expedition of sorts, whereby they investigated the heritage sources to draw a sketch of the social relations of the founding society as governed by its material and symbolic structures. This project of historicization involves an interpretive effort guided by a grid of reading focused on power practices, relations of domination, and political strategies. Within this framework, we are offered an understanding of Muhammad's relations with the Companions, the wars of the nascent state, gender relations, and so on. This constitutes a departure from the classical accounts as well as from the narratives of the early modern biographers. By definition, historicity negates claims to transcendence and, as such, it is not possible to posit a past which exists outside of history.

The historicization of the early Islamic history and the life of Muhammad presents tensions and challenges similar to those faced by Christian writers in the nineteenth century who pursued knowledge and sought to record the life of the historical Jesus. Once located in his time, there was a risk that Jesus would appear alien to the modern Christian faith. As observed by J. W. Burrow, "the more fully known the historical Jesus became, the more firmly located he became in the messianic, eschatological context of the first century."[52] This was not the intended outcome of Christian historicist authors like Albert Schweitzer whose purpose was to defend the historical Jesus against mythological images of him, viewing such a defense as necessary for reconciling faith with modern ideas of progress.[53] Neither reconciliation nor defense is the aim of the historicizing narrative of Muhammad's life. In this respect, the project of these historical revisionists is distinct from Christian historians who investigate the "historical Jesus." The revisionists' aim is not to find the "historical Muhammad"—in fact the aim is not primarily historical truth as such. Rather, the overriding purpose is one of a critical engagement with the presentation of the foundational period as found in Islamist and official discourses with the aim of diminishing the hold that the "golden age" retains over projects aimed at reforming the present.[54]

Finally, 'Abd al-Karim and Qimni's rereadings raise the issue of the status of Revelation. That is, where does Revelation stand in their overall interpretations of the early period? At the heart of this question is the matter of what it means to historicize the Text. Does it simply mean that the Text should be read and interpreted in reference to the context of Revelation? Or, does it imply that we read the Text independent of Revelation, from the premise of denial of its truth? Clearly, historicization projects, such as the ones discussed here, challenge claims that the Text applies to all time and space. In these projects, Revelation is subordinate to historicity. But is Revelation denied by historicity? Certainly, neither 'Abd al-Karim nor Qimni are explicitly advancing a position of denial. However, it is a conclusion that may be drawn from Qimni's al-Hizb. This conclusion is possible because of a particular textual construction. Qimni, as pointed out above, argues that the spiritual and intellectual climate of pre-Islamic Mecca was opportune for the development of a religion. As a source of evidence, he uses the poetry of the time which conveyed and articulated messages similar to those of the Qur'an. This could be read to mean that Muhammad reworked the existing language as expressed in poetic verse. Further, Qimni concludes with a verse attributed to Yazid ibn Mua'wiyya to the effect that Hashim sought and attained power, but there was no message and there was no revelation. Both Qimni and 'Abd al-Karim have been charged with blasphemy and with kufr (infidelity). It is to the reception of their work that I now turn.

The Politics of Reception

An analysis of the reception of these works is necessary in order to gain an understanding of the boundaries of the said and the thought of, and the dialogic nature of the revisionist enterprise.

Who, then, are the receivers of these texts? For the present purposes, I will focus on the religious establishment as represented by al-Azhar, on the intellectuals and the Islamist activists. Finally, I will look at how the "general public" is constructed by these receivers.

Initially, al-Azhar remained silent and did not take a stand on the books. It subsequently moved to a position of outright condemnation and then recommended the banning of the books. The banning recommendations came from *Majma' al-Buhuth al-Islamiyya* (Islamic Research Academy) in al-Azhar. In the case of Khalil 'Abd al-Karim, he was also charged with representing the prophet as a tribal man who established a tribal state and, as such, he was deemed to be denying Muhammad's prophetic status and portraying him as nothing more than a social reformer.[55] The reports contended that the author attributed *Jahiliyya* characteristics to the Companions. According to the Academy's report on *The Society of Yathrib*, the usage of the name *Yathrib* is in itself an offense.[56] It argued that the name applies neither to Muhammad's era nor to the Caliphal period since these two periods are Islamic. Further, the description of that society's sexual mores and ethical values is seen to be distortive.[57] The idea that Muhammad established a Qurayshite state and not an Islamic state is deemed insulting to Muhammad.[58] Other accounts in *The Society of Yathrib* were found to be insulting to the Companions, particularly to 'Umar ibn al-Khattab and Sa'd ibn Ibada. A similar assessment is made in the report on *Shadw*, where it is contended that the book contains grave insults to the first generation of the Companions.[59] The two reports conclude by recommending the banning of the books on the grounds that they insult the Prophet and the Companions and all Muslims.

In conjunction with banning orders, the authors were subject to interrogations by state security. In the case of Qimni, he was brought to court by the Security Board in relation to another book entitled *Rab al-Zaman* (God of the Time). The interrogations followed the same line of charges made in the reports of the Islamic Research Academy in al-Azhar. Further, Qimni was brought before the North Cairo Lower Court where the judge acquitted him of the charges. The judge dismissed the allegations made against Qimni by the Academy. Here, we should note the strategy of the Academy for dealing with what it sees as transgressions against Islam. The Islamic Research Academy reports contend that the writings contain errors and distortion and are misrepresentations of "what is known to be true in Islam."[60] At the same time, the Academy refuses to publish the reports or to release them for public consultation.[61] The justification of the Academy for this is that it needs to preserve the anonymity of the reports' authors. More importantly, the Islamic Research Academy's *'ulama* do not consider the issues at stake to be open for public discussion, believing the public to be incapable of making sound judgments on these matters.[62] That is, these issues are only subject to review by the *'ulama* and not the ordinary Muslim.

The reaction among intellectuals is indicative of the differing positions that structure Egyptian politics today. Support came from the left, mainly authors associated with the leftist party *al-Tajammu'* (Progressive Unionist Party) and its publication *al-Ahali*. On the other hand, Islamist writers went on the attack, inciting readers by issuing charges of *takfir* against the authors. Fahmi Huwaidi, a writer with *al-Ahram*, had earlier attacked Qimni's Hashimite thesis on the grounds that it constituted an insult to Islam and recommended that intellectuals refrain from dealing with the sacred.[63] Others joined the chorus of condemnation. In one instance, a writer suggested that someone shut Qimni up.[64] A book responding to Qimni's entire body of works was published in 1997 with an introduction by Shaykh Yahya Isma'il, former head of the al-Azhar 'Ulama Front. The book highlights factual errors and misuse of sources on the part of Qimni.[65] However, the introduction is a statement of takfir and a call on Muslims to punish this offense.

Qimni was also the target of a negative press campaign. He was depicted as a person seeking fame,[66] as an ultra-Egyptian nationalist, as anti-Arab, and as an anti-Muslim intellectual.[67] The media commotion surrounding his book Rab al-Zaman and his press interviews brought him a great deal of public attention and, as a result of the takfir charges, there were fears that his life was in danger. He subsequently went into hiding for a period of time in 1998. The attackers included Dr. 'Abd al-Mu'ti Bayumi, Dean of the al-Azhar University's Faculty of the Fundamentals of Religion, along with many other leading Azhar scholars.[68] Some announced that Qimni had committed intellectual suicide. His ideas were construed as mere musings not amounting to systematic thought. More importantly, these intellectuals confirmed that the fixed fundamentals of the umma are not subject to investigation or negation.[69]

Some Islamist activists, on the other hand, condemned the writings but opposed the book ban. For example, Abu al-Ila Madi, the former Secretary of the Engineers Syndicate Board, held the view that these works should be challenged in the intellectual arena. At the same time, he stated that there were certain core principles of the Muslim community that should not be challenged, as this was likely to cause offense to the average Muslim.[70] From this perspective, the only effect revisionist writings are likely to have would be to stir the sentiments of Muslims against the authors themselves. It is deemed that the ordinary Muslim would not accept that his/her sacred symbols be put into question.

Al-Azhar's reaction and the predominant intellectual reaction proceed from a number of premises. First, that they are the guardians of the absolute truth. Any challenge to the claims to power and authority made in the name of orthodoxy must be stamped out. Second, as guardians, they are better qualified than the ordinary believer to judge and respond to the challenge. As such, the believer should not be involved in this debate. It is assumed that he/she will react only at the emotional level, being incapable of reacting at the intellectual level. These various assumptions give rise to a particular construction of the "general public" as receiver of the revisionist texts. The accuracy of this construction is difficult to gauge. However, it does not change the fact that the revisionists' interventions represent a politics of contestation and their writings attempt to create a space for debating issues previously banned from public discussion. What, then, is the likely impact of the revisionist writings on official Islam and militant Islamism?

Assessment by Way of Conclusion

At a preliminary level, the revisionist authors aim to break Official Islam's monopoly on research dealing with the founding period—a monopoly historically claimed on the basis of religious learning. Thus, the sources used to produce the official narratives are subjected to a new reading which produces counternarratives and, by extension, subverts claims to authenticity and truth. These counternarratives exist as forms of contestation of the official story, rivaling it in the task of instructing Muslims about their histories. At a higher level, it institutes an historical perspective on the heritage which aims to undermine a core principle of "orthodoxy," a claim to transcendence, and a position of standing outside of history.

The main challenge posed to militant Islamism is that of unhinging their idealized image of the founding period and raising for consideration the idea that the golden society was not golden. Again, by putting their counternarrative into the public sphere, the revisionists put into question not only the model society, but also the political imaginary which is deployed around the ideas of that model.

From this brief assessment, it is evident that the revisionist project differs considerably from the Reformation model. It is true that the revisionists challenge established religious authorities and defy clerical monopoly on religious knowledge. It is also true that they aim to implicate the ordinary Muslim in reinterpreting her/his religious heritage. In this respect, like the Reformation thinkers, their project contributes to widening the sphere of debate and to reshaping public opinion. However, the comparison of this project with the Christian Reformation remains of limited benefit given the extent to which the revisionist project differs in objectives and methods from those of the Reformation and given the specificities of the historical context in which revisionist authors operate. The objective of historicizing the heritage does not proceed from a view of upholding religious truth or a desire to recapture the fundamentals of religion. Indeed, we find that there are no theological debates on the position of the believer in relationship to the Divine—a subject of central concern in Reformation thought. The recovery of human responsibility in the notion of "vocation" articulated in Protestant thinking was driven by a desire to assert a particular view of the faith. Further, it is noted that pastoral, liturgical, and confessional aims were at the heart of Reformation writings. For example, the Reformation pamphlets were replete with prayers, blessings, and curses.[71] This theological dimension is not found in the revisionist writings discussed here. In effect, by situating the revisionist project within its discursive field and paying attention to its dialogic dimension, we find that it aims to counter what the revisionist authors view as the mythologized narrative of the early Islamic period put forth by both Islamists and representatives of Official Islam. This aim is political and is inscribed in modern concerns about the nature of political authority and its sources of legitimacy.

In my own reading, what lies at the heart of the revisionist challenge is a project of secularization of the Islamic identity by instituting a historicizing perspective on the religious heritage. In other words, the revisionist writings offer Muslims a new approach for dealing with and positioning themselves from the foundational period of the religion. This approach does not reject the heritage or deny it, but rather affirms it in its historicity. It follows that if the heritage is to inspire or guide the Muslim in his/her present, it will do so in light of an understanding of the historical context in which it developed and with a critical mind as to how this can link up with the present.

Notes

1. The main texts discussed in this chapter are Mahmud Sayyid al-Qimni, *al-Hizb al-Hashimi wa Ta'sis al-Dawla al-Islamiyya* (The Hashemite Faction and the Foundation of the Islamic State) (Cairo: Madbuli al-Saghir, 1996); Khalil 'Abd al-Karim, *Quraysh min al-Qabila ila al-Dawla al-Markaziyya* (Quraysh from Tribe to Central State) (Cairo: Sina, 1997) and *Shadw al-Rababa bi-Ahwal Mujtama' al-Sahaba: Muhammad wa al-Sahaba*, vol. 1 (The Fiddle's Chants on the Ways of the Society of the Companions: Muhammad and the Companions) (Cairo: Sina, 1997). The chapter will also draw on 'Abd al-Karim's *Mujtama' Yathrib* (The Society of Yathrib) (Cairo: Sina, 1997).

2. Numerous contemporary studies of the European Reformation(s) refute this all too common misunderstanding. For an overview, see Carter Lindberg's study, *The European Reformations* (Oxford: Blackwell, 1996).

3. A representative of the first endeavor is the work of Muhammad 'Abid al-Jabiri. For example, see his *Nahnu wa al-Turath* (We and the Heritage) (Casablanca: al-Markaz al-Thaqafi al-'Arabi, 1985). The objective of developing a historical perspective on the Islamic heritage is central to Muhammad Arkoun's work. See his *Tarikhiyyat al-Fikr al-'Arabi al-Islami* (The Historicity of Arab Islamic Thought) (Beirut: Markaz al-Inma al-Qawmi, 1987).

4. The traditional account holds that history remained in the service of religious controversy during the Reformation period. However, that view has been revised in more recent studies. For example, Irene Backus's research reveals that "historical scholarship during the Reformation era had two main components. One of these was a genuine interest in the past; the other was a concern to affirm confessional identity by privileging a particular historical method." See *Historical Method and Confessional Identity in the Era of the Reformation* (Leiden: Brill, 2003).

5. The main works in this literature on Muhammad include Muhammad Husayn Haykal's *Hayat Muhammad* (Life of Muhammad) (Cairo: Maktabat al-'Arab, 1935), 'Abbas Mahmud al-'Aqqad's *'Abqariyyat Muhammad* (The Genius of Muhammad) (Cairo: al-Maktabah al-Tijariyyah al-Kubra, 1942), Tawfiq al-Hakim's play *Muhammad* (Cairo: Matba'at Lajnat al-Ta'lif wa al-Tarjamah wa al-Nashr, 1936), and Taha Husayn's *Ala Hamish al-Sira* (On the Margins of the Tradition of the Prophet) (Cairo: Dar al-Ma'arif, 1946-1947). Further, al-'Aqqad wrote a series of biographies, entitled *al-'Abqariyyat*, dealing with the successors of the Prophet. Haykal's *Islamiyyat* works include biographies of the first three successors.

6. See Israel Gershoni and James P. Jankowski, *Redefining the Egyptian Nation, 1930-1945* (Cambridge, England: Cambridge University Press, 1995). To gain a sense of the varying interpretations of the motivations and objectives of these writings see Charles D. Smith, "'Cultural Constructs' and Other Fantasies: Imagined Narratives in Imagined Communities; Surrejoinder to Gershoni and Jankowski's 'Print Culture, Social Change and the Process of Redefining Imagined Communities in Egypt,'" *International Journal of Middle East Studies* 31 (1999): 95-102; and Israel Gershoni and James Jankowski, "Print Culture, Social Change and the Process of Redefining Imagined Communities in Egypt," *International Journal of Middle East Studies* 31 (1999): 81-94.

7. Zahia Ragheb Dajani, *Egypt and the Crisis of Islam* (New York: Lang, 1990), 2.

8. Negative and antagonistic narratives of Muhammad's life, presenting a demonized view of his character, were the norm in western accounts during the medieval period. According to some orientalists and modern scholars, this view persisted in modern accounts of Muhammad. See Jabal Muhammad Buaben, *Image of the Prophet Muhammad in the West: A Study of Muir, Margoliouth and Watt* (Leicester, England: The Islamic Foundation, 1996).

9. See al-'Aqqad's *Ma yuqal 'an al-Islam* (That which is being said about Islam), cited in Dajani, *Egypt and the Crisis of Islam*.

10. Dajani, *Egypt and the Crisis of Islam*, 13.

11. E. S. Sabanegh, *Muhammad, le Prophète: Portraits Contemporains, Égypte 1930-1950* (Muhammad, the Prophet: Contemporary Portraits, Egypt 1930-1950) (Paris: Librairie J. Vrin, 1981).

12. See Albert Hourani, *Arabic Thought in the Liberal Age 1798-1939* (Cambridge, England: Cambridge University Press, 1983), and Sabanegh, *Muhammad*.

13. Donald, M. Reid, *Cairo University and the Making of Modern Egypt* (Cambridge: Cambridge University Press, 1990).

14. See Sabanegh, *Muhammad*.

15. The first three decades of the twentieth century saw an expansion in the volume of writings on Muhammad. For a review of this literature see Maxime Rodinson, "A Critical Survey of Modern Studies on Muhammad," in *Studies on Islam*, ed. and tr. Merlin L. Swartz (New York: Oxford University Press, 1982), 23-85.

16. Taha Husayn was to join the Wafd in the mid to late-1930s. See Charles D. Smith, "The 'Crisis of Orientation': The Shift of Egyptian Intellectuals to Islamic Subjects in the 1930's," *International Journal of Middle East Studies* 4 (1973): 408.

17. Smith, "The Crisis," 400.

18. Gershoni and Jankowski, *Redefining the Egyptian Nation*, in particular, chapters 3 and 4.

19. Gershoni and Jankowski, *Redefining the Egyptian Nation*, 69.

20. For a discussion of modern western writings on Muhammad see Buaben, *Image of the Prophet Muhammad in the West*.

21. Smith, "The Crisis," 402.

22. Sabanegh, *Muhammad*.

20. According to Sabanegh, Taha Husayn was the exception in that he viewed miracles as the affirmation of spiritual knowledge which defies reason. Smith, however, concurs with Peter Caccia that Taha Husayn found that the traditional tales contained in their irrational content the proof of their questionable veracity. Smith, "The Crisis," 394.

24. Smith, "The Crisis," 405-7.

25. ʻAbd al-Karim, *Quraysh*, 89, 104, 130.

26. ʻAbd al-Karim, *Quraysh*, 52.

27. ʻAbd al-Karim, *Quraysh*, 54.

28. Montgomery Watt, *Muhammad: Prophet and Statesman* (Oxford, England: Oxford University Press, 1964).

29. ʻAbd al-Karim, *Quraysh*, 69. Sources used here are Ibn Saʻd's *Tabaqat*, Jawad Ali and al-ʻAqqad.

30. ʻAbd al-Karim, *Quraysh*, 141.

31. ʻAbd al-Karim, *Quraysh*, 78.

32. Qimni, *al-Hizb al-Hashimi*, 97-105.

33. Qimni, *al-Hizb al-Hashimi*, 109-27.

34. In this book, Husayn raised doubts about whether certain poems attributed to the pre-Islamic period did, in fact, predate Islam. For a discussion, see Dajani, *Egypt and the Crisis of Islam*.

35. See L. Wiederhold, "Blasphemy against the Prophet and his Companions (Sab al-Rasul wa Sab al-Sahaba): The Introduction of the Topic into Shafiʻi Legal Literature and its Relevance under Mamluk Rule," *Journal of Semitic Studies* 63 (1997): 39-73.

36. Muhammad Saʻid al-ʻAshmawi, *al-Khilafa al-Islamiyya* (The Islamic Caliphate), 3rd ed. (Cairo: Madbuli al-Saghir, 1996); Faraj Fouda, *al-Haqiqa al-Gha'iba* (The Missing Truth) (Cairo: Dar al-Fikr lil-Dirasat wa al-Nashr wa al-Tawziʻ, 1988).

37. Khalil ʻAbd al-Karim, interviewed by author, Cairo, April 1998.

38. See Salwa Ismail, "Confronting the Other: Identity, Culture, Politics and Conservative Islamism in Egypt," *International Journal of Middle East Studies* 30 (1998): 199-235. Reprinted in Salwa Ismail, *Rethinking Islamist Politics: Culture, the State and Islamism* (London: I.B. Tauris, 2003).

39. Khalil ʻAbd al-Karim, interviewed by al-Dustur. *al-Dustur*, 28 January 1998.

40. It should be noted that these traditional works of Arabic historiography are the sources used by Western historians working on the early period. The sources are problematic according to some of these scholars. Crone has noted that they contain inconsistencies, literary inventions, and anachronisms. Patricia Crone, *Slaves on Horses: The Evolution of the Islamic Polity* (Cambridge, England: Cambridge University Press, 1980).

41. For a discussion of Jawzi's writings on Muhammad and the founding period of Islam see Tamara Sonn, "Bandali al-Jawzi's *Min Tarikh al-Harakat al-Fikriyyat fi'l-Islam*: The First Marxist Interpretation of Islam," *International Journal of Middle East Studies* 17 (1985): 89-107. See Maxime Rodinson, *Marxism and the Muslim World*, tr. Jean Matthews (New York: Monthly Review Press, 1981). A materialist account of the rise of Islam and of Islamic ideas and societies is also found in Husayn Muruwwa, *al-Nazaʻat al-Madiyya fi al-Falsafa al-ʻArabiyya al-Islamiyya* (The Materialist Tendencies in Arab Islamic Thought), 2 vols. (Beirut: Dar al-Farabi, 1978-79).

42. The field of Muhammad research is characterized by two contradictory impulses. On one hand, it is thought that a reconstruction of the life of Muhammad and his mission was achieved by modern Western scholars at the turn of the twentieth century, and there is nothing new to add. The social, political, and religious systems of pre-Islamic western Arabia were extracted from the traditional sources and no new discoveries are to be made. On the other hand, revisionist writings of both Western and Muslim scholars have sought to question some of these constructions, providing different interpretations of that period. On this, see F. E. Peters, "Jesus and Muhammad: A Historian's Reflection," *The Muslim World* 86 (1996): 334-41.

43. Watt's writings on the nature of Meccan trade have been subject to a critical assessment by Patricia Crone in *Meccan Trade and the Rise of Islam* (Princeton: Princeton University Press, 1987). She questions the thesis that Mecca was a thriving commercial center. According to Crone, the commodities involved in this trade (leather, clothing, animals, and food-stuffs) were of a modest nature and the volume of trade could not have been very significant.

44. Crone contends that the tribal setting of Northern Arabia is the starting point for understanding the rise of Islam.

45. In interview with ʿAbd al-Karim, he indicated that he was not familiar with Crone's work. Author's interview, April 1998.

46. Muhammad Arkoun, *Rethinking Islam Today* (Washington, D.C.: Center for Contemporary Arab Studies, Georgetown University, 1987) and *Tarikhiyyat al-Fikr al-ʿArabi al-Islami.*

47. Arkoun, *Tarikhiyyat*, 17.

48. Arkoun, *Tarikhiyyat*, 16.

49. Arkoun, *Tarikhiyyat*, 17.

50. Arkoun, *Tarikhiyyat*, 18.

51. Arkoun, *Tarikhiyyat.*

52. J. W. Burrow, *The Crisis of Reason: European Thought, 1848-1914* (New Haven: Yale University Press, 2000), 206.

53. Burrow, *The Crisis of Reason*, 206. See also Albert Schweitzer, *The Quest for the Historical Jesus: A Critical Study of its Progress from Reimarus to Wrede* (New York: Macmillan, 1961).

54. For an overview of the history of writings on the historical Jesus, see Gregory W. Dawes, *The Historical Jesus Question: The Challenge of History to Religious Authority* (Louisville, Ky.: Westminster John Knox Press, 2001).

55. *al-Ahrar,* 4 March 1998.

56. "Majmaʿ al-Buhuth al-Islamiyya, al-Idara al-ʿAmma lil-Taʾlif wa al-Tarjama, Taqrir ʿan Kitab *Mujtamaʿ Yathrib*" (Report on the Book *Mujtamaʿ Yathrib*), 1 January 1998.

57. "Taqrir ʿan Kitab *Mujtamaʿ Yathrib.*"

58. "Taqrir ʿan Kitab *Mujtamaʿ Yathrib.*"

59. "Majmaʿ al-Buhuth al-Islamiyya, al-Idara al-ʿAmma lil Taʾlif wa al-Tarjama, Taqrir ʿan Kitab *Shadw al-Rababa Bi-Ahwal Mujtamaʿ al-Sahaba, al-Safar al-Awal, Muhammad wa al-Sahaba*" (Report on the Book *Shadw al-Rababa*), 3 January 1998.

60. A summary of the Majmaʿ report on *Rab al-Zaman* is contained in the text of the Court Ruling on the same book. See *Mahkmat Shamal al-Qahira al-Ibtidaʾiyya, Jalsat,* 15 September 1997.

61. A formal request on my part to the Majmaʿ to consult the reports was refused. The position of the Majmaʿ was explicitly stated in a personal communication with Majmaʿ officials, including Mr. Shukri Muhammad, Director, the Committee of Writing and Publication, April 1998.

62. This position was expressed by Mr. Shukri Muhammad.

63. Fahmi Huwaidi, "al-Taʿdud la al-Taʿdi," (Plurality, Not Transgression), *al-Ahram,* 23 March 1989, reprinted in Qimni, *al-Hizb al-Hashimi*, 31-37. Huwaidi's comments pertained to a magazine article by Qimni. The article was the basis of his book *al-Hizb al-Hashimi.*

64. Muhammad Ahmad al-Masir, "Fada'ih al-Fikr al-Siyasi," (The Scandals of Political Thought) *al-Nur*, 29 July 1992 and 5 August 1992, reprinted in Qimni, *al-Hizb al-Hashimi*, 39-47.

65. 'Umar 'Abd Allah Kamil, *al-Ayat al-Bayyinat: li-ma fi Asatir al-Qimni min al-Dalal wa al-Khurafat* (The Clear Verses: On the Deviation and Myths in Qimni's Legends) (Cairo: Maktabat al-Turath al-Islami, 1997).

66. "Dr. 'Abd al-Sabur Marzuk Yaktub li al-'Arabi Radan ala Mashru' al-Qimni" (Dr. 'Abd al-Sabur Marzuk writes for *al-'Arabi* a Response to Qimni's Project), *al-'Arabi*, 23 March 1998: 11.

67. *al-'Arabi*, 23 March 1998.

68. See *al-'Arabi*, 30 March 1998: 9.

69. *al-'Arabi*, 20 March 1998.

70. Abu al-'Ila Madi, interview by author, Cairo, May 1998.

71. See Peter Matheson, *The Rhetoric of the Reformation* (Edinburgh: T&T Clark Ltd., 1998), 47.

6

In Search of a Counter-Reformation: Anti-Sufi Stereotypes and the Budshishiyya's Response[1]

Mark Sedgwick

If there was a reformation in the Islamic world during the nineteenth century, the historian should be able to identify significant parallels between the processes of religious change in the Islamic world and in Europe during the European Reformation. The historian should also be able to identify significant parallels between the consequences of these processes. The oft-repeated regret of Western pundits that Islam has not had a reformation (and, by implication, badly needs one) would, however, seem to suggest that parallels between consequences, between the post-Reformation West and the post-reformation Islamic world, are lacking.

This chapter examines parallels between both processes and consequences. It considers one important parallel between processes: the intellectual impact of contact with an alien culture. Turning to consequences, it then argues that there are signs of a counter-reformation in at least one part of the contemporary Islamic world, Morocco. "Counter-reformation" is here loosely defined as an attempt by the formerly dominant religious authorities to respond to the new circumstances created by a reformation, to reestablish in modified form something of that which was lost during a period of reformation.[2]

Counter-reformation must be distinguished from Enlightenment, a distinction which is clear in European history but is less easily visible elsewhere. Pundits who wish for a "reformed" Islam, for example, perhaps by conscious or unconscious parallel with "Reformed" Judaism, are actually hoping for an Enlightened Islam. It was the Enlightenment, not the Reformation, that produced tolerant liberalism in the West; the Reformation gave rise to such phenomena as Calvin's Geneva, a society that was neither tolerant nor liberal. Despite its name, "Reformed" Judaism resulted not from a process in any way analogous to the European Christian Reformation, but from a very different process that this chapter does not afford the space to explore.

It is generally accepted that the greatly increased familiarity with classical culture—especially Greek culture—resulting from the Renaissance played a significant part in the process of the European Reformation. Today, classical Greek culture is commonly considered part of Western culture, but in pre-Reformation Catholic terms classical Greek culture was an alien culture, despite the elements of it that had earlier found their way into Christianity. Just as the intellectual world of pre-Reformation Europe was altered by the contact with alien culture, so the intellectual world of much of the nineteenth-century Islamic world was altered by contact with an alien culture—that of Europe or, more specifically, that of Paris. So far as process is concerned, then, this chapter examines one aspect of that contact: the impact of French historiography. This impact is considered in the context of its relation with one of the most significant changes in Islam during the nineteenth and early twentieth centuries: the eclipse of Sufism.

The change in the status of Sufism in most Arab countries between 1800 and today is very striking. In 1800, Sufism flourished—as it had for centuries—among the elites and among the masses, to the extent that it can be seen as then being an integral part of the religion of Islam. In contrast, Sufism in the Arab world is today indisputably in eclipse, at least among the elites. This is not the case in non-Arab parts of the Islamic world, especially in sub-Saharan Africa, nor is it the case to anything like the same extent among the poor—less touched by the processes we are examining—but it is very clearly the case among the elites of the Arab countries upon which this chapter focuses.[3]

The eclipse of Sufism during the late nineteenth and early twentieth centuries is itself an important parallel between the European Reformation and the process of religious change in the Islamic world, in two respects. One of the clearest consequences of the European Reformation was the eclipse of the authority of the Catholic Church in newly Protestant areas of Europe. A parallel is visible in the Islamic world. It is of course less easy to identify the location of religious authority in eighteenth-century Islam than in pre-Reformation Catholicism. I have argued elsewhere that established authority in the Sunni world before 1800 was embodied in the *madhhabs* (schools of jurisprudence) as the equivalent in non-hierarchically organized Sunni Islam of the Church in hierarchically organized Catholic Christianity.[4] Hierarchical organization can, however, be found within Sunni Islam as well as in Catholicism—it can be found in Sufism. In late Ottoman Islam, Sufi *shaykhs* represented established religious authority, in some ways even more than the non-Sufi *'ulama* did. The authority of the Sufi *shaykh* necessarily vanished with the eclipse of Sufism, part of a general eclipse of previously established structures of religious authority, of which the most striking element was the widespread abandonment of *taqlid* (following) of the *madhhabs* in favor of various forms of *ijtihad* (independent judgment).[5] This, then, is one parallel with the European Reformation, a parallel of process visible in its consequences. A second parallel, this time of consequences, is that the eclipse of Sufism has entailed an important modification in the beliefs and practices of many Muslims. This is important because the European Reformation was not just about the demolition of the authority of the Catholic Church, but also had dramatic consequences for the beliefs and practices of Protestant Christians. Unless the historian can demonstrate some similar consequences in the case of Islam—some significant change in the beliefs and practices of Muslims in countries or social classes where a reformation is alleged to have occurred—any reformation argument falters. The eclipse of Sufi beliefs and practices in the Islamic world, I argue, parallels the eclipse of central elements of Catholic belief and practice in early Protestantism.

A third parallel, also of consequences, would be a counter-reformation. This was defined above as "an attempt by the formerly dominant religious authorities to respond to the new circumstances created by a reformation, to reestablish in modified form something of that which was lost during a reformation." The Budshishiyya, the important Moroccan Sufi order which is the focus of the second half of this chapter, has since the later 1960s attempted with remarkable success to reestablish Sufi practices and beliefs among Arab elites. As such, it has been identified by one scholar as one of the very few Sufi orders to break through into "modernity."[6] This breakthrough might equally be described as a successful, if limited, counter-reformation. It will be argued that this success stems ultimately from classic Sufi techniques such as emphasizing the charisma of the *shaykh*, and from concentrating on essentials rather than inessentials. These classic Sufi techniques can only be brought to bear, however, once the anti-Sufi stereotypes that are the consequence of the earlier Islamic reformation have been disarmed, and it is upon these stereotypes—their origins and the Budshishiyya's response—that this chapter focuses.

A second respect in which the Budshishiyya may be seen to be conducting a successful counter-reformation is that it has reestablished the close and cooperative relationship between major Sufi orders and the state that was often found before the nineteenth century but has since become rare. This important aspect of the Budshishiyya's activities became clear only after my fieldwork was completed, however, and so will receive only passing attention in this chapter.[7] Although this chapter focuses on the Budshishiyya and so on Morocco, there are indications that similar counter-reformation activity is taking place elsewhere as well, though further research is needed to confirm this.

The Reformation and Antipathy to Sufism

The common view of Sufism held by the elite in the Arab world at the end of the twentieth century is well illustrated by the illusions that a Moroccan Sufi, Zakia

Zouanat, attempted to dispel in two mainstream French-language Moroccan magazines in 2000. Sufism, she explained, is not "deviationism," and Sufis are either nonpolitical or members of regular political parties (that is, they are not Islamists). "Sufism is not an archaism that people are trying to revive," she wrote, "nor an obscurantism that people are trying to install, nor [is it] an anachronism."[8]

The anti-Sufi stereotypes she was challenging are widespread, a significant and important consequence of the processes that I believe constitute an Islamic reformation, and a consequence also of some related later developments. Sufism is today generally seen by educated Moroccans and other Arabs as a deviation from Islam, or as linked to radical Islamism in its fanaticism, or is thought to be archaic and obscurantist in comparison with modern rationality, or an anachronism in the modern age, the age of socialism and nationalism. Similar views in Egypt, for example, have been documented by Valerie Hoffman in her *Sufism, Mystics and Saints in Modern Egypt*,[9] and are confirmed by my own experiences teaching students at the American University in Cairo (AUC), the institution of choice among the contemporary Egyptian elite. Today's AUC students' grandparents are probably somewhat familiar with Sufism, and many of their great-grandparents were surely Sufis, but the students themselves generally know nothing of Sufism except that it is un-Islamic, involves the worship of tombs and ignoring the *shari'a*, and is somehow associated with drug use among the poor. When an AUC student has any other view of Sufism than this, it often derives from the West, from what Colin Campbell called the "cultic milieu,"[10] and may be associated with an interest in pendulums or in Idries Shah.

Today's anti-Sufi stereotypes developed over more than a century. In the Arab world outside the Arabian peninsula, this development may be divided into three stages—the process in the Arabian peninsula was a different one, dominated much earlier by Wahhabism, a movement that precedes the Islamic reformation. Though it had significant consequences after the Islamic reformation, Wahhabism (and so also the Arabian peninsula) falls outside the scope of this chapter. Before examining in detail certain aspects of the three stages experienced in the Arab world outside the Arabian peninsula, I will briefly review them.

In the first stage, which I will call the "reformation stage," a world-view that had sustained Sufism through many centuries was replaced—largely as a result of "modern" education—with a rationalistic world-view among elites that was incompatible with many of the understandings on which Sufism is based. This change was an important part of the Islamic reformation, but one that this chapter will not explore very far, for lack of space. The most important religious response to the arrival of the rationalistic world-view, a response which I will loosely label "Salafism," then made things worse (from a Sufi point of view) in two ways. Firstly, it reached an accommodation with the new rationalistic world-view instead of challenging it. Secondly, it promoted a historical analysis that blamed Sufism for much of the "backwardness" (relative to Europe) of the

Islamic world. This first, reformation, stage is the origin of the stereotypes of "archaism" and "obscurantism" that Zouanat denies.

During the second stage, which I will call the "ideological stage" and date from about 1919 to about 1967, new enthusiasms from nationalism to socialism (and even including variations on national socialism) briefly marginalized Islam as a whole, and so also marginalized Sufism. At much the same time, the social and economic transformation of Arab societies disrupted the networks which had previously linked Arab elites to circles in which Sufism was known and understood. The result was increasing ignorance of Sufism among the elites, deriving from the lack of any first-hand experience of it. This second, ideological stage may be associated with the stereotype of "anachronism" that Zouanat denies.

During the third stage, which I will call the "reformed stage," the religious revival that swept the Arab world from the 1970s (and continues today) condemned Sufism even more firmly than Salafism had during the first (reformation) stage, producing Zouanat's "deviationism." In addition, as a result of the growth of radical political Islamism, Arab elites became highly suspicious of all forms of Islamic organization, including Sufi orders. This was a paradoxical development, given that the Islamists were the strongest exponents of the stereotype of Sufis as deviationists, and a paradox that was only possible because of the ignorance of Sufism that derived from the disruption of networks during the second (ideological) stage.

We will now look more closely at the most interesting features of these three stages, concentrating on the reformation stage. This stage is familiar to all in outline, even though views of its meaning differ, but some of the sources of its analyses are less well known, and its implications for Sufism are rarely fully appreciated.[11]

During the second half of the nineteenth century, throughout the Arab world, modernizing rulers and colonial masters alike introduced new systems of education on European models. These educational systems were rarely explicitly secularizing, but displaced the 'ulama and Sufis from the dominant positions they had previously enjoyed, and also displaced established Islamic disciplines from the education of future members of the elite. Established and aspiring elite families were obliged to put their children through these modern systems of education to equip them for the new career paths created by modernizing and colonial states. The education given at venerable institutions such as the Azhar in Cairo or the Qarawiyyin in Fez had for centuries been the path to position and respect, but with modernity led only to increasingly ill-paid and low-status occupations.

Many of these "modern" schools produced graduates who were more at ease reading English or French than Arabic, and who were familiar with the thinkers of the European Enlightenment and the conclusions and methods of nineteenth-century natural science. An ever increasing proportion of upper- and upper-middle-class Arabs thus came to value reason and rationality almost as highly as their nineteenth-century French counterparts did, and so rejected as "superstition" much of the unseen and unseeable world that is central to Sufism. The search for *baraka* (grace) and stories of *karamas* (miracles) had inspired generations of Sufis, but seemed as far from reality to the educated, "modern" Arab of the late nineteenth century as such phenomena did to progressive Europeans of the same period.

Salafism, the nineteenth and early twentieth-century reform movement that was in many ways a response to these conditions, failed to challenge the growth of rationalism. Some, such as the unusually well-informed Amir 'Abd al-Qadir al-Jaza'iri (who had spent five years in France after the defeat of the state he had created in Algeria) saw the dangers that rationalism posed to religion,[12] but the more typical—and certainly the more influential—response was that of the preeminent Salafi, Muhammad 'Abduh. 'Abduh's response was clear: rather than being irrational as its European critics charged, Islam was the apogee of rationality. Reason was not incompatible with religion—rather, true religion (Islam) was rational, and reason was Islam. Islam contained the foundations not only of a truly rational morality, but also of a truly rational social order. Indeed, Europe owed its own advanced civilization to its acquisition of reason from the Islamic world, an acquisition which 'Abduh dated to the Crusades.[13] This is an unusual choice of date, and one that lies uneasily with 'Abduh's other views, but—as we will see—it is a choice than can be easily explained.

The significance of Salafism for anti-Sufism was not just that instead of combating rationalism it accepted and even encouraged it, but that it was also actively anti-Sufi. 'Abduh may have looked sympathetically on Sufism in his youth—the story of his Sufi uncle is well known[14]—but he and other Salafis were, in their later years, uniformly hostile to Sufism. It is important that they were hostile to Sufism as a phenomenon, not just to aspects of Sufi practice, as was the case with earlier anti-Sufis. Ibn Taymiyya (1263-1328) is the classic anti-Sufi reformer of pre-reformation Islam, but was actually hostile less to Sufism as an institution than to specific practices favored by many Sufis,[15] as was another pre-reformation reformer often seen as anti-Sufi, the Ottoman jurist Kadizade Mehmed (died 1635).[16] Ibn Taymiyya and Kadizade were anyhow more the exception than the rule among pre-reformation Islamic reformers: many more reformers accepted Sufism, or were even themselves Sufis. One of the most important reform movements of the eighteenth century, the Tariqa Muhammadiyya movement, was essentially Sufi,[17] and the first self-proclaimed "Salafis"—those of early nineteenth-century Damascus—were also predominantly Sufis.[18]

Sufi reformers were of course no threat to Sufism. Even Ibn Taymiyya and Kadizade were less of a threat to Sufism than the Salafis, since their criticisms were based on different readings of the *shari'a*, and so could (at least in theory) be addressed on that level. 'Abduh's anti-Sufism, in contrast, was harder to address, since it was based less on a particular reading of the *shari'a* than on a particular variety of historical analysis, strengthened by the radical nature of 'Abduh's whole reform project.

'Abduh is not remembered primarily for his historical analysis, but—like his early mentor Jamal al-Din al-Afghani—he took a keen interest in the work of one of the leading historians of the early nineteenth century, François Guizot (1787-1874).[19] Guizot is now almost forgotten, his books out of print not only in English but even in French, yet he was once hugely influential. As well as being a historian he was an active politician and, at one point, the French premier.[20] Crucial elements of the thought of not only John Stuart Mill but even of Karl Marx have been traced to his lectures.[21] Given Guizot's impact on his European contemporaries, it is not surprising that Arab and Persian intellectuals who knew his work—such as 'Abduh and Afghani—should also be affected by his theories.[22]

Guizot's central preoccupation was the rise of European "civilization," especially the development of nineteenth-century conceptions of individual and political liberty. The European Reformation, which Guizot saw as "the insurrection of the human mind against absolute power in the intellectual order,"[23] played a central part in his analysis. 'Abduh applied Guizot's pattern to Islamic history. The place filled by the obscurantist pre-Reformation Roman Catholic Church in Guizot's reading of European history was allotted, in 'Abduh's understanding of Islamic history, to the Sufi orders. For 'Abduh, the advent of the Sufi orders during the late 'Abbasid period played a key role in the termination of the Golden Age of Islamic civilization, replacing reason with mere obedience, quelling the vaunting human spirit, and spreading that unfortunate passivity which many critical nineteenth-century European observers saw as characteristic of Islamic societies.[24] That 'Abduh also saw reason as being transmitted from the Islamic world to Europe during the Crusades is clearly inconsistent with this in terms of chronology, but again 'Abduh was following Guizot, for whom the shock of cross-cultural encounters during the Crusades helped to establish reason in Europe.[25]

'Abduh, then, introduced a view of the poisonous nature of Sufism that became increasingly widespread, though of course its true origins (Guizot's lectures at the Sorbonne) remained generally unrecognized. But even without Guizot, 'Abduh's Salafism would surely have been anti-Sufi. As a radical religious and social reformer, 'Abduh necessarily rejected established religious authority. There is an element of circularity in my logic here, since one definition of radical reform depends on its relationship to established authority—the more authority is rejected, the more radical the reform. It is, however, very clear that 'Abduh rejected the key repository of authority in Islam, the *madhhabs*, and so—for reasons discussed above—Sufism was also a natural and even an inevitable target for him and other Salafi reformers.

The anti-Sufi stereotypes created during the reformation stage, then, were of Sufism as irrational, and as a prime cause of Islamic backwardness and passivity, a major obstacle to rational reform and national revival.[26]

The second stage of the development of anti-Sufi stereotypes was the growth in popularity of ideologies that marginalized Islam and, with it, Sufism. In Morocco, for example, socialism became increasingly popular among the Francophone elite, as it did among intellectuals in France—the worlds of Moroccan and French progressive intellectuals were by then barely distinguishable. With socialism came materialist explanations of religion that typically saw Sufi *shaykhs* as exploiters of the people. Such views were to be found among Arab intellectuals as far away from Morocco as the Sudan. In Egypt, where the influence of socialism was somewhat less than in Morocco, nationalism was more important. Arab nationalism was not inherently anti-Sufi (except to the extent that it embraced 'Abduh's view of the causes of national decline), but at the least it tended to exclude other preoccupations.

Equally important during this second, ideological stage was the disruption of social networks caused by rapid urbanization and social transformations, such as those resulting from the 1952 revolution in Egypt. The new networks that were established by new elites in urban contexts did not link them to older social structures such as the Sufi orders, of whom the new elites became increasingly ignorant. Sufism came to be associated with the village—and not in any idealized way. Although the village was not forgotten by the new urban elites and was often visited on major festivals and remembered with some affection, it did not represent any Arcadian ideal. The village was seen as backward, as an "other" to be left behind. Sufism was seen likewise.[27] A further consequence of these social changes was that any members of the Arab elite who somehow encountered a Sufi order would feel as if they were among aliens—social differences being much more pronounced in the Arab world than in the West, only the most exceptional AUC student (for example) can mix comfortably with the lower classes, and none can feel at all at home among them.

The third and final stage in the eclipse of Sufism continues to the present day. This is the reformed stage, which should logically follow on the reformation stage, but in practice may be dated from the start of the religious revival that swept the Arab world after the 1967 defeat by Israel made the failure of nationalist utopianism plain for all to see. The Islam revived during this period was for the most part post-Salafi Islam, called by some neo-Salafism,[28] which I prefer to label "reformed Islam." It contained not only the hostility toward Sufism of the original Salafis, but also a Wahhabi emphasis on the extirpation of *bid'a* (unjustified innovation), and—most importantly—Wahhabi definitions of *bid'a*. These, like those of Ibn Taymiyya, originally condemned many individual practices characteristic of Sufism rather than Sufism as such, but reformed Islam came (in practice if not in theory) to view Sufism as a whole as one vast *bid'a*. Reformed Islam, then, was even more resolutely anti-Sufi than the original Salafism of Abduh had been during the reformation stage.[29]

The reformed religious revival also saw the rise of radical, political Islamism. The roots of Islamism go back to the nineteenth century, but it was only in the last quarter of the twentieth century that Arab elites were faced with Islamist movements that appeared as a threat to the elites themselves—a threat to the established order in general, and also a threat to the elites' way of life. Islamism appeared a real threat to the elites' way of life in countries such as Morocco. While the lifestyles of some Arab elites (such as the Egyptian and Syrian) had remained relatively conservative, the Moroccan elite had adopted many aspects of French culture with regard to female fashion, social mixing across gender lines, and even sometimes the consumption of alcohol. As has already been remarked, elite reactions against Islamism tended (paradoxically) to include reactions against the group that Islamists themselves condemned: Sufis.

Sufi orders such as the Budshishiyya in Morocco, then, faced numerous obstacles in any attempt to attract members of the Arab elites to Sufism. On the one hand, there was the gulf of understanding resulting from the growth of rationalism in the reformation stage and the disruption of networks in the ideological stage. On the other hand, there were the stereotypes of Sufism as an irrational contributor to the decline of Islamic civilization (from the reformation stage), as irrelevant and exploitative (from the ideological stage), and as un-Islamic (from the reformed stage). Finally, the emergence of the Islamist threat to established order made not only elites, but also regimes and their security apparatuses, nervous and suspicious of all forms of Islamic organization, Sufi orders included.

The Budshishiyya's Counter-Reformation

One of the few Sufi orders that has managed to attract members of Arab elites despite these obstacles is the Budshishiyya, which has since the 1960s been unusually successful in recruiting members of Morocco's intellectual and social elites. This order is a Moroccan branch of the Qadiriyya, first established among the Berber tribes of the Beni Snassen Massif (northeast Morocco) in about 1942 by Abu Madyan ibn Munawar al-Budshish (died 1956).[30]

Like many *shaykh*s whose followers later attract large followings of their own, al-Budshish himself had only a small circle of followers. He was the grandson of a Qadiri who had fought the French under the Amir 'Abd al-Qadir, and came of a Qadiri lineage established since the sixteenth century among the Beni Snassen, where it had arrived from Baghdad via Algeria. His own most important *shaykh*s, however, were first Tijani and then Darqawi, the last *shaykh* being the Darqawi *wali* (saint) Muhammad al-Hulw, a tanner in Fez who had taken the order from 'Ali al-Darqawi himself. Al-Hulw restored al-Budshish to *baqa* (spiritual sobriety); he had been in a state of *fana* (spiritual union with the divine) since a meeting with the *qutb* (pole, *axis mundi*), also in Fez.[31] Although the Budshishiyya is a Qadiri order, then, its more immediate origins are in the eighteenth-century Sufi explosion, and—in the case of the Tijaniyya—in the Tariqa Muhammadiyya movement, briefly mentioned above.

Al-Budshish's successor, under whom the first expansion of the Budshishiyya took place, was Abu al-'Abbas ibn Mukhtar, not a Berber but an Arab, a first cousin of al-Budshish through his father.[32] The initial breakthrough of the Budshishiyya into elite Francophone circles is said to have been in the 1960s, when 'Abd al-Salam al-Wali, a prominent socialist intellectual, went to the order's *zawiyya* (lodge) at Madagh (Oujda province, Beni Snassen Massif) to combat the growing devotion there to Abu al-'Abbas, a mission of enlightenment typical of the ideological stage of the development of anti-Sufism. Rather than convincing the deluded to mend their ways, however, al-Wali turned from socialism to Sufism, becoming a Budshishi himself, in which he was followed by a number of his political associates.[33]

However the breakthrough occurred—and the elements of *karama* in the above story cast some doubt on its historical accuracy—once some intellectuals had joined the Budshishiyya, the writings of some seven or ten Budshishi authors, and the normal tendency of an order's membership to spread across family and social networks, meant that a growing number of intellectuals entered the order. The most important Budshishi writer was Taha 'Abd al-Rahman, whose *al-'Amal al-Dini wa Tajdid al-'Aql*[34] brought many to the Budshishiyya. Another well-known Budshishi was Ahmad Tawfiq, a professor at Morocco's leading university (Muhammad V in Rabat), a counselor of King Hasan II, and director of the Moroccan National Library,[35] and from 2003 Morocco's minister of Religious Affairs. Here we see the restoration of networks linking the elite to Sufism, with new networks replacing those destroyed during the ideological stage of the development of anti-Sufism, and the restoration of close and cooperative relations between at least some Sufis and the state.[36]

Early twenty-first century states are, of course, very different from early nineteenth-century states, and so caution is called for whenever close relations between a contemporary state and a Sufi order are encountered. A "chicken and egg" problem arises: is the state recognizing an important order, or is the order important because the state has recognized and supported it? When dealing with the early nineteenth century, it can usually be safely assumed that both were to some extent true, that a symbiotic relationship existed. When dealing with the early twenty-first century, such as assumption is less safe. In the case of the Budshishiyya, however, it is clear that the steady growth of the order's size and influence preceded its recognition by the Moroccan state.

Elite or "educated" membership of the Budshishiyya was a well-established phenomenon by the time of Abu al-'Abbas's death in 1971, and was further encouraged under his son, Hamza ibn Abu al-'Abbas, who—like his father and al-Budshish himself before him—was far from the "modern" elite by background and education.[37] By the year 2000, perhaps half of the order's approximate membership of at least 25,000 were "educated" Moroccans.[38] Many of these were young men and women, sometimes school-leavers. Many came from the Islamic Studies departments that proliferated in Moroccan universities after 1979,[39] and so were more from the educated than the Francophone classes, less elite but still modern.

Recruitment from Islamic Studies departments is a remarkable achievement, given the prevalence of reformed Islam and of radical, political Islamism in such places. One factor here may be that pointed to by Tozy, who argued that the Budshishiyya's high-quality educational activities were especially important in an era when state control had robbed other sources of Islamic education of much of their quality and legitimacy. Tozy described himself as "astonished" by the quality of the Budshishiyya's educational activities.[40] Building on the order's existing membership, Shaykh Hamza appointed a number of university professors from various fields as his *muqqadams* (lieutenants) in many of Morocco's major cities,[41] a variety of appointment that shows an informal awareness of these men's central positions in various networks. In 1976 Shaykh Hamza instituted an annual "summer university" for Islamic studies at Oujda (the provincial capital for Madagh), taught by scholars who were mostly themselves Budshishis. Around 1993 children's classes were added, and in 2000 about 1,600 adults (men and women equally) and about 100 children attended the two sessions of a fortnight each, studying the classical Islamic sciences: *hadith*, *fiqh*, *sira*, and *usul*.[42]

As time passed, the Budshishiyya increasingly sponsored further "outreach activities" such as public lectures and performances of "Sufi singing." By 2000 there was at least one such event almost every month, often held at universities in Morocco's major cities. These events—in contrast to the "summer university"—were not usually overtly Budshishi. Their purpose, it may be deduced, was to reach beyond existing networks, to circumvent the anti-Sufi stereotypes of those parts of the elite that could not be reached through academic and intellectual networks.

A similar objective evidently inspired the foundation of a journal, entitled *al-Ishara*, established in 1998 to address the general public rather than Budshishis (who since 1993 already had their own publication, *al-Murid*). In 2001-02, the Budshishiyya went on to the Internet, with two websites, both in French. The first, tariqa.org, is overtly Budshishi, and is relatively small; its mailing list, in 2002, occasionally distributed "thoughts for the day" from Shaykh Hamza. The other, soufisme.org, is not overtly Budshishi, and corresponds to a magazine published in France by the Budshishi *muqaddam* there, Faozi Skali—*Soufisme d'Orient et d'Occident*. This site is bigger, and is addressed indiscriminately to Francophone *internautes* (web-surfers) in France and Morocco; it also emphasizes Guénon, discussed below. There is also a third site, isthme.org, but this is addressed only to a French audience, and deals purely with Skali's French activities, including the café "Le Derviche" in Marseilles.[43]

The success of all these outreach activities is clear from the occasional coverage the Budshishiyya receives in the mainstream Francophone press. After a "round table" held by two Budshishis at the Casablanca bookshop "Art et Culture" in June 2000, for example, one of the Budshishis (Dr. Zakia Zouanat) was interviewed (as a "specialist on Sufism") in the "Maroc société" column of the magazine *Demain*,[44] and at about the same time she herself published an article describing her *shaykh* in the most lyrical terms—and yet in terms calculated to appeal to her peers—in *Le Journal*,[45] Morocco's leading French-language news magazine (until it was closed down about a year later for publishing an article accusing the prime minister of high treason). Shaykh Hamza "inspires . . . a feeling of reverential fear" to the point where "my fingers tremble on the keys of my computer." "He is like a living archetype, escaped from the most splendid ages of our culture. Surrounded by his disciples, he brings to mind miniatures showing a Jalal al-Din al-Rumi surrounded by his Mevlevi dervishes." His "oeuvre," however, is "a work of ethical realization inspired by Sufism and adapted to the times." Shaykh Hamza is "in favor of the protection of women against abuses" and "in favor of openness and comprehensive tolerance." "Sufism," she explained to the readers of *Demain*, "has that universal dimension that puts it in touch with what is most profound in man's inspiration toward freedom, in the search for the absolute." Her careful presentation even glosses *karamat* as "spiritual virtues," a gloss which is technically justified, even though the word would normally (and more accurately) be translated as "miracles."[46]

Zouanat's presentation directly addresses the reformation stereotype that associates Sufism with decline: Shaykh Hamza is from "the most splendid ages of our culture." In assuring the reader that the Budshishiyya is modern and far from intolerant, she is addressing both the stereotypes of the ideological stage and the fears of those feeling threatened by Islamism. She does not attempt to address the reformed stereotype of Sufism as un-Islamic, but this can hardly be done at the same time as addressing those afraid of Islamism, and probably few Islamists were expected to read her article anyhow.

In addition to these presentational factors, the triumph over stereotypes of the Budshishiyya has clearly also been helped by a factor the Budshishis themselves point to, the general discrediting of socialism in intellectual circles over the last quarter of twentieth century, a process accelerated—in Morocco as elsewhere—by the dissolution of socialist eastern Europe.[47] An even more important external factor was the spread among the Moroccan Francophone elite of the ideas of René Guénon (1886-1951), a French antimodernist writer. Guénon never visited Morocco nor came into contact with the Budshishiyya (though he knew of the Darqawiyya), and wrote not for Francophone Moroccans but for Europeans. His works, however, directly challenge the rationalism that Muhammad 'Abduh accepted. Though Guénon's challenge was not to 'Abduh but to the original, European model, his critiques can have as devastating effect on rationalist Salafism as on European modernism. For Guizot, the Reformation ushered in the glorious age of European civilization; for Guénon, the Renaissance heralded the virtual extinction of all that was truly valuable, leaving Europe barely worthy of the name of "civilization."[48]

Guénon is little known in North America, but is better known in France, Italy, and Spain—and, increasingly, in Russia, Turkey, and Iran—and is familiar to many "spiritual seekers" everywhere. In his denial of the supremacy of reason and his emphasis on the validity of premodern myth and symbol, he might be identified as a precursor of postmodernism. He has something in common with C. G. Jung, but much more in common with Mircea Eliade, whose whole approach to religion in fact derives directly from Guénon's. Alternatively, because of the later applications by others of his work to politics and society— areas in which Guénon himself was little interested—he is often seen as a dangerous Fascist, a "key thinker of the New Right."[49] The political applications of Guénon's philosophy are, however, unknown in the Arab world (with the minor exception of a small number of extremist Israeli settlers in Hebron). Finally, he is the accidental founder of what in the end amounted to a new religious movement in the form of an important (and until very recently, an entirely secret) Sufi order led by a European *shaykh*, Frithjof Schuon, who was finally seen by some of his followers as a divine incarnation bringing a new religion at the end of time. These events, however, took place in Europe and the United States, and Schuon's order never had more than a handful of followers in the Arab world, and only a few in Morocco. Just as Guénon was innocent of the political applications made of his work, he was also innocent of Schuon's applications, denouncing them as soon as they came to his notice in the late 1940s, shortly before his own death.

Guénon's central thesis is that truth is to be found not through human reason but in tradition, which is why the movement deriving from him is often known as "Traditionalism." Guénon's own understanding of "tradition" derives ultimately from the *Corpus Hermeticum* ascribed to Hermes Trismegistos, and from the "perennial philosophy" of the Renaissance via nineteenth century American and French esotericism,[50] but his concept has generally been understood in the Arab world in more orthodox Islamic terms, and often equated to *din* (religion), sometimes that of the Hanif, pure but pre-Islamic monotheists such as Abraham.[51] Guénon initially identified tradition—and so truth—with the East, and identified modernity—degeneration and the loss of Tradition—with the West. Although twenty years' residence in Egypt led Guénon to modify this view, which is in some ways no more than a variation on the Orientalism to which Edward Said so eloquently objected, it is a view with obvious appeal for Arab Muslims.

Much of the power of Guénon's work, however, derives from a different and more unusual thesis, that humanity is regressing rather than progressing.

This view leans most heavily on Hindu conceptions of cyclical time, but is compatible with certain classic Islamic conceptions. The apparent achievements of Western civilization, then, are purely apparent. In fact, when the improvements in technical skill are placed against the losses in spiritual knowledge, it is clear that the net result is severe decline. That the apparent (gain) is the opposite of the real (loss) is characteristic of the modern age, an instance of "inversion." Modernity is full of similar inversions: churches that teach irreligion, promised freedoms that in fact enslave, alleged individualism that is in reality only atomization and enforced uniformity. Whatever the outside observer may think of these theses, they have over the last seventy-five years appealed to countless Westerners who found themselves estranged from Western modernity without really knowing why, from Eliade to Thomas Merton and Huston Smith, from Albert Camus and E. F. Schumacher (author of *Small Is Beautiful*) to Britain's Prince Charles. There are probably more Moroccans who feel estranged from Western modernity than there are Westerners, and—to return to our main subject—Guénon's Traditionalism has found many enthusiasts within the Moroccan Francophone elite.

Guénon's works enjoyed two periods of popularity in France, the first before the Second World War when they were being written, and the second during the 1960s and 1970s, when they were popularized by several "alternative" writers, most importantly Louis Pauwels, owner of a short-lived but far-reaching alternative French-based media empire. Although Guénon's books were known to individual French residents of Morocco before and during the Second World War—it was in Morocco that Camus discovered them, for instance—it was not until the late 1960s that Francophone Moroccans began to read them in quantity, along with the works of Camus and Sartre.[52]

Guénon has continued to be read by Francophone Moroccans until today. While his books, mostly published by the up-market Parisian house Gallimard, are too expensive for many Moroccan bookstores to keep permanently in stock, they can easily be ordered. Most bookstores routinely stock books by followers of Guénon, issued by less expensive publishers, which refer to Guénon, and would easily lead the interested reader back to Guénon himself. The "religion" sections in Francophone bookstores in Casablanca inevitably reflect the reading tastes of the French public, and thus give much more space to Sufism than to other aspects of Islam, in marked contrast to Arabic bookstores. In Morocco as in France, followers of Guénon are prominent among the authors of the most widely read French-language books on Islam, and also prominent among French translators of classic Islamic works.[53] One popular author of French books on Sufism, whose books are generally prominent in any Moroccan display of books on "religion," is himself a Moroccan and also a Budshishi: Faozi Skali (born 1953), the *muqaddam* referred to above. His most important book is *La voie soufie*.[54] Skali is very much a Moroccan of the Francophone elite, and discovered Sufism and the Budshishiyya as a result of reading Guénon while a student in Paris.[55] This, according to another Budshishi *muqaddam*, Ahmad

Qustas (born 1952), is typical. In his view, the writings of Guénon have played some part in the coming to the order of nearly all those originating in the Francophone milieu.[56]

As well as examining the Budshishiyya's success in attracting "modern" Moroccans, we also have to explain the order's success in retaining such people once they have been first attracted to it. This derives in part from the widely acknowledged charisma of Shaykh Hamza, to which all the Budshishis with whom I spoke testified. Another quality to which Ahmad Qustas drew attention was that Shaykh Hamza was adroit in "tying up the arrogance of the intellectual." The Budshishiyya's success in retaining elite recruits, however, also results from a pragmatic approach to the application of the *shari'a*, from the "purity" of its practices, and from internal organization that makes excellent use of preexisting networks.

Shaykh Hamza stresses the importance of following the *shari'a*, often saying that "our order is built on the Book and the Sunna."[57] In this he is in part addressing reformed stereotypes of deviationism, and in part echoing the Tariqa Muhammadiyya movement and many other earlier great *shaykhs*. However, he and his lieutenants do not consider adherence to every detail of the *shari'a* an urgent issue, especially for people such as university students and Frenchmen. Thus women who arrive at the *zawiyya* at Madagh wearing fashionably tight jeans rather than covering their hair may be requested to modify their dress a little out of deference to the sensibilities of less Westernized Budshishis, but they are never told to cover their hair because that is what the *shari'a* requires. Zouanat herself not only does not cover her hair but is even distinctly glamorous, which must reassure actual and potential female Budshishis of her own class and culture. This "openness" (as it is seen by many of the Francophone elite) is in part the logical extension of the order's general outreach activities—it would make little sense to attract a "modern" Francophone Moroccan woman to an artistic event only to drive her away with immediate demands to veil her nakedness. It also reflects a variety of pragmatism well-established among Sufis since the earliest days of Sufism. Senior Budshishis explain that the view is that people will come to the details of the *shari'a* in their own way, and at their own time.

Thirdly, the Budshishiyya's practices are—in comparison to the Moroccan norm—"pure." Three standard aspects of contemporary Moroccan Sufism are often—though not always—conspicuous by their absence from the Budshishiyya: visits to tombs, a dramatic form of *dhikr* (communal repetitive prayer), and the function of the *shaykh* as patron and intermediary in political and economic affairs (though it remains to be seen how well this will resist the pressures created by increasing Budshishi presence in government). Visiting tombs of saints in search of *baraka* or some form of intercession is a well-established aspect of popular practice throughout the Islamic world, and one generally endorsed by Sufis, whose past *shaykhs* are often the saints whose tombs are visited. It has always been a controversial practice, and is today especially controversial. The Budshishiyya does not encourage such visits, and its annual *mawlid* (anniversary celebration) at Madagh celebrates the birth of the Prophet, not of one of its own *shaykh*s. Similarly, the standard form of the Budshishi *dhikr* is restrained in comparison to the Moroccan norm, which makes use of music and drums, and frequently involves participants beating their chests or even using whips[58]—an interesting transfer of Shi'i practice to a country far from the centers of Shi'ism. None of these features are to be found at the standard Budshishi *dhikr*, and Shaykh Hamza also eschews the standard patronage aspects of the role of most Moroccan *shaykh*s. By a process of elimination, then, practices such as the order's liturgy are emphasized more than in most other orders. It is unclear whether these departures from the Moroccan norm date from as late as the 1960s or from much earlier, and the extent to which they are found today is in dispute,[59] but if they date from the 1960s they would be a classic example of counter-reformation. An early origin is however possible, since this variety of "pure" practice is characteristic of the eighteenth-century Tariqa Muhammadiyya movement which lies at the order's origins.

A fourth factor in retaining elite Budshishis is the deliberate building of networks within the order that correspond to, and so are reinforced by, other preexisting networks. Put differently, the environment of the Budshishiyya is one in which a member of the Moroccan elite can feel at home. In the bigger cities, *dhikr* sessions are organized by district, so that Budshishis tend to meet their neighbors, usually people of similar backgrounds. I joined one such session in a well-appointed villa in a prosperous part of Fez, attended mostly by evidently well-to-do men in their fifties and above. Other sessions in other places, I was told, would attract a predominantly younger congregation (the age profile of the order in fact tends toward the young). The *dars* (lesson) was on this occasion given by Ahmad Qustas, the local *muqaddam*, whose person is in some ways symbolic of the order as a whole. As a one-time professor of Islamic studies at the Qarawiyyin, he was well qualified to speak on Islam. As a long-time follower of a *shaykh* whose greatness is generally acknowledged, he was well qualified as a *murshid* (spiritual guide). As a trilingual graduate of the University of Maryland and the driver of a Mercedes, he was well qualified to mix with the elite. He has since become the *chef de cabinet* (a sort of under-secretary) at the ministry of Religious Affairs,[60] and his future career will be interesting to watch.

The separation of Budshishis by background is not exclusive to the Budshishiyya, nor is it absolute. Many other Moroccan orders have similar local networks.[61] All Budshishis also meet twice a week in the order's main local *zawiyya* for *dhikr*, as well as in smaller groups in their own districts; and most Budshishis meet most others once a year on the Prophet's Birthday in Madagh. Budshishis are also divided according to their spiritual status, with most *dhikr* sessions remaining open to all, and special *taqwin* (strengthening) sessions of all-night *dhikr* being reserved for those more advanced students who are selected for the purpose. This division is not related to what may be called "retention strategies," but is rather an aspect of the functioning of the order as an order.

Conclusion

The Budshishiyya, then, has addressed reformed and reformation anti-Sufi stereotypes very effectively, to the extent that its activities can be seen as an instance of something very like a counter-reformation. The Budshishiyya itself is a relatively new order, but is clearly representative in type of what I termed "the formerly dominant religious authorities." It has certainly responded to new circumstances, and it has succeeded in reestablishing—at least among the elites—"something of that which was lost" during the previous century, the period that I see as an Islamic reformation. It is also showing signs reestablishing the former cooperative relationship that major Sufi orders often enjoyed with the state. To what extent the Budshishiyya is an isolated example, and to what extent it will become evident as part of a wider trend, remains to be seen. If there is a wider trend, the Budshishiyya might be associated in it with the Nurcus, in Turkey, an area that falls beyond the scope of this chapter.

If a wider counter-reformation is not yet an established consequence of a reformation that parallels the European experience, the eclipse of Sufi beliefs and practices in much of the Arab world is more of an established fact. It is an eclipse which parallels similar eclipses in Europe. This chapter has traced the origins of this eclipse, origins that have not been established with complete certainty, but which 'Abduh's use of Guizot, the emphases in the writings of Zakia Zouanat, and the nature of the Budshishiyya's response all make most plausible.

It has been argued that the earliest origin of these anti-Sufi stereotypes was in the period that I characterize as the reformation, when Sufism's position was first weakened and then assailed. Resistance to Sufi practices had existed before this period, but was neither particularly widespread nor particularly influential. Sufism was initially weakened by the spread among the elites of a rationalistic world-view that was "incompatible with many of the understandings on which Sufism is based." There is, admittedly, an element of circularity here—such a major change is almost more of a reformation than a cause of one—and this transformation requires some further demonstration. It is, however, clear that European-style rationalism was very present among the Moroccan elites in the latter part of the twentieth century, since otherwise they could have had little interest in a René Guénon, one of whose main targets was European-style rationalism. The same test is not available for countries where the elites do not read French,[62] but the indications are that the situation was little different elsewhere in the Arab world.

The means by which Sufism's position, once weakened, was then assailed are clearer. The influence of François Guizot can be easily traced, establishing the association between Sufism and civilizational decline, an association addressed by Zouanat's counter-association of Sufism with Islam's days of glory.

The development of contemporary anti-Sufi stereotypes, stereotypes which closely parallel certain Protestant stereotypes of Rome, was not just the consequence of rationalism and Guizot. There were at least two further stages, the "ideological" and the "reformed," stages that are easier to sketch than to prove.

Guizot and Guénon are of course only two aspects of the intellectual impact on the Islamic world of contact with an alien culture, but both are clearly visible and likely to be representative. Guizot was of the Enlightenment—although much later than the classic Enlightenment philosophers, he deserves to be called an Enlightenment writer if only on account of his optimism. Guénon was representative of what may be called the post-Enlightenment, whether in its modern or postmodern forms—and indeed (as has been said) Guénon's thought can be seen as a precursor of contemporary postmodernism.

One last aspect of the model outlined in this chapter needs to be addressed: the subaltern role by implication assigned to the Islamic world. Paris invents reason, and Muslims respond; Paris sees the problems with reason, and the Muslims again respond. This would seem to deprive Muslims themselves of agency, a view which is not only insulting but also historiographically dubious. The nineteenth century, however, was the period of human history in which the interconnections between different regions of the world first became such that one can properly speak of "globalization." In examining such an era, it is not possible to ignore the existence of global centers of intellectual production, among which Paris was for a long time preeminent. Both Guizot and Guénon had an important impact in Moscow; why not then in Casablanca?

Notes

1. This chapter is based on a paper given at the annual meeting of the American Academy of Religion in Toronto, November 23-26, 2002. My thanks to the American University in Cairo for a research grant that made possible my fieldwork in Morocco. My thanks also to three anonymous reviewers for the *International Journal of Middle East Studies*, who read an earlier draft of this chapter before it was withdrawn to appear in this book, and to the editors of *IJMES* for their understanding when they lost an article on which work had already started.

2. The European Counter-Reformation was, of course, not just a reaction to the European Reformation, but also an independent response to some of the factors that resulted in the Reformation.

3. Algeria may to some extent be an exception. See Ahmed Rouadjia, *Grandeur et Décadence de l'État Algérien* (Grandeur and Decadence of the Algerian State) (Paris:

Karthala, 1994). Possible state-sponsored exceptions in Uzbekistan, Syria, and Egypt are discussed in note 36.

4. Mark Sedgwick, "Sects in the Islamic World," *Nova Religio* 3 (2000): 195-240. A revised version of this article is forthcoming as Sedgwick, "Establishments and Sects in the Islamic World," in *New Religious Movements: The Future of New Religions in the 21st Century*, ed. Phillip Lucas and Thomas Robbins (New York: Routledge, 2003).

5. This is a development that this chapter does not afford space to examine.

6. For the only previous scholar to have studied the order so far, Mohammed Tozy, this is its main significance. Tozy also remarks that the Budshishiyya has demonstrated the limits of the power of the Moroccan state in religious affairs. Mohammed Tozy, "Le Prince, le Clerc et l'Etat: La Restructuration du Champ Teligieux au Maroc" (The Prince, the Cleric, and the State: The Reconstruction of the Religious Field in Morocco), in *Intellectuels et Militants de l'Islam Contemporain* (Intellectuals and Militants in Contemporary Islam), ed. Gilles Kepel and Yann Richard (Paris: Du Seuil, 1990), 71 and 86.

7. This chapter also ignores Karim Ben Driss, *Sidi Hamza al-Qadiri Boudchich. Le Renouveau du Soufisme au Maroc* (Paris: Albouraq, 2002), of which I learned only as this chapter was in press. Readers may also care to consult Mostafa Amrous, "Les Confréries Religieuses et l'Islamisme au Maroc du Dix-Neuvième au Vingtième Siècle" (unpublished thesis, University of Paris X, 1989). My thanks to Rafael Medel for drawing my attention to Amrous's thesis, which I have not yet been able to consult.

8. Zakia Zouanat, "Sidi Hamza, le Saint Vivant," *Le Journal* (Casablanca) (27 May 2000): 55; and Thami Afailal, "René Guénon: Un Modèle Soufi du XXème Siècle" (René Guénon: A Sufi Model of the 20th Century), *Demain* (1 July 2000): 17.

9. Valerie J. Hoffman, *Sufism, Mystics and Saints in Modern Egypt* (Columbia: University of South Carolina Press, 1995).

10. Colin Campbell, "The Cult, the Cultic Milieu and Secularization," *A Sociological Yearbook of Religion in Britain* 5, ed. Michael Hill (London: SCM Press, 1972): 119-36.

11. See, however, Carl W. Ernst, *The Shambhala Guide to Sufism* (Boston: Shambhala, 1997), 205-10.

12. Itzchak Weissman, *Taste of Modernity: Sufism, Salafiyya, & Arabism in Late Ottoman Damascus* (Leiden: Brill, 2001), 164-65.

13. Muhammad 'Abduh, *Risalat al-Tawhid* (The Theology of Unity) (Cairo: Dar al-Hilal, 1963).

14. "Shaykh Darwish" (which seems unlikely to have been his real name) was given credit by Rashid Rida for helping the young 'Abduh back on to the Islamic path after he had dropped out of the courses he was taking at the Ahmadi mosque in Tanta. See Albert Hourani, *Arabic Thought in the Liberal Age, 1798-1939* (Cambridge: Cambridge University Press, 1983), 131.

15. For Ibn Taymiyya and Sufism, see George Makdisi, "Ibn Taimiya: A Sufi of the Qadiriya Order," *American Journal of Arabic Studies* 1 (1973): 118-29. Another interesting article is Eric Geoffroy, "Le Traité de Soufisme d'un Disciple d'Ibn Taymiyya: Ahmad 'Imad al-Din al-Wasiti, m. 711/1311" (The Sufi Treatise of a Disciple of Ibn Taymiyya: Ahmad 'Imad al-Din al-Wasisti, d. 711/1311), *Studia Islamica* 82 (1995): 83-101.

16. See Madeline C. Zilfi, *The Politics of Piety: The Ottoman Ulema in the Postclassical Age (1600-1800)* (Minneapolis: Bibliotheca Islamica, 1988).

17. This movement has been much discussed by scholars in recent years, and a clearer picture is beginning to emerge. See chapter two of my *Saints and Sons: The Making and Remaking of the Rashidi Ahmadi Sufi Order, 1799-2000* (Leiden: Brill, forthcoming).

18. See Weissman, *Taste of Modernity*.

19. Hourani, *Arabic Thought*, 114.

20. Guizot was also minister of education 1832-37, then ambassador to London, then foreign minister in 1840 and finally prime minister until the revolution of 1848.

21. Larry Siedentop, "Introduction to François Guizot," in *The History of Civilization in Europe* (London: Penguin, 1997), xxx-xxxvii.

22. More than 'Abduh and Afghani knew Guizot. 'Abduh lectured on Guizot's theories, and the *History of Civilization* was published in Arabic in 1877. Hourani, *Arabic Thought*, 114.

23. Guizot, *History of Civilization*, 197.

24. 'Abduh, *Risalat al-Tawhid.*

25. Guizot, *History of Civilization,* 144-45.

26. Of course, it was still not entirely clear what constituted "the nation," but its revival was anyhow the objective.

27. I have little scientific evidence for these conclusions, but the dislocations referred to are very obvious today, and can hardly have resulted from any earlier period. Though he is concerned with lower social classes, 'Abd al-Hakim Qasim gives an interesting insight into the process in his excellent novel *Ayyam al-Insan al-Sab'a* (The Seven Days of Man) (Cairo: Dar al-Kitab al-'Arabi, 1969).

28. For example, Reinhard Schulze, *Islamischer Internationalismus im 20. Jahrhundert: Untersuchungen zur Geschichte der Islamischen Weltliga* (Leiden: E. J. Brill, 1990).

29. The origins and course of the mixture of Salafism with Wahhabism lie beyond the scope of this chapter, but the role of Rashid Rida is clearly central.

30. The surname "Budshish" is a form of the nickname Abu Dashish, *dashish* being a soup made of barley, a staple food of the Moroccan poor once often distributed at Sufi *zawiyya*s.

31. Ahmad Qustas, *Nibras al-Murid fi Tariqa al-Tawhid* (The Lamp of the Novice on the Path of Unity) (Fez: al-Murid, 1993), 34-38.

32. Mukhtar was, like his brother Munawar (the father of al-Budshish), a Qadiri; he had led a *jihad* against the French in the north east of Morocco between 1906 and 1908. See Qustas, *Nibras al-Murid*, 34-38.

33. Interviews with Budshishis in Fez, January 2001. Where no other source is given, information on the Budshishiyya derives from such interviews.

34. Taha 'Abd al-Rahman, *al-'Amal al-Dini wa Tajdid al-'Aql* (Religious Practice and the Renewal of Reason) (Casablanca: al-Markaz al-Thaqafa al-'Arabi, first published 1989; third edition 1997).

35. He was well enough known to be the first writer on Sufism to come to the mind of Mazruq al-'Arabi, a ticket inspector at Fez railway station with whom I fell into conversation while awaiting a train.

36. Some observers have seen similar developments elsewhere, and there has also been much speculation about the encouragement of Sufism by various states as an

antidote to radical political Islamism. This subject would require a separate study to explore properly. In both Algeria and Uzbekistan, Sufis are reported to have benefited from official patronage, but my feeling is that state sponsorship of Sufism is often more the dream of some Sufis than an established reality. That the current Mufti of the Republic in Egypt is a Khalwati is more accident than design, for example; his Sufi identity is downplayed rather than central (my thanks to Rachida Chih, the leading contemporary authority on the Egyptian Khalwatiyya, for her illuminating comments on this point). The favored position of the Naqshbandiyya in Syria probably owes much to Mufti Kuftaru's personal relations with leading circles within the Alawite leadership; see Annabelle Böttcher, *Syrische Religionspolitik unter Asad* (Syrian Religious Politics Under Asad) (Freiburg: Arnold-Bergsträsser-Institut, 1998). The true extent of the political influence of the Naqshbandiyya in Turkey is unclear, but may have been exaggerated by the fears of Turkey's secularist elite.

37. He studied at the *madrasa* in Oujda, the local provincial capital for Madagh. His son Jamal, however, was in 2001 preparing a Ph.D. at the Department of Shari'a at the Qarawiyyin University.

38. The estimate is from Ahmad Qustas, and is based on an attendance of 20,000 at the 2000 *mawlid* celebrations at Madagh. Marc Boudet estimates an attendance of 15,000-20,000, which would reduce Qustas's estimate. See Boudet, "Embarquement pour Madagh," *Soufisme* 5 (2000): 5. An outsider estimated a total following of not 20,000 but 200,000, and Mohammed Tozy quotes a Budshishi source as estimating 100,000, but says that he has no way of judging this estimate himself. See Tozy, "Le prince, le clerc et l'État," 83. The size of Sufi orders is notoriously difficult to estimate, and is also a question of definition: what exactly makes someone a "follower" rather than a sympathizer?

39. Youth was emphasized by my Budshishi sources. For recruitment in *lycées* and universities, see Tozy, "Le Prince, le Clerc et l'État," 81 and 85.

40. Tozy, "Le prince, le clerc et l'État," 82-84, 72-77, and 89-90.

41. For example, Muhammad Dashimi in Fez, and Muhammad ibn 'Aqid in Casablanca (a professor of law).

42. Ahmad Qustas, interview, January 2001.

43. Sites visited in September 2002.

44. Afailal, "René Guénon."

45. Zouanat, "Sidi Hamza."

46. Afailal, "René Guénon" and Zouanat, "Sidi Hamza."

47. This is the conclusion I arrived at in my interview with Ahmad Qustas.

48. The work in which Guénon expresses these ideas most clearly is *La Crise du Monde Moderne* (Paris: Bossard, 1927; Paris: Folio, 1999). See also *Orient et Occident* (Paris: Payot, 1924; Paris: Guy Trédaniel, 1993). The most recent English translations of these two books are *The Crisis of the Modern World* (Ghent, NY: Sophia Perennis et Universalis, 2001) and *East and West* (Ghent, NY: Sophia Perennis et Universalis, 2001).

49. Denis Paillard, "Encouragée par des Activistes Occidentaux: L'Inquiétante Renaissance de l'extrême droite," *Le Monde Diplomatique*, January 1993.

50. For the earlier history of Traditionalism, see chapters 1 to 3 of my *Against the Modern World: Traditionalism and the Secret Intellectual History of the Twentieth Century* (New York: Oxford University Press, forthcoming 2004). Where no other source is given for information concerning Traditionalism outside Morocco, see this book.

51. Conclusions based on discussions with Moroccan, Algerian, Turkish, and Iranian followers of Guénon.

52. Ahmad Qustas, interview, Fez, January 2001.

53. These comments are based on visits to a selection of bookstores in Casablanca in January 2001 and discussions with the manager of the Livre Service bookstore.

54. Faouzi Skali, *La Voie Soufie* (The Sufi Way) (Paris: Albin Michel, 1993; first published 1985). It was followed by four others: *Futuwwa: Traité de Chevalerie Soufie, Jésus dans la Voie soufie, Traces de Lumières,* and *Le Face à Face des Doeurs: le Soufisme Aujourd'hui. Futuwwa* is almost an academic work. *Jésus dans la Voie Soufie* was written with Eva de Vitray-Meyerovitch, the translator of the Rumi text which had been influential on the younger Skali. The subject matter of this book may reflect Vitray's concerns more than Skali's. Vitray had become Muslim long before she met Skali, but it was Skali who introduced her to the Budshishiyya, which she later took from Shaykh Hamza. See Skali, "Eva de Vitray." *Traces de Lumières* is a series of dialogs between a master and a disciple based on Ibn Ata Allah. *Le Face à Face des Coeurs* is an edited collection of Skali's lectures. See Bruno Hussein, Review of Skali's *Face à Face, Soufisme* 5 (2000): 39.

55. Faozi Skali, interview, Fez, January 2001.

56. Ahmad Qustas, interview, Fez, January 2001.

57. Quoted in Qustas, *Nibras al-Murid,* 42.

58. Earle Waugh, personal communication (Cairo, September 2002), based on fieldwork in Morocco during visits from 1995 to 1999. My thanks to Dr. Waugh for first pointing out to me the various differences from the norm discussed in this section.

59. There are no known accounts of earlier Budshishi practice, and different observers disagree as to the prevalence of the "pure" and of the more normal Moroccan forms of the *dhikr.* I was not able to visit enough *dhikrs* to form a view myself.

60. Rafael Medel, email to the author, May 2003.

61. Earle Waugh, personal communication.

62. Guénon has only very rarely been translated into Arabic, and though there are many English translations, he is less well known in Anglophone intellectual circles than in Francophone ones.

7

Primitivism as a Radical Response to Religious Crisis: The Anabaptists of Münster in the 1530s and the Taliban of Afghanistan in the 1990s

Ernest Tucker

In 1957, Norman Cohn identified five characteristics of salvation common to the millenarian sects and movements that proliferated in Europe between 1250 and 1600 CE. He found that these groups commonly saw salvation as collective, terrestrial, imminent, total, and miraculous.[1] Cohn's work spawned studies of millenarian projects in diverse cultures and times that envisioned idealized futures promising deliverance from current problems.[2] He noted the persistence of the utopian dream into the modern era of a "final, exterminatory struggle against 'the great ones'; and of a perfect world from which self-seeking would be forever banished."[3] Numerous observers have described many versions of this "pursuit of the millennium" at various turning points in the histories of all parts of the world. Perhaps one of the most striking such eras occurred as Europe was overtaken in the sixteenth and seventeenth centuries by a series of upheavals during the Protestant Reformation. Scholars of many millenarian movements in other cultures have adapted insights from this European epoch and applied them to a wide variety of other episodes of millennial aspirations around the globe in different eras.

Islamic societies have certainly experienced numerous millennial movements, among which were the twelfth-century Nizari/Isma'ili Assassins, charismatic religious coalitions with nomadic tribal followers like the Safavids in fifteenth-century Iran, and various messianic leaders who arose at pivotal moments across the Islamic world, such as the nineteenth-century Sudanese *mahdi*.

Since Islam is a faith in which "right practice" (orthopraxy) is as important as "right belief" (orthodoxy), millennial sentiments in the Islamic world have often focused as much on the creation of a just terrestrial order as an anticipation of a Day of Judgment.[4] Although salvation and the forgiveness of sin are clearly basic goals for Muslims who, like Christians, confront such a final time of moral and ethical reckoning, the establishment of justice ('*adl*) in a God-given terrestrial realm is equally important and has shaped Muslim millennial concepts as much as apocalyptic expectations. Christian millennialism, by contrast, has often been more driven by the expectation and hope of imminent salvation.

Given this general difference, perhaps little could be found to link such Muslim phenomena with the long sequence of Christian providential projects beyond the common quest of all such movements for a better future through divine intervention. This chapter will argue that two radical millennial movements, one Christian and one Islamic, might profitably be compared to reveal parallels between the broader epochs of religious change and crisis in which they both figured. Comparison of the extreme ways by which both purposefully abandoned long-held norms of their respective faiths can shed light on the similar magnitude of political, social, and economic transformations occurring during their respective eras.

Although the Anabaptists of Münster (called the "Münsterites" in this chapter) in the 1530s and the Afghan Taliban in the 1990s produced two millenarian movements that many observant Christians and Muslims would rather forget, their millennial expectations came to be transformed into action in similar ways during crises. Both movements asserted religious legitimacy not only through extreme words, but extreme deeds, in order to restore "authentic" versions of their faith traditions as they saw them. Their harshness and intensity may also have arisen from a similar need to eradicate the uncertainties of their complex times. Ultimately, despite the fact that Münster in the early sixteenth century was not physically in such dire straits as Afghanistan in the twentieth and that many more Christians have disowned the Münsterites than Muslims have disavowed the Taliban, both groups have come to be widely regarded as erroneous failures by their coreligionists, particularly those trying to discern new spiritual pathways.

George Williams contrasted the "Radical Reformation" of the Anabaptists, Spiritualists, and Rationalists with the "Magisterial Reformation" of Lutherans and other more mainstream Protestant groups that were formed in sixteenth-century Europe. He perceived the focus of the latter group to have been the more conservative goal of *reformatio* (reformation of the existing religious order), an agenda at odds with the radical goal of the former group: *restitutio* (restitution of what was perceived to have been the original order of the faith community).[5] From his perspective, the radical reformers wished to "recreate" their version of what the original religious community had been based on their reception of scripture, while the magisterial reformers wanted only to "reform" the existing order to correct its problems and deficiencies, not destroy it. In the modern Islamic case, there are similar arguments over "reform" and "restitution" with respect to existing religious norms.[6] In the context of the present comparison, it is interesting to note how the Taliban, like the Anabaptists, placed more emphasis on "restitution" than "reformation" as defined by Williams.

Of course, it could also reasonably be asserted that even among groups who promoted the radical renewal or reformation of Christianity and Islam at various times, both the Münsterites and the Taliban were essentially anomalies. More sustained and less radical reformation and renewal movements among other contemporary religious activists might be presented as more useful objects of study, since they better reflected broader, more gradual trends. It is also only fair to admit that the differences between the political, historical, economic, and social contexts of these two places and times might make them truly impossible to compare. This essay will argue that these two crisis episodes are worth comparing, though, because of an important parallel between them: their reductionist primitivism. The Münsterites and the Taliban, despite their myriad differences, pursued millennial dreams. They both used unprecedented violence to depart radically from long-established religious custom and impose religious understanding based on a simplified, purified, and reductionist version of faith. Both arose at comparable crisis points for two monotheisms struggling to come to terms with global contexts that had rapidly changed and threatened traditional norms.

The two groups went beyond most other contemporary reformation projects of their respective faiths in at least four ways. They emphasized the symbolic destruction of existing religious and cultural treasures with an intensity that far transcended their fellow religious reformers. The Taliban and Münsterites were led by figures who emerged from obscurity such as Mulla Muhammad Omar and Jan Bockelson van Leyden. These men based their authority less on formal demonstrations of religious understanding or knowledge than on proofs of mystical connection to God through dreams and visions. The two groups administered justice and enforced moral strictures with unprecedented harshness, singling out women in particular for suppression. Finally, the two groups became quite alienated from other contemporary groups in their faith traditions that advocated religious reform—an alienation that united otherwise mutually hostile groups against them.

Ultimately, the Taliban and the Münsterites are most comparable as consciously unschooled attempts to "get it right": to follow the perceived "true" commandments of scripture by relying on purity and naïveté in contrast to the perceived hypocritical sophistication of those around them. Their stridency came to be viewed as dangerous both by defenders of traditional versions of their faiths and other fellow religious reformers. A brief comparison of the histories and fates of the two groups thus can shed light on broader struggles to redefine relationships between religious truth and worldly life that engulfed Christianity and Islam at these particular times.

Contexts of the Two Groups

Despite considerable differences between the settings in which the two movements arose, their contexts reveal interesting points of comparison. Sixteenth-century northern Germany and the Low Countries were being transformed by the rise of early modern industry and commerce, a trend that paralleled the erosion of a feudal order that had dominated and organized this region for many centuries. New classes of tradesmen and craftsmen along with groups of deracinated peasants, none of whom fit neatly into the established feudal order, began to crowd into the growing cities. Tensions were further exacerbated by the growing importance of money in the society: a development that affected all social classes and groups. These trends accompanied a rising sophistication and religious knowledge among the common people of northern Germany and the Low Countries, a development sped up by a swift increase in the number of printed books after the turn of the sixteenth century.

Even prior to the formal fragmentation of the Christian community that took place during the Reformation, these changes promoted a new focus on "evangelism," defined by Williams in this particular historical context as the "widespread outcropping of an undogmatic, ethically serious combination of medieval piety and humanistic culture."[7] This new consciousness developed in many different forms across Europe, but it helped create social change by facilitating novel interpretations of religious beliefs that would have great impact on traditional structures and patterns of life.

The medieval inquisition of heretics had traditionally suppressed such new interpretations through a network of inquisitorial monitoring established in the thirteenth century designed to bolster officially endorsed religious doctrines and practices. The rising trend of this new "evangelism," though, began to question certain specific practices, such as the long-established sale of indulgences. When the church needed more cash for its operations, it began to promote the sale of indulgences, sparking Martin Luther's 1517 declaration of his "Ninety-Five Theses" and indirectly ushering in a wave of popular uprisings throughout northern Germany in the 1520s. In previous times, the Church might have quickly crushed and silenced Luther, but he now escaped punishment for his statements—sheltered by northern German nobles—elector Frederick III of Saxony (1463-1525) and his brother John (1468-1532). Many princes in northern Europe began to see in Luther and other church reformers ways to assert political independence if they supported assertions of theological independence.

Luther's statements ignited smoldering resentments among peasants and townspeople that had built up during the twilight of medieval German feudalism. This unrest erupted in the Peasants' War of 1524-1525, an uprising led by Luther's former follower Thomas Müntzer who was agitating for economic reforms and social justice. Luther strongly condemned this violent outburst, since his main goal was not to overthrow the church and existing social order, but to bring it back to principles that he thought had been abandoned.

The suppression of the Peasants' War, though, only marked the end of one of the first episodes of growing popular pressure for religious reform. The 1520s also witnessed a rapid increase in Anabaptism: a new movement that called for Christians to be rebaptized as adults only when they could fully understand and accept the meaning and importance of baptism. This aggravated social tensions because denial of infant baptism had long been regarded as a clear sign of treason to the established order. It was a form, however, of defiance easily practiced by the laity that was very hard to suppress. Anabaptism was perceived as a direct attack on the church's legitimacy because baptism had always been considered one of the key sacraments that its priests administered. Any act of rebaptism thus called into question the efficacy of the church's main sacrament and, by implication, the very legitimacy of the church's authority.

The rise of the Anabaptist movement in the wake of violent peasant uprisings eventually provoked sharp reactions both from the established church and from contemporary religious reformers. Luther himself denounced the Anabaptists in 1527 with the statement, "Let everyone believe what he likes. If he is wrong, he will have punishment enough in hellfire."[8] Holy Roman Emperor Charles V formally declared on January 4, 1528, that anyone who had been baptized again as an adult or did not have newborn children promptly baptized would be considered a criminal warranting death.[9] Other rulers, such as England's Henry VIII, burned many Anabaptists at the stake.[10]

In this atmosphere of rising religious tension, the prosperous north German city of Münster attempted to insulate itself and focus on commerce through the 1520s. It mostly succeeded in avoiding overt religious controversy because, until the early 1530s, a truce prevailed between the Protestant townspeople and the Catholic prince-bishop in the city. This goal of this peace was to promote commerce. With this agreement, Münster became a stronghold of stability within fortified walls in the midst of a rural area in a time of transition and upheaval, when suppression of Anabaptists in many other areas caused refugees to flow into the city.

Perhaps in part due to the intense persecution to which they had been subjected beginning in the late 1520s, the Anabaptists had a more apocalyptic view of a coming last judgment than other Protestants who had taken refuge in Münster. This helped spark a messianic Anabaptist uprising against Münster's prince-bishop in 1534. Anabaptist groups in Münster suddenly seized control of the city and proclaimed that they were going to impose God's will on earth and set the stage for the second coming of Christ. After amassing a large army and laying intermittent siege to the city for nearly two years, the prince-bishop finally overthrew this movement by the late spring of 1536 and reestablished his control of the city, although clandestine cells of militant Anabaptists lingered in north Germany for several decades.

Later Anabaptists came to view the Münsterite regime as a failed, sinful, and disastrous mistake. Anabaptism became well established over the next two centuries as a pacifist and quietist movement, despite the fact that others tarred them with the brush of the Münsterites and fought against them for the next few centuries. Notable Anabaptist groups like the Mennonites and Old-Order Amish, who still separate themselves to differing degrees from their contemporary worldly surroundings in order to maintain their purity and simplicity as faithful believers, often remain conscientious objectors to the military draft or secular state service of any kind. Governments in many countries have persecuted and discriminated against Anabaptists because they have stood aloof from secular political, judicial, and economic systems. Later Anabaptists avoided worldly entanglements perhaps bearing in mind what had happened in Germany in the early sixteenth century.

In a different time and place, Afghanistan by the 1990s had become fragmented by two decades of unremitting conflict beginning with the Soviet invasion of 1979, a period of war that had far more severe effects than any of the upheavals of sixteenth-century Germany, but had effects similar to them in how it unraveled the existing social structure. Through the 1980s, Afghan *mujahidin* battled Soviet forces both because the Russians were foreign invaders, against whom Afghans fought in support of their traditional tribal and national rulers, and were infidels, against whom it was permissible to conduct military *jihad* or holy war.[11]

Neither the Islamic nor the ethnic component of anti-Soviet resistance in Afghanistan proved capable through the 1980s of uniting the people there, though. After the 1989 Soviet withdrawal and the fall of its puppet Communist regime, the country was wracked by the endless settling of scores and remained broken into many separate territories dominated by warlords.

In this chaotic setting, a movement of religious students mostly of the Pushtun ethnic group called the Taliban started a movement in 1994 to proclaim a "true" Islamic government based on *shari'a* Islamic law that would supersede all previous attempts to establish Islamic rule in Afghanistan. Despite its rise during a time of turmoil in which Afghanistan existed as a "failed state," the Taliban movement had deeper roots in a large network of Deobandi *madaris* (schools) that originated with the Darul Uloom *madrasa* in Deoband. The Darul Uloom was a school founded in the late nineteenth century as a way to regroup after the debacle of the Indian Mutiny and the imposition of direct British rule in India.[12] It spawned Pakistani branches in Peshawar and Nowshehra in the twentieth century.

The Darul Uloom and these successor schools were devoted to reviving traditional Islam as envisioned by Shah Valiullah of Delhi (1703-1762), who saw his mission as ridding Islam in a puritanical fashion of practices and beliefs that he believed were later additions to it.[13] Two Pakistani clerics trained in these institutions, Fazlur Rahman and Samiul Haq, later became leaders of two factions of the Jamiat-e-Ulama-e-Islam organization who developed strong links with the Taliban government in Afghanistan. The Taliban movement had mostly been organized by Afghan students who had studied in these Pakistani *madaris* for many years beginning when Afghanistan was a monarchy. The Deobandis in

Pakistan historically had been in opposition to the Muhammad Ali Jinnah's Muslim League since before the founding of Pakistan as a nation in 1947.

The political activism of these Afghani students took a distinctively secondary place to their study of Islamic law and theology in Deobandi *madaris* until the 1980s, when the deterioration of Afghani society as a result of the Soviet invasion of 1979 caused large numbers of religious students to seek refuge across the border in Pakistan. Upon the crumbling of Afghanistan in the late 1980s and early 1990s into separate warlord enclaves, the Taliban emerged as a movement that saw itself as bound only by a harsh and uncompromising version of Islamic law. The Taliban movement ruled as the ad hoc government of large parts of Afghanistan from 1995 through the end of 2001, even though it was never recognized as such by the U.N. and in fact secured formal diplomatic recognition only from three other nations: Pakistan, Saudi Arabia, and the United Arab Emirates. The current status of many former Taliban supporters remains unclear, but some appear to have taken refuge in neighboring Pakistan and other countries. Both the Taliban and the Münsterites thus controlled governments for similarly limited but similarly memorable periods of time.

Destruction of Religious and Cultural Icons

Both the Münsterites and the Taliban built their identities by destroying religious and cultural symbols. The Taliban became famous around the world for their detonation of the faces of the ancient Buddha statues of Bamiyan in the spring of 2001. This act was condemned as a sign of religious fanaticism by most Muslim governments and high-ranking clerics, such as the mufti Shaikh Nasr Farid Wassel, an eminent Egyptian Muslim scholar.[14] Even Iran, the only other country to have successfully carried out an Islamic revolution, quickly issued a statement denouncing this act.[15] It appears that the Taliban carried this out partly as a way to signal their claim of authority to execute Islamic commandments however they interpreted them: an interpretation that could change quite suddenly.

The Taliban leader Mullah Muhammad Omar had first ruled that the statues could be preserved as long as they were not worshiped, but then changed his mind, stating that all idols should be smashed, just like Muhammad had smashed idols in the Ka'ba. Omar's response to the international outcry was to assert: "All we are breaking are stones."[16] The impetus for the Taliban to carry out this destruction appears to be its desire to carry out a symbolic act at a particular moment, perhaps partly as a strike against the Bamiyan area whose Hazara inhabitants were largely Shi'i Muslims, but mostly to assert their prerogative.[17] Although Islamic fundamentalists in other countries had attacked tourists at ancient monuments, such as in the 1998 attack on Japanese visitors in Luxor, they did not stage similar acts of monumental destruction of sites sacred to existing religious groups such as Buddhists.

The Taliban did not limit attacks to the destruction of religious icons that could be seen to represent obvious anathemas to them. In 1998, Mullah Omar approved of the destruction of 55,000 books from the cultural center of Nasir-e Khusraw in northern Afghanistan.[18] Although the Taliban probably regarded Khusraw as an Islamic heretic, he was so highly regarded for centuries throughout the Persian-speaking world as a great literary stylist and writer by adherents of various groups of Muslims that the gratuitous destruction of these works can be viewed as part of an attempt to eradicate even *Islamic* traditions that did not conform to the narrow Taliban view of religious truth.

This is reminiscent of the 1534 decision taken by Jan Matthias, the first leader of the Anabaptist uprising in Münster, to burn every book that he found except the Bible. His edict included all books of Christian theologians such as Augustine, Aquinas, and Luther.[19] Reminiscent of the Taliban in Bamiyan, the Münsterites set out to deface the central cathedral in February of that year, smearing religious paintings there with excrement, smashing ancient tombs, and scattering remains and coffins all around. Matthias announced: "We preach the separation of the world. The state is to be used to destroy the [existing] state."[20] The Taliban stated in a November 1996 decree "the Religious Police (*Munkrat*) have the responsibility and duty to struggle against . . . social problems and will continue their effort until evil is finished."[21] Both groups viewed the destruction of longstanding cultural and religious symbols as part of their relentless campaigns to define in a theatrical way their conflict with all existing norms save the scriptures they recognized.

Choice of Leaders: Jan Bockelson and Mullah Muhammad Omar as Naifs

Both the Taliban and the Münsterites ended up with leaders for whom formal religious training was not the only or even the most important quality for righteous leadership, in societies in which religious learning and the ability to display it were of paramount importance in establishing someone's legitimacy to discuss Holy Scripture. Jan Bockelson van Leyden and Mullah Omar both projected a reticence and a naïveté designed to show how God truly had called them, a truth verifiable only through stories of supernatural approval. A lame goldsmith Johann Dusentschur testified in Münster in front of the twelve elders (as the Anabaptist governors of the city were called) that God had told him in a vision that Jan van Leyden would be their new David, cast down the mighty, and raise the lowly.[22] Taliban soldiers reported to a correspondent that the prophet Muhammad had come to Mullah Omar in a dream in 1994 and told him to rid Afghanistan of its warlords and had helped him secure the country in miraculous ways. When the reporter asked if Mullah Omar had performed any miracles lately, the response was "He's still alive, isn't he? Isn't that miracle enough, when the mightiest nation on earth is trying to kill him?"[23] They also said that angels had been seen accompanying the Taliban in battle. None of this folkloric wisdom is unusual or surprising. What is noteworthy is the degree to which Jan and Omar avoided projecting any airs of intellectual authority based on religious education, a striking departure from traditional models of religious wise men in both contexts.

The Treatment of Women

Both groups treated women very harshly as they sought to enforce their programs and interpretations through rules derived from novel interpretations of scripture. Jan van Leyden dissolved all existing marriages and forced all women to marry new husbands. Polygamy was encouraged to follow the example of Old Testament prophets. A wife's resistance to her husband's commands could be punished by death.[24] The Taliban issued several decrees in 1996 confining women to their houses and empowering family elders to punish them severely if they disobeyed.[25] In both cases, those in charge set rules that made only oblique references to specific scriptural passages: mere assertions of naïve spiritual authority. Although it could be asserted that such rules ultimately arose from the reinterpretation of existing religious traditions, the extreme ways they were implemented were designed to prove, through their severity, the righteousness of those who had imposed them.

Relationships with Other Religious Movements and Organizations

Some contemporary reform groups were sympathetic to these regimes because they shared many ideas. In the Taliban case, the good relationship between the global Islamist al-Qaʻida movement and the Taliban has been well documented. Many fellow-traveling Anabaptists tried to come to Münster from various parts of northern Europe, but were stopped by the forces of the Prince-Bishop and his allies besieging the city.

Ultimately though, the Münsterites and the Taliban also made unlikely allies of those who opposed them. The Münsterites brought together Catholics and Protestants who had been and would continue to fight and oppose each other for many more decades after the fall of Anabaptist Münster in 1536. Luther remarked that the Münsterite regime was the work of a "young ABC devil or schoolgirl devil who does not yet know how to write."[26] In the struggle against the Taliban, the United States intermittently cooperated with Iran in a similarly unlikely alliance.[27] Iran issued continuous official statements during the 1990s denouncing the Taliban government as anti-Islamic and fought against it on several occasions.

Perhaps the root cause of this unlikely alliance of forces against the Münsterites and Taliban was similar: the two regimes' focus on otherworldly salvation made them less interested in any political compromises to establish stable temporal governments. Thus, they marked similar challenges to both their fellow reformers as well as to defenders of the existing order.

Conclusions

During the counterreformation of the late sixteenth century, Münster became more overtly Catholic in orientation with the expansion of a Jesuit presence there. Afghanistan, after the intervention of the United States and its allies there, is now in the process of trying to regain a stability designed to be reminiscent of how the country operated several decades ago, but with unclear long-term prospects. Comparison of these periods of Münsterite and Taliban rule is primarily useful as evidence for how some Muslims and Christians reacted to similar periods of change in similar ways by attempting to "purify" and "cleanse" religious truth of worldly evils. They adopted such consciously naïve and extremist versions of religious doctrine that they changed, in parallel ways, the terms of debate about religious doctrine even for those who completely opposed them and disagreed with them.

Despite all the intriguing similarities discussed above, the two movements ended very differently. Ultimately, the Münster experiment was terminated in 1536 when the Anabaptists were crushed by the troops of the Prince-Bishop. The Taliban, although now discredited by many Muslims, militarily defeated, and dispersed, continue to be favorably regarded by a substantial proportion of their coreligionists. It is worth noting, though, that although the Münster experience lasted for only a few years in the 1530s, it could later be seen as part of the beginning of a much longer period of uncertainty as European religious beliefs and practices adjusted to the uncertainties of a world transformed from the late medieval period. It is now too early to predict what might follow the Taliban episode as the Islamic world adjusts to vast global changes on a much greater scale. However, it seems only prudent to examine the process of Islamic transformation taking place right now in light of the perspective afforded by looking back at a similar period of change in Christianity.

One place to begin such an examination might be with such movements as the Anabaptists and the Taliban, who by avowedly rejecting complexity and subtlety in reformed interpretations of scripture in similar ways, both shed light on movements such as those occurring among contemporary Islamic and Christian communities, where the reformational aspects might be seen less clearly.

Notes

1. Norman Cohn, *The Pursuit of the Millennium* (New York: Oxford University Press, 1970), 13.

2. For examples, see Jeffrey Kaplan, *Radical Religion in America: Millenarian Movements from the Far Right to the Children of Noah* (Syracuse: Syracuse University Press, 1997).

3. Cohn, *Pursuit of the Millennium*, 286.

4. There have been numerous discussions about the relative importance of orthodoxy and orthopraxy in Islam. Some have asserted that Islam favors orthopraxy over orthodoxy and others have characterized them as equally important. See John Esposito, *Islam: The Straight Path* (Oxford: Oxford University Press, 1998), 68; W. M. Watt, *A Short History of Islam* (Oxford: One World, 1996). I agree with two Muslim imams who recently held them to be equally important. See "Interview with Imam Faisal Abdul Rauf" (March 2002), *Frontline*, www.pbs.org/wgbh/pages/frontline/shows/muslims/interviews /feisal.html (9 December 2002) and "Interview with Akbar Muhammad" (March 2002), *Frontline*, www.pbs.org/wgbh/pages/frontline/shows/muslims/interviews/akbar.html (9 December 2002).

5. George Williams, *The Radical Reformation* (Philadelphia: The Westminster Press, 1962), xxvi.

6. One aspect of this in Islamic discourses is the perceived difference between "Islamism" and Islamic "fundamentalism" or "neo-fundamentalism." For discussion of this point in the Taliban context, see Olivier Roy, "Has Islamism a Future in Afghanistan?" in William Maley, ed., *Fundamentalism Reborn? Afghanistan and the Taliban* (New York: New York University Press, 1998), 199-201.

7. Williams, *Radical Reformation*, 2.

8. Martin Luther in Roland Bainton, *Here I Stand* (New York: Abingdon-Cokesbury Press, 1950), 294.

9. John Horsch, *Mennonites in Europe* (Scottdale, Penn.: Mennonite Publishing House, 1942), 300.

10. Anthony Arthur, *The Tailor-King* (New York: St. Martin's Press, 1999), 10.

11. For the historical context of Afghanistan during this period, see Larry Goodson, *Afghanistan's Endless War* (Seattle: University of Washington Press, 2001).

12. *Encyclopedia of Islam*, 2nd ed., s.v. "DEOBAND."

13. Khaled Ahmed, "The Grand Deobandi Consensus," *The Friday Times of Pakistan* (4-10 February 2000).

14. "Al-Azhar Scholars to meet Taliban," *Dawn* (11 March 2001) www.dawn.com/2001/03/11/int1.htm (9 December 2002).

15. Former Iranian president Akbar Hashemi Rafsanjani called the destruction of pre-Islamic statues by Afghanistan's Taliban regime "ugly. . . . Look at what the Taliban is doing in Afghanistan. They are destroying the ancient statues . . . and this deed today, is not a good deed, it is an ugly deed, and there is no logic to it." *Agence France Presse* (report dated 7 March 2001).

16. Haroon Siddiqui, "No Foundation in Islam for Taleban Rampage on Statues," *Toronto Star* (4 March 2001).

17. It should be noted that the Taliban conducted a hard-fought war against the Hazara in 1998-1999 in the Bamiyan region. See Ahmed Rashid, *Taliban: Militant Islam, Oil, and Fundamentalism in Central Asia* (New Haven: Yale University Press, 2000), 68.

18. Latif Pedram, "Afghanistan: The Library is on Fire," *Autodafe: The Censored Library* 1 (Autumn 2000), www.autodafe.org/autodafe/autodafe_01/art_03.htm (2 December 2002).

19. Arthur, *Tailor-King*, 53.

20. Arthur, *Tailor-King*, 38.

21. Rashid, *Taliban*, 218.

22. Arthur, *Tailor-King*, 109.

23. Tim McGirk, "Thanksgiving with the Taliban," *Time Magazine* (3 December 2001).

24. Arthur, *Tailor-King*, 92-93.

25. Rashid, *Taliban*, 217-18.

26. Arthur, *Tailor-King*, 187.

27. See "America and Iran are Allies," *International Herald Tribune* (25 November 2002).

8

Islamic Fundamentalism and the Trauma of Modernization: Reflections on Religion and Radical Politics

Nader A. Hashemi

> It is not the consciousness of men that determines their being, but, on the contrary, their social being that determines their consciousness.
>
> —Karl Marx

The *al-Qaʿida* terrorist attack against the United States on the morning of September 11, 2001 was a transformative moment in global politics. It definitively resolved a debate that had surfaced after the end of the Cold War about new and emerging threats to international peace and security. From the outset Islamic fundamentalism was a leading candidate for the position.[1] Influential journals such as *The Economist, The Atlantic Monthly, Time,* and *Foreign Affairs* were busy debating this topic, influenced by Western leaders such as Jacques Chirac, Helmut Kohl, Daniel Quayle, and Yitzhak Rabin who collectively were warning in scattered statements that the "green peril" of Islam had replaced the "red menace" of Communism as the chief threat to Western civilization.[2] Samuel P. Huntington's thesis on the "Clash of Civilizations" gave this debate a stamp of academic respectability.

Public opinion in the United States was not far behind elite opinion on this issue. In 1993, a comprehensive nationwide poll found that 42 percent of Americans agreed with the statement that "there should be restrictions on the number of Muslims allowed to immigrate to the U.S." and 43 percent concurred with the view that Muslims "tend to be religious fanatics."[3] Dramatic events in the Middle East during the last two decades of the twentieth century are arguably responsible for these attitudes.

A partial listing of the emotionally charged and defining images that have shaped both public opinion and U.S. foreign policy toward the Arab and Islamic world include: the 1979 revolution in Iran and the concomitant seizure of the U.S. embassy in Tehran, the assassination of Anwar Sadat in 1981, the 1983 bombing of the U.S. embassy and marine barracks in Lebanon (the largest single death toll of American troops since Vietnam), the *fatwa* imposed a death sentence against Salman Rushdie in 1989, the annexation of Kuwait by Saddam Hussein and subsequent Gulf War in 1991, the rise and misogynist rule of the Taliban in Afghanistan throughout the 1990s, two Palestinian Intifadas and a wave of suicide attacks against Israeli civilians in 2000, and finally and most dramatically, the suicide missions in 2001 against the twin towers in New York and the Pentagon in Washington, D.C.

Some of the understandable and challenging questions that emerge from these events are: why those veils, burqas, and the oppression of women? Why such hatred and bitterness toward the West? Why those scowling faces, dreary beards, and calls for assassination? Why so many manifestations of conservatism and violence? Why is there so much anger and political conflict in the Islamic world? Are all these things inherent in Muslim societies, in their culture and religion? Is Islam incompatible with liberty, democracy, human rights, gender equality, and other emancipatory principles?

To date most of the mainstream journalistic and scholarly treatment of these questions has focused on the inner doctrines of Islam and the unique peculiarities of Muslim civilization as the leading explanatory variable. Few studies, however, have attempted to explore the phenomenon of Islamic fundamentalism both historically and comparatively.[4] This chapter seeks to depart from convention by taking the long view of history. It will focus on lessons to be learned from key moments in European modernization that shed light on contemporary political conflict in Muslim societies. It will be argued that the actual content of Islamic fundamentalist thought is less important than the process of rapid modernization of traditional societies that produces a radical interpretation of religion as a response to social dislocation and uncertainty. Islamic fundamentalism is much more complicated a social phenomenon than is generally appreciated and its long-term effect may carry latent benefits for political development.[5]

Comparing Histories: Islam and Christianity

Well over a decade ago Gregg Easterbrook suggested that Islam was in the same space as Christianity, in the High Middle Ages and Early Modern Period, in terms of the ebbing and flowing of religious passions. He wrote:

> Ought Islam to be considered barbarian because the religion sometimes sparks rioting and has followers who endorse that internally contradictory concept, the 'holy war?' Neither speaks well of Islamic values, but consider an intriguing historical parallel. Today's Moslem extremism is occurring about 1,300 years

after the death of Mohammed, in 632 A.D. The low ebb of Christianity—the Inquisition, followed by decades of mutual slaughter among Catholics and Protestants—began approximately the same number of years after the death of Christ. A low point of Judaism—the final loss of the Holy Land to the Romans—came in 70 A.D., a few centuries more than a thousand years after Moses led the flight from Egypt. This could be nothing but coincidence. But perhaps major religions, involving as they do deep-seated webs of philosophy, emotion and politics, require a millennium to shake themselves out.[6]

To compare religious traditions is not to equate them. The study of history, however, would be rendered meaningless unless one can draw upon relevant historical analogies to illuminate contemporary phenomena. Marc Bloch has in fact suggested that one of the principal purposes of historical comparison is the identification of differences.[7] It is a major assumption of this chapter that the similarities between Islam and Christianity—and the radical protests movements they have spawned at approximately the same time and for many of the same reasons—are significant to merit a comparison.[8]

The Muslim world today is at the beginning of the fifteenth century of the *hijra*,[9] approximately a century before Martin Luther nailed his "Ninety-Five Theses" to the door of the Castle Church in Wittenberg. Christendom in the early sixteenth century, like Islam at a similar age in its historical development, was marked by intellectual, political, and religious upheavals.

In 1516, Sir Thomas More published his *Utopia*, a book that reflected new Renaissance thinking by posing fundamental and heretofore unexamined questions about the relationship between church, state, and society. A year later Martin Luther launched his protest against the sale of "indulgences" by the Catholic Church, an event which unofficially marked the beginning of Protestantism. Early sixteenth century Europe also witnessed the emergence of a wide range of scientific discoveries and overseas exploration as the era of modern capitalism and colonialism began in earnest. The printing press created a media revolution bringing new ideas, partisan rhetoric, and a spirit of inquiry to the people. Most significantly it made the Bible accessible to the masses in the local vernacular. Soon the Reformation and Counter-Reformation were to engulf Europe dividing the continent both religiously and politically.[10]

Similarly, the latter half of the twentieth century ushered in profound social and political changes for Muslim societies. The ending of the era of colonialism saw the emergence of many nominally independent Muslim majority states that have been marked by an abundance of military *coups d'état*, interstate wars, revolutions, an oil boom, foreign interventions, high rates of population and urbanization, and growing socioeconomic inequality.[11] The forces of economic and cultural globalization have significantly transformed the traditional way of life in Muslim societies and, coupled with a general absence of democracy, they have produced numerous social pathologies, the most significant being the rise of Islamic fundamentalism.

Social scientists who have studied this period note that religiously inspired rebellions were common in the early phases of European modernization.[12] In other words it was a sign of, and a reaction to, the changing times. Similarly, the emergence of radical Islamist movements at the end of the twentieth century can be understood in the same social and historical context. The parallels between the two time periods are worth emphasizing as a counterpoint to the generally accepted view that interprets Islamism as a *sui generis* ideology rooted in the cultural essence of Muslim societies.

When comparing religiously inspired protest movements in Europe in the sixteenth century with those in the Middle East in the late twentieth century, two observations are worth noting. Democracy and human rights in the West did not emerge from documents but rather from struggle, in particular from contentious and disputatious politics of which religion was central point of conflict. Europe has indeed traveled a long way in terms of its own political development in the previous 500 years. Any objective attempt to explore the problems of democracy and political development in non-Western societies, particularly Muslim societies, requires a rethinking of the development of democracy in the West and an appreciation that road has been extremely bumpy with many potholes and detours along the way.

Secondly, we should be wary of the tendency to read history backwards instead of forwards. There is an implicit assumption in much of the commentary about the Muslim world today that, in comparison, the West has always been liberal and democratic and that one can draw a straight line from Plato and Socrates in ancient Greece to Isaiah Berlin and John Rawls in late twentieth century England and the United States. As historian Mark Mazower observes in *Dark Continent: Europe's 20th Century*, it is wrong to see "Europe as the natural home of freedom and democracy." Rather, in the last 100 years it was "frequently a nightmarish laboratory for social and political engineering, inventing and reinventing itself through war, revolution and ideological competition."

Communism and Fascism, Mazower argues, "should be regarded not as exceptions to the general rule of democracy, but as alternative forms of government that attracted millions of Europeans by offering different solutions to challenges of the modern world. By 1940 the prospects for democratic government looked bleak, and Europe's future seemed to lie in Hitler's hands."[13] These are sobering reminders for a Western audience struggling to understand international affairs in the aftermath of September 11, 2001.

Islam, Modernization, and Development

The rise of Islamic fundamentalism at the end of the twentieth century was a baffling development for many observers of the Middle East. It seemed to confirm the worst prejudices and stereotypes about Islam and Muslims. How could large numbers of people, in the age of secular reason, at the end of the twentieth century, identify in such a profound way with a militant version of religion as the primary source of their identity? This not only challenged the received wisdom of both the Enlightenment and social science theory but it gave credence to an essentialist interpretation of Muslim politics. Bernard Lewis, Ernest Gellner, and Martin Kramer are three prominent representatives of this school of thought.

The prevailing interpretation as to why fundamentalism has emerged in the Muslim world instead of liberal democracy is often cast as a function of the unique peculiarities of Islamic civilization. Despotism—according to this theory—was at the very core of the Muslim faith, as it demanded submission both to God and to those who ruled in his name.[14] In an oft-cited Orientalist cliché, Islam does not recognize a separation between religion and politics but is a total way of life, the implication being that a totalitarian system was the natural state of affairs.[15] Bernard Lewis explains that one reason for the absence of liberal democracy in the Muslim world is that Islam discouraged the formation of independent groups that might have challenged despotic rule. In what is today a standard Orientalist trope, the problems of Muslim society can be located in medieval Muslim history. "Islamic law," Lewis writes, "knows no corporate legal persons; *Islamic history* knows no councils or communes, no synods or parliaments, nor any other kind of elective or representative assembly. It is interesting that the jurists never accepted the principle of majority decision—there was no point, since the need for a procedure of corporate decision never arose."[16] Delving deeper into the history of medieval Islam to explain the contemporary absence of democracy, Lewis adds: "the political experience of the Middle East under the caliphs and sultans was one of almost unrelieved autocracy, in which obedience to the sovereign was a religious as well as a political obligation, and disobedience a sin as well as a crime."[17]

Ernest Gellner, a towering figure in the social sciences, similarly locates the modern problems of political development in the Muslim world in a cultural essence located deep in the annals of Muslim history.[18] The "High Culture" of the urban 'ulama (clergy) and bourgeoisie, which was characterized as scriptural and puritanical and which according to Gellner is normative for the urban life of the entire Islamic world, under modern conditions is appropriated at the mass level due to political centralization, urbanization, and mass education. Islamic fundamentalism is thus "the demand for the realization of this norm, and the popular support it enjoys stems from the aspiration to the High Culture by the newly urbanized masses." This explanation of Muslim politics, argues Gellner, is "entirely congruent with the requirements of industrialisation and of political modernity, contrary to the previously dominant assumptions of social theory that modernity requires secularization."[19] In short, rise of Islamic fundamentalism in the late twentieth century is an authentic representation of the totality of Muslim society.

Martin Kramer is the most recent author of repute who works within the above ideological framework when writing about Muslim societies. In a discussion about modern Middle Eastern history he wrote, "of the many fundamentalisms that have emerged within Islam during recent years, perhaps none has had so profound an impact on the human imagination as Hizbullah— 'the Party of God.'" In attempting to explain their political behavior he notes that "more than any other fundamentalist movement in recent history, Hizbullah evoked the memory of the medieval Assassins, who had been feared in the West and Islam for their marriage of fierce militancy with destructive deeds."[20] The linking of the activities of Hizbullah—a late twentieth century Islamist group— with the twelfth century Assassins is a typical interpretation of modern events used by this genre of scholars as if to suggest that the more complex modern forces of demographic shifts, economic disparity, cultural transformation, and foreign interventions are not worth taking into account.

Juan Eduardo Campo, in an incisive and acerbic response to Kramer, noted: "One can only imagine the objections that would be raised if a respected American Studies scholar were to interpret Chicano or African American gang activity in American cities in terms of ancient Aztec or African warrior religions, while neglecting to discuss the immediate social, cultural, and economic causes."[21] Campo's comment on the modern socioeconomic crisis of state and society in the Middle East and its relationship to the emergence of religious fundamentalism merit some investigation as an alternative reading of the problems of Muslim political development.[22]

The Malaise of Modernity and Political Islam

While fundamentalism is often considered an exclusively Muslim phenomenon it is important to acknowledge that all the major religions have experienced this form of militant religious piety.[23] The fact that it first emerged in the West (recall the story of the Anabaptists in Münster, Germany) is not accidental, given that it was in Europe and later the United States where the process of modernization had its initial and most consequential impact.

The momentous transformation of society and culture over the last two centuries has profoundly altered the way human beings relate to one another and view the world around them. In the twentieth century in particular, there has been a discernible shift away from large extended families and a group-based identity toward a more individual centered existence. This passing of traditional society has also included a weakening of parental authority, greater political rights for women, and the questioning and challenging of religious authority. While these trends are not visible in equal magnitude in every country, they do exist to varying degrees across most societies and are intimately connected to what Charles Taylor has termed the "Malaise of Modernity."[24]

Modernity has also been identified with an increase in social problems such as higher divorce and crime rates, alcohol and drug addiction, nerve disorders, and family breakdown. This social miasma has given rise in troubled times to questions of "identity" that can help navigate the individual and his/her community through the troubled waters of the modern age.

Throughout human history during times of great social transformation and political turmoil, a natural concomitant is the revival of religion. During the Mongol occupation of Russia (1237-1480), for example, the Orthodox Church experienced one of its greatest periods of growth.[25] A similar phenomenon occurred in the United States in the mid-nineteenth century with the onset of the Industrial Revolution.[26] Stated simply, social upheaval engenders a reaction where one seeks stability and security by a return to the basic and the familiar. Muslim societies are no different in this regard. Writing specifically about the Muslim reaction to modernity, James Piscatori perceptively observes:

> Muslims are in a sense looking for what Daniel Bell called "new rites of incorporation" which link today's deracinated individual to a community and a history. And yet, in another sense, they are looking, rather, for *old* rites of incorporation that appear to be new even as they are familiar. Religion, precisely because in the past it answered questions about life and death and provided its followers with moral links to each other, becomes the means by which individuals hope to answer the new question of what it is to be modern, and, in so doing, to gain perhaps a reassuring, common world-view. In this respect, born-again Christians and veiled-again Muslims are responding to the same broad phenomenon.[27]

A common target for all fundamentalist groups is secularism, in particular the consumer-oriented culture and materialism that is identified with our secular age. These movements are all literalist when it comes to interpreting scared scripture and critical readings of the religious texts are generally viewed as heretical. To quote from a popular saying among Islamist activists: *kullu bid'atin dallalah* (all innovation is forbidden/on the path of loss).

What fundamentalist groups seek to do is drag God from the sidelines and place religion at the center of social and political debate. "Every fundamentalist movement I have studied," notes Karen Armstrong, "in Judaism, Christianity and Islam, is rooted in a profound fear of annihilation—a conviction that the liberal, secularist establishment wants to wipe out religion. This is true of the militant Christian groups in the United States as it is of Muslim extremists in Egypt and Iran." The need to "defend Islam" is a common refrain espoused by Muslim fundamentalists, indicating a sincere belief that their faith is under assault. "Fundamentalists believe they are fighting for survival, and when people feel that their backs are to the wall, they lash out violently like a wounded animal."[28]

Secondly, fundamentalist movements are all evangelists whose primary audience consists of members of their own faith who are deemed to have gone astray and lack sufficient piety at attain personal salvation. They are against the idea of pluralism in matters of faith while firmly believing that there is only one correct school of interpretation of scripture, religion and law.

Significantly, it is important to point out that these movements are not traditional in terms of trying to roll back the clock to a pristine age and disengage completely with modern society like Amish Christians or Hasidic Jews. Rather they are modern both in terms of the values they are reacting against and in terms of their use of modern technology, support for post secondary training, and urban lifestyle. This is most apparent in the educational backgrounds of many of their adherents who tend to come disproportionately from the applied sciences, engineering, and medicine where the answers are precise and the formulas exact.[29] Ambiguous meanings, multiple correct responses, shades of grey, and an appreciation for nuance are not part of their intellectual or professional training. Their response to contemporary social and political questions is informed by this cognitive rigidity. Reflecting on the new millenarian movements, John Sigler perceptively writes that "there are those . . . who have a need for clear rules and directions, for right and wrong, and that modern culture, with its relativism, and uncertainties, clearly fails to provide this needed direction. These new militant movements provide not only inerrant scriptural authority, but new families and support in an age of loneliness and exaggerated individualism." Sigler adds: "these movements offer alternatives to the major cultural trends of modernity. They emphasize stability, security, solidarity and community. Many people find it hard to face the harsh realities of modern life without some sense of order."[30] The stable and supportive communities that these groups offer are a source of attraction to many people in our modern and postmodern age.

In commenting on the parallel processes of religious resurgence in disparate societies, two scholars make the important observation that the "resurgence of 'fundamentalistic' promotion of particularistic ideologies and doctrines," should be seen as the "recent globe-wide assertion of particularist ideas," and should be comprehended in the context of "increasing *globality*."[31] Globalization, in other words, based on fundamental changes in technology, from the media age to the information age, has through the media revolution greatly heightened awareness among previously segmented and isolated populations. The concept of "identity" is, at its core, relational, in that individuals and groups define themselves in relation to other individuals and groups in society. The more we are aware of others, the more this forces the question—what is distinct about me and my community in a globalized world.

In a widely read book, *Jihad vs. McWorld*, Benjamin Barber argued this point that the rise of ethno-religious nationalism in the late twentieth century is a reaction to the increasing political, economic, and cultural interdependence of our planet.[32] In short, the rise of particularist identities is a natural concomitant to globalization.

The above political, cultural, and sociological insights suggest a need for a longer term perspective on the rise of religious fundamentalism particularly as it relates to problems of democracy in the Muslim world. In pursuit of this end I would like to draw upon Fernand Braudel's concept of the *longue durée*.[33]

Fernand Braudel and the *Longue Durée*: The Modernization of Muslim Societies

Fernand Braudel is one of the most widely cited and influential historians of the twentieth century. He belongs to the *Annales* school of historians that have made significant contributions to historical research and theory. Departing from traditional historical approaches, the *Annales* historians assume that history needs to be comprehended in the context of forces that underlie human behavior and not as a simple recalling of conscious human actions. Braudel was one of the first historians to suggest that history should synthesize data from the social sciences, in particular economics, and thus provide a broader historical overview of human societies.

Braudel's concept of the *longue durée* (the study of history as a long duration) should be understood in contrast with *l'histoire événementielle* (the history of events), such as battles, revolutions, and the actions of great people.[34] The *longue durée* extends the perspective of historical space as well as time. Until the *Annales* school, historians had taken the juridical political unit of the nation-state, duchy, or principality as their starting point. Yet, when large time spans are considered, geographical features, economic systems, or political processes may have more significance for human populations than national borders. In his doctoral thesis, a seminal work on the Mediterranean during the reign of Philip II, Braudel treated the geohistory of the entire region as a "structure" that exerted a myriad of influences on human life since the first settlements on the shores of the Mediterranean Sea. "By *structure*," Braudel wrote, "observers of social questions mean an organization, a coherent and fairly fixed series of relationships between realities and social masses" that affect the flow and outcome of history.[35] For example, the study of mercantile capitalism in Europe between the fourteenth and eighteenth centuries would be a phase of history that lasted over the *longue durée* and could be studied on its own. "Despite all the obvious changes which run through [this period]," Braudel notes, "these four or five centuries of economic life had a certain coherence, right up to the upheavals of the eighteenth century and the industrial revolution. . . . These shared characteristics persisted despite the fact that all around them, amid other continuities, a thousand reversals and ruptures totally altered the face of the world."[36]

Returning to the case of the Muslim world, I would like to draw upon Braudel's concept of the *longue durée* to assess the political process of modernization in the Middle East and its connection to Islamic fundamentalism.

In the same way that Braudel is critical of the "current event" approach to history (*l'histoire événementielle*) because of its limited explanatory value, focusing exclusively on the phenomena of religious fundamentalism in Muslim societies—in particular its doctrinal component—also carries an analytical cost in terms inhibiting a deeper understanding of the obstacles to political development in the Muslim world. In this context, several points are worth noting.

Modernization and Its Discontents in Muslim Societies

Modernization is a traumatic process. The West took several hundred years to develop its secular and democratic institutions and much of it by trial and error. The war of religions, political persecution, genocide, the Industrial Revolution, the exploitation of workers, the rise of nationalism, and two world wars resulted in a profound change in all spheres of life—political, economic, intellectual, and religious. Today we are witnessing a similar process of transformation in developing countries with concomitant destabilizing effects.[37]

It is important to appreciate that the modernization process in the Muslim world has been very different in many respects. Unlike in Europe where it was largely an indigenous process, in the case of Muslim societies, modernization began as a direct result of the colonial encounter with Europe. Instead of innovation, their modern experience was one of imitation in an attempt to play catch up with the West. Muslim countries in the postcolonial era have been split unhealthily into two camps: an elite, who have received a Western-style education and internalized secular values, and a large majority who have not. Many regimes are ruled by a gerontocracy of aging men while the majority of their populations are under the age of thirty. Most political change since the era of formal independence has been forced top-down on society in an accelerated manner, not bottom-up via an indigenous process of social evolution and democratic bargaining. In 1935, for example, Reza Pahlavi (the father of the last Shah) ordered his troops to go into the streets of Tehran to forcibly remove—at bayonet point—the veil from women's heads. These policies were matched in neighboring Turkey by Mustafa Kemal Atatürk's harsh secularization and Westernization of Turkish society. Two generations later, in the same authoritarian way that the Pahlavi monarchy forcibly removed the veil, Ayatullah Khomeini and his Islamic revolutionaries imposed it on Iranian women with equal determination and rigor. Similarly, the rise of political Islam in Turkey can partially be explained as a counterreaction to Kemalist secularist policies that lack indigenous social roots. It is against this backdrop that we should situate and explore the emergence of Islamic fundamentalism as a historical phenomenon.

This is not the first time societies undergoing intense periods of social change have encountered militant religious movements seeking stability and order. Western observers of the Muslim world need to overcome their amnesia about their own history and recognize distinct parallels between what is happening today in the Middle East and the early phases of modernization of the West. In the post-September 11 euphoria about the superiority of Western values, it needs to be repeatedly stated that Western history did not begin with human rights, democracy, and free markets but rather the origins lay elsewhere. Michael Walzer, who has been a long-time participant in the polemics of the American Jewish community against the Arab world, wrote his doctoral dissertation at Harvard on the Puritan Revolution in England in the seventeenth century, a period of civil war and intense turmoil. He provided a comprehensive framework for understanding what he called "The Revolution of the Saints" and "A Study in the Origins of Radical Politics."[38] It is this thesis and its relevance for Muslim politics that we turn our attention to next.

The Walzer Thesis: The Revolution of the Saints and Radical Politics

The early modern period in England was a time of intense social transformation marked by population growth, rural to urban migration, and a receding of feudalism.[39] Writing on this period, Michael Walzer describes the following social problems that provided a fertile soil for the emergence of Puritanism in England in the sixteenth century.

The "problem of rural 'depopulation,' vagabondage, and extensive . . . poverty" due to "rapid population growth [and] . . . the dislocation of men from the old rural society set thousands of beggars wandering the roads." For over a century "these beggars quite literally formed a distinct social group, completely alienated from the work-a-day world on whose fringes they dwelt. . . . Other men, driven from the land, poured into the cities . . . where they were newly subject to the calamities of depression and urban unemployment."

Secondly, the "problem of rapid urbanization . . . with its intensification of the dangers of plague and fire . . . brought new men into London who could not be absorbed by the existing civic institutions." In the midst of this turmoil "Puritanism flourished also in the city and especially in the suburbs: in the records of the bishop's court recent immigrants turn up often as members of sectarian religious groups. Deprived of village solidarity, disoriented in the great crowds, many men must have found solace in Puritan faith and even Puritan discipline."

On a related point, Walzer discusses the "the problem of the religious vacuum left by the slow decay and then abrupt collapse of the old church. At a fairly early point, both in London and the country, this vacuum began to be filled by Puritanism" as "once again, for many men, Puritanism provided an alternative set of social and spiritual activities."

"Finally . . . there was the basic problem of social organization raised by the
. . . end of rural 'housekeeping,' the disappearance of urban confraternities and
the weakening of guild ties, the increased rate of social and geographic mobility,
the creation of the urban crowd and the urban underworld. How were men to be
reorganized, bound together in social groups, united for co-operative activity
and emotional sustenance? It was in response to such questions," Walzer
observes, "that there emerged, in the course of the sixteenth and seventeenth
centuries, so many new forms of organization and relationship, so many theories
of contract and covenant. Debate over the precise nature of the new
organizations—and especially the Puritan organization—makes up considerable
part of the tractarian literature of the period."[40]

The political order of the time was ripe with corruption, nepotism, and
anarchy. Driven by a militant religious fervor the Puritans and their Calvinist
ideology sought to bring order and stability to their society by overthrowing the
corrupt establishment and beheading the king. These "saints," as Walzer calls
them, were motivated by two things: "a fierce antagonism to the traditional
world and the prevailing pattern of human relation and a keen and perhaps not
unrealistic anxiety about human wickedness and the dangers of social disorder.
The saints attempted to fasten upon the necks of all mankind the yoke of a new
political discipline."[41] In assessing their behavior in the context of a changing
Europe, Walzer describes the Puritans as "an agent of modernization, an
ideology of the transition period."[42]

Near the end of his book, Walzer attempts to link his case study of English
Puritanism to other cultural contexts and societies undergoing intense social
change. He writes that the "Puritan concern with discipline and order . . . is not
unique in history. Over and over again, since the days of the saints, bands of
political radicals have sought anxiously, energetically, systematically to
transform themselves and their world." The key development that gives rise to
militant religious piety is the breakdown of the old order. The choice of
sainthood in such circumstances, observes Walzer, "seems reasonable and
appropriate" and in light of the above discussion, "given similar historical
circumstances, Frenchmen and Russians would predictably make similar
choices. Englishmen became Puritans and then godly magistrates, elders, and
fathers in much the same way and for many of the same reasons as eighteenth-
century Frenchmen became Jacobins and active citizens, and twentieth-century
Russians [became] Bolsheviks."[43] Echoing sentiments discussed above about the
rise of political Islam in the Middle East, Walzer writes:

> In different cultural contexts, at different moments in time, sainthood will take
> on different forms and the saints will act out different revolutions. But the
> radical's way of seeing and responding to the world will almost certainly by
> widely shared whenever the experiences which first generated that perception
> and response are widely shared, whenever groups of men are suddenly set loose
> from old certainties.[44]

Puritanism, therefore, "provided what may best be called an *ideology of transition* [Walzer's emphasis]. It was functional to the process of modernization not because it served the purposes of some universal progress, but because it met the human needs that arise whenever traditional controls give way and hierarchical status and corporate privilege are called into question."[45]

During more tranquil times when a semblance of peace is restored, the radical ideology of the saints no longer has a popular appeal and they gradually disappear from society. In the context of seventeenth century England, Walzer writes, "after the Restoration, its energy was drawn inward, its political aspirations forgotten; the saint gave way to the nonconformist. Or, Lockean liberalism provided an alternative political outlook." This suggests "only that these problems were limited in time to the period of breakdown and psychic and political reconstruction. When men stopped being afraid . . . then Puritanism was suddenly irrelevant."[46]

Summarizing his theory of radical politics based on the history of English Puritanism, Michael Walzer concludes that his "model may serve to reveal the crucial features of radicalism as a general historical phenomena and to make possible a more systematic comparison of Puritans, Jacobins, and Bolsheviks (and perhaps other groups as well)."[47]

The main points of his model are:

1. At a certain point in the transition from one or another form of traditional society (feudal, hierarchical, patriarchal, corporate) to one or another form of modern society, there appears a band of "strangers" who view themselves as chosen men, saints, and who seek a new order and an impersonal, ideological discipline.

2. These men are marked off from their fellows by an extraordinary self-assurance and daring. The saints not only repudiate the routine procedures and customary beliefs of the old order, but they cut themselves off from the various kinds of "freedom" . . . experienced amidst the decay of tradition. The band of the chosen seeks and wins certainty and self-confidence by rigidly disciplining its members and teaching them to discipline themselves. The saints interpret their ability to endure this discipline as a sign of their virtue and their virtue as a sign of God's grace.

3. The band of the chosen confronts the existing world as if in war. Its members interpret the strains and tensions of social change in terms of conflict and contention. The saints sense enmity all about them and they train and prepare themselves accordingly.

4. Men join the band by subscribing to a covenant which testifies to their faith. Their new commitment is formal, impersonal, and ideological; it requires that they abandon older loyalties not founded upon opinion and will— loyalties to family, guild, locality, and also to lord and king.

5. The acting out of sainthood produces a new kind of politics.

6. Within the band of the chosen, all men are equal. . . . The activity of the chosen band is purposive, programmatic, and progressive in the sense that it continually approaches or seeks to approach its goals.
7. The violent attack upon customary procedures set the saints free to experiment politically. Such experimentation is controlled by its overriding purposes and the right to engage in it is limited to the chosen few who have previously accepted the discipline of the band. It is not a grant of political free-play, but it does open the way to new kinds of activity, both public and secret. The saints are entrepreneurs in politics.
8. The historical role of the chosen band is twofold. Externally, as it were, the band of the saints is a political movement aiming at social reconstruction. It is the saints who lead the final attack upon the old order and their destructiveness is all the more total because they have a total view of the new world. Internally, godliness and predestination are creative responses to the pains of social change. Discipline is the cure for freedom and "unsettledness."
9. [This is a transitional movement.] One day . . . [when] security becomes a habit and zeal is no longer a worldly necessity. Then the time of God's people is over. . . . Once that order is established, ordinary men are eager enough to desert the warfare of the Lord for some more moderate pursuit of virtue. Once they feel sufficiently secure as gentlemen and merchants, as country justices and members of Parliament, they happily forgo the further privilege of being "instruments." Hardly a moment after their triumph, the saints find themselves alone; they can no longer exploit the common forms of ambition, egotism and nervousness; they can no longer convince their fellow men that ascetic work and intense repression are necessary.
10. [While the saints] helped carry men through a time of change; they had no place in a time of stability. They had been elements of strength in an age of moral confusion and of cruel vigor in an age of vacillation. Now it was suggested that saintly vigor had its own pathology and conventionalism its own health.[48]

Conclusion

It is a main argument of this chapter that political modernization in the Muslim world has produced a similar form of radical politics akin to English Puritanism, French Jacobinism, and Russian Bolshevism. The case of the Islamic Republic of Iran, where currently there is a profound and important debate taking place between former revolutionary radicals (who are now championing pluralism, tolerance, and democracy) and conservative clerics (who are trying to maintain the revolutionary status quo) is a perfect illustration of this point.[49]

During the 1960s and 1970s Iran experienced a state-led modernization process that dramatically affected existing social relationships, cultural patterns, and economic life. The land reform program disrupted the ebb and flow of rural life leading to massive migration into the major cities with its concomitant destabilizing effects on urban life. In discussing this period, Ali Mirsepassi writes that the Shah's "modernization programs did not, however, encompass change in the political power structure, nor did they introduce cultural and political modernity. On the contrary, through the modernization process, a more structured and powerful autocratic state power was built."[50]

It was during this time that religion in Iran became politicized in large part due to the destabilizing effects of rapid modernization on a traditional society and also as a reaction to the authoritarian policies of the state. Said Amir Arjomand, in his comparative treatment of the Iranian revolution, observes that the "reaction of privileged groups and of autonomous centers of power against the expansion and centralization of the state is a major source of most if not all the early modern European revolutions." Throughout this period a common thread that consistently reappears in Spain, Portugal, the Netherlands, France, and Britain is that "estates and corporations reacted when their autonomy and inherited privileges were threatened by the state; and they usually found allies in Calvinist preachers and iconoclasts." The Shi'a *'ulama* in Iran, Arjomand suggests—demonstrating the relevance of the Walzer paradigm—were the equivalent of the Calvinist preachers who played a similar role in the early phases of European modernization.[51]

To the extent that Walzer's model is valid for understanding the process of modernization in Muslim societies, this would suggest that the actual content of the ideology is less important than the enveloping socioeconomic context which produces a transitional force of saints during a time of turmoil. One of the added benefits of recalling Walzer's thesis is that it provides an alternative framework to the Bernard Lewis-Samuel Huntington paradigm that emphasizes the "sacred rage of Islam" and the inherent "clash of civilizations" due to an alleged inherent Islamic hatred for the West. It also forces Western social scientists to recall their own history of political development where violent periods marked the transition from tradition to modernity.

Notes

I am indebted to John Trumpbour, Emran Qureshi, and Ausma Khan for feedback on this chapter.

1. While I use the terms "Islamic fundamentalism," "Islamism," and "political Islam" interchangeably throughout this chapter, I am in broad agreement with the reservations of some scholars who note that the term "Islamic fundamentalism" is more accusatory than descriptive. In my utilization, the term refers to any group that places Islam at the center of their political platform. In his deconstruction of the concept, Juan Eduardo Campo writes "that rather than referring to an objective set of phenomena, . . . [Islamic fundamentalism] has been created to serve as a key element in European and

American hegemonic discourses about these societies in order to subordinate and control them. This means that it is of little explanatory value; does not facilitate rendering modern amalgamations of religion and politics more intelligible—unless it is seen first in reference to the scholars and institutions who have actually invented and used it." Eduardo Campo, "The Ends of Islamic Fundamentalism: Hegemonic Discourse and the Islamic Question in Egypt," *Contention* 4 (Spring 1995): 168. John Esposito discusses the etymology of the word "fundamentalism" and makes a case for its non-use in relation to Muslim societies. See his *The Islamic Threat: Myth or Reality?* (New York: Oxford University Press, 1992), 7-8, for a brief discussion. Similarly, Joe Stork and Joel Beinin prefer the term "political Islam" to "Islamic fundamentalism." For an explanation see their insightful essay, "On the Modernity, Historical Specificity and International Context of Political Islam," in Joel Beinin and Joe Stork, eds., *Political Islam: Essays from Middle East Report* (Berkeley: University of California Press, 1997), 3-25.

2. For a representative sample of elite opinion consider the remarks of Willy Claes, Secretary-General of NATO, who warned in 1995 that Islamic fundamentalism "is at least as dangerous as communism was. Please do not underestimate this risk." Cited in "NATO chief warns of Islamic extremists," *Globe and Mail* (3 February 1995). I explore this issue in "From the Red Menace to the Green Peril: International Security and the Chimera of an 'Islamic Threat'" (M.A. Research Essay, Carleton University, 1995). References for the journals cited and the quotations from Western statesmen can be obtained from this.

3. John Zogby Group International, Inc., "American Attitudes towards Islam: A Nationwide Poll," *The American Journal of Islamic Social Sciences* 10 (Fall 1993): 403-7.

4. A recent notable exception is L. Carl Brown, *Religion and State: The Muslim Approach to Politics* (New York: Columbia University Press, 2000). Also in this genre see Ellis Goldberg, "Smashing Idols and the State: The Protestant Ethic and Egyptian Sunni Radicalism," in Juan R.I. Cole, eds., *Comparing Muslim Societies: Knowledge and the State in a World Civilization* (Ann Arbor: University of Michigan Press, 1992), 195-236. See note 24 for further references.

5. For a recent contribution to this debate see Francis Fukuyama and Nadav Samin, "Can Any Good Come of Radical Islam?" *Commentary* 114 (September 2002): 34-38.

6. Gregg Easterbrook, "Death and Dogma: Behind the Moslem Fury at 'Satanic Verses'—The West's Enduring Ignorance of Islam," *Washington Post* (19 February 1989).

7. Marc Bloch, "Towards a Comparative History of European Societies," in Frederic C. Lane and Jelle C. Riemersma, eds., *Enterprise and Secular Change: Reading in Economic History* (Homewood, IL: R.D. Irwin, 1953), 489-521. I borrow this idea from Norman G. Finkelstein, *Image and Reality of the Israel-Palestine Conflict* (London: Verso, 1995), 89.

8. One of the critical differences is that radical protest movements in the Muslim world are shaped by the impact of Western imperialism.

9. *Hijra* refers to a specific event in Muslim history where Muhammad migrated from Mecca to Medina in September 622. This coincides with the first year of the Islamic era.

10. Saad Eddin Ibrahim, "From Taliban to Erbakan: The Case of Islam, Civil Society, and Democracy," in *Civil Society, Democracy, and the Muslim World*, ed. Elisabeth Özdalga and Sune Persson (Istanbul: The Swedish Institution, 1997), 35.

11. To cite just one example, the number of Moroccans living in absolute poverty has risen in less than a decade from 28 percent to 45 percent. Hrair Dekmejian, "Islamic Revival: Catalysts, Categories and Consequences," in Shireen Hunter, *The Politics of Islamic Revivalism* (Indianapolis: Indiana University Press, 1988), 8.

12. Rodney Stark and Williams Bainbridge, *The Future of Religion: Secularization, Revival and Cult Formation* (Berkeley: University of California Press, 1985), George Huntston Williams, *The Radical Reformation*, 3rd edition (Kirksville, Mo.: Sixteenth Century Journal Publishers, 1992), and Lewis W. Spitz, *The Renaissance and Reformation Movements* (Chicago: Rand McNally, 1971).

13. Mark Mazower, *Dark Continent: Europe's 20th Century* (New York: Alfred A. Knopf, 1999). This excerpt is from the dust jacket.

14. David Pryce Jones, *The Closed Circle* (London: Paladin, 1990). Karl Wittfogel, *Oriental Despotism: A Comparative Study of Total Power* (New Haven: Yale University Press, 1957) locates the roots of state authoritarianism in the organization of irrigation works.

15. This thinking is echoed by Islamic fundamentalist theoreticians such as Sayyid Qutb and Abu al-A'la Mawdudi.

16. Emphasis added. Bernard Lewis, *The Middle East and the West* (New York: Harper Torchbooks, 1964), 48. Cited by Yahya Sadowski, "The New Orientalism and Democracy Debate," in *Political Islam*, 35.

17. Sadowski, "The New Orientalism."

18. Ernest Gellner, *Muslim Society* (Cambridge: Cambridge University Press, 1983) and *Postmodernism, Reason and Religion* (London: Routledge, 1992).

19. Sami Zubaida summarizing Gellner in *Islam, the People and the State: Political Ideas and Movements in the Middle East* (New York: I.B. Tauris, 1993), xiv-xv. For concise overview of Gellner on this topic, see Dale Eickelman, "From Here to Modernity: Ernest Gellner on Nationalism and Islamic Fundamentalism," in John A. Hall, *The State of the Nation: Ernest Gellner and the Theory of Nationalism* (Cambridge: Cambridge University Press, 1998), 258-71.

20. Martin Kramer, "Hizbullah: The Calculus of Jihad," in *Fundamentalisms and the State: Remaking Politics, Economics, and Militance*, Martin E. Marty and R. Scott Appleby, eds. (Chicago: University of Chicago Press, 1993), 539.

21. Juan Eduardo Campo, "The Ends of Islamic Fundamentalism: Hegemonic Discourse and the Islamic Question in Egypt," *Contention* 4 (Spring 1995), 174-75. Campo, while praising Kramer for including some valuable information about Hizbullah in his article, notes that "it unfortunately neglects to discuss in any meaningful way the most immediate cause for the rise of the organization: the 1982 Israeli invasion and American complicity with it." This is typical of all Orientalist scholars and political modernization theorists. The role of West in the internal affairs of the Third World is always considered helpful at best, benign at worst.

22. For a lengthy response to the essentialist interpretation of Muslim politics by Orientalist scholars, see Zubaida, *Islam, the People and the State*, 121-82.

23. Hindu fundamentalism has largely escaped any critical scrutiny by most Western analysts. For example V. S. Naipaul suffered no negative press after he endorsed the destruction of the Ayodhya mosque while describing Hindu fundamentalism as a "mighty creative process." See his interview with Dilip Padgoankar, "'An Area of Awakening,'" *Times of India* (July 18, 1993). For an exhaustive treatment of the subject see the five volumes of "The Fundamentalism Project," edited by Martin E. Marty and R. Scott

Appleby and published by the University of Chicago Press: *Fundamentalisms Observed* (1991), *Fundamentalisms and the State: Remaking Polities, Economies and Militance* (1993), *Fundamentalisms and Society: Reclaiming the Sciences, the Family and Education* (1993), *Accounting for Fundamentalism: The Dynamic Character of Movements* (1994), and *Fundamentalisms Comprehended* (1995).

24. Charles Taylor, *The Malaise of Modernity* (Concord, Ontario: Anansi Press, 1991).

25. Charles J. Halperin, *Russia and the Golden Horde* (Bloomington: Indiana University Press, 1985).

26. After the attack on the World Trade Center on 11 September 2001, it was widely reported in the press that church attendance in the United States had increased. See Laurie Goodstein, "As Attacks' Impact Recedes, a Return to Religion as Usual," *New York Times* (21 November 2001).

27. James Piscatori, *Islam in a World of Nation-States* (Cambridge: Cambridge University Press, 1986), 31.

28. Karen Armstrong, "Is A Holy War Inevitable?" *Gentlemen's Quarterly* (January 2002): 98. For a thoughtful treatment and elaboration on this subject see her book *The Battle for God* (New York: Alfred A. Knopf, 2001).

29. Saad Eddin Ibrahim, "Anatomy of Egypt's Militant Islamist Groups," *International Journal of Middle East Studies* 12 (1980): 423-53, and Charles Kurzman, "Bin Ladin and Other Thoroughly Modern Muslims," *Contexts* 1, no. 4 (2002): 13-20.

30. John Sigler, "Understanding the Resurgence of Islam: The Case of Political Islam," *Middle East Affairs Journal* 2 (Summer/Fall 1996): 86.

31. Roland Robertson and JoAnn Chirico, "Humanity, Globalization, and Worldwide Religion Resurgence: A Theoretical Exploration," *Sociological Analysis* 46 (1985): 233. Cited by John Voll, *Islam: Continuity and Change in the Modern World*, 2nd edition (Syracuse: Syracuse University Press, 1994), 376.

32. Benjamin Barber, *Jihad vs. McWorld* (New York: Ballantine Books, 1995). I am indebted to John Sigler for this insight.

33. Also helpful in regard is the concept of historical and political trajectories employed by Perry Anderson and Jean-Francois Bayat. For a short summary of their views as it applies to the developing world see John Martinussen, *Society, State and Market: A Guide to Competing Theories of Development* (London: Zed Books, 1997), 179-80. For a more detailed discussion see Perry Anderson, *Lineages of the Absolute State* (London: Verso, 1979) and Jean-François Bayart, "Finishing with the Idea of the Third World: The Concept of the Political Trajectory," in *Rethinking Third World Politics*, ed. James Manor (London: Longman, 1991), 51-71.

34. Fernand Braudel, "La Longue Durée," in *Écrits sur l'Histoire* (Writings on History) (Paris: Flammarion, 1985), 41-83.

35. Braudel, "La Longue Durée," 50.

36. Braudel, "La Longue Durée," 54.

37. L. Carl Brown observes that a "case can be made that the Muslim world today is seized with the equivalent of all such factors plus more. Not only are the increases in literacy, publications, rural to urban migration, and economic interdependence greater for today's Muslims than for Europeans of the Reformation period. Not only is the time involved squeezed down for today's Muslims to a few decades as opposed to at least a century and a half, if not more, for Reformation Europe." Brown, *Religion and State*, 137.

38. Michael Walzer, *Revolution of the Saints: A Study in the Origins of Radical Politics* (Cambridge: Harvard University Press, 1965). For Walzer's views on the Arab world, see his exchange with Edward Said in *Grand Street* in 1986. This is partially reproduced by William D. Hart, *Edward Said and the Religious Effects of Culture* (Cambridge: Cambridge University Press, 2000), 176-99. I am indebted to John Sigler for introducing me to Walzer's thesis and its relevance to the Islamic world.

39. J. M. Roberts, *The Penguin History of the World* (New York: Penguin, 1990), 484.

40. Walzer, *Revolution of the Saints*, 201-3.

41. Walzer, *Revolution of the Saints*, 302.

42. Walzer, *Revolution of the Saints*, 300.

43. Walzer, *Revolution of the Saints*, 310. In this context Walzer draws a comparison between Lenin and Oliver Cromwell. See page 310, footnote 14.

44. Walzer, *Revolution of the Saints*, 311.

45. Walzer, *Revolution of the Saints*, 312.

46. Walzer, *Revolution of the Saints*, 316.

47. Walzer, *Revolution of the Saints*, 317.

48. Walzer, *Revolution of the Saints*, 317-20.

49. See "Intellectuals in Post-Revolutionary Iran," a special issue of the *International Journal of Politics, Culture and Society* 15 (Winter 2001).

50. Ali Mirsepassi, *Intellectual Discourse and the Politics of Modernization: Negotiating Modernity in Iran* (Cambridge: Cambridge University Press, 2000), 73.

51. Said Amir Arjomand, "Iran's Islamic Revolution in Comparative Perspective," *World Politics* 38 (April 1986), 390.

Conclusion

An Islamic Reformation?
Some Afterthoughts

Fred Dallmayr

Historical analogies are always hazardous. There may indeed be superficial historical parallels; but their occurrence is often peculiarly twisted and their significance counterintuitive. A main reason resides in the lack of linearity: the fact that history is a dense fabric of multiple strands whose status and inter-relation are open to multiple interpretations and reinterpretations. Even if one strand at a given time and place should be comparable with a similar strand elsewhere, the immense complexity of historical contexts would thwart any simple analogy. The difficulty is compounded or accentuated in the case of cross-cultural or cross-civilizational studies—where the terms "culture" or "civilization" stand for inherited frames of meanings and ways of life shared among larger groups of people. Although perhaps not impossible, any attempt to move laterally beyond or across such frames is likely to be suspect on epistemic as well as experiential grounds. The suspicion is bound to be particularly strong among historians whose professional training tends to alert them more to concrete particularities than to bland uniformities, more to fine nuances than to glib abstractions. Even nonhistorians, however, can see the problem: there is no prima facie evidence for assuming that the histories of cultures—and the stories of their people—are synchronized or readily convertible.

Historical comparison thus dictates prudence. Nowhere is such prudence more desirable than in the case of "the Reformation" and parallel historical applications of that term. It is now widely recognized, and historians firmly insist, that the so-called Reformation in sixteenth-century Europe was not one single event but a series of different, though interconnected "reformations"—each of which, in turn, displayed a welter of religious, social, and political dimensions. In the words of Roland Bainton, the Reformation which unfolded in sixteenth-century Europe was a combination of multiple strands: including doctrine-theological, moral, and sociological facets.[1] Moreover, the complex meaning of "Reformation" is further refracted in the diversity of geographical locations or contexts. Thus, it is possible, and even customary, to distinguish between a German Reformation, an English Reformation, a Scottish Reformation, a Swiss Reformation, and so on. Hence, the historian's delight in concreteness can find satisfaction in a seemingly endless plethora of contextual details and particularities. All these factors augur ill for the ready transfer of "the Reformation" from one country to the next—and, *a fortiori*, from one civilizational frame of reference to another. Unsurprisingly, serious doubts have been raised—both by Muslims and non-Muslims—regarding the plausibility or feasibility of an Islamic Reformation or even a Reformation-like development in Muslim countries. The present volume on numerous occasions makes reference to such skeptical arguments or outright denials, voiced sometimes by leading Muslim scholars and intellectuals in our time.

Although mindful of the historian's reticence and the obvious need for caution, I cannot quite go along with the simple rejection of historical parallels. One main reason has to do with a central strand of "the Reformation," however one may contextualize it: namely, its religious or spiritual dimension. Overshadowing all other (social and geographical) considerations is the immense religious fervor and commitment of the great historical Reformers. This aspect is well accentuated by Filipe Fernández-Armesto and Derek Wilson when they write that the Reformation was above all "a spiritual movement: spiritual in the sense of being a convulsion of the human spirit; spiritual also in strengthening the ties that bind individuals and society to the divine spirit."[2] Such "convulsion," however, cannot be fully stabilized, just as the "divine spirit" cannot be domesticated or imprisoned. Differently phrased: religion as the "bonding" with the divine spirit necessarily needs to be constantly renewed and respiritualized, to prevent it from sliding into humdrum conformism and routinization. This aspect has been clearly recognized by the Reformed Christian Church in its traditional motto: "*ecclesia reformata semper reformanda est*" (the reformed church must constantly be reformed)—a motto that was taken over later by the Second Vatican Council in its affirmation "*ecclesia semper reformanda.*"[3] As a religion, and not merely a compendium of legal precepts, Islam likewise has to honor the deeper demand of spirit: the demand for a continuous reform, renewal, and transformation of human life. At least in this sense, a historical parallel is bound to assert itself among all religions, including Islam.

There are additional and perhaps still more weighty reasons, however, for affirming historical parallels or the transfer of the "Reformation" category across civilizational boundaries. A basic factor in this regard is the process of globalization. As is well known, the sixteenth century in Europe is also called the "Age of Discovery," an age marked by far-flung explorations of new lands beyond the oceans and also by new discoveries and inventions in communications, astronomy, and the art of warfare. Curiously, Martin Luther's proclamation of his "Theses" was separated only by a few decades from the great Copernican revolution which redefined the place of humanity in the universe. Discoveries and innovations of this kind paved the way for the upsurge of modern science, based on empirical-experimental methods, which in turn prepared the ground for the "Age of Enlightenment" wedded to a rigorous testing of traditional assumptions and beliefs by the standard of critical reason. Further corollaries of the unfolding of European modernity were a series of political revolutions, designed to topple autocratic regimes, and even more far-ranging social and economic changes steadily transforming agrarian cultures into industrial and urbanized societies anchored in capital-fueled market economics. Complementing these changes, the twentieth century brought telecommunications, jet travel, and the technological streamlining of all modes of production. Under the auspices of globalization, all these features of European modernity are dislodged from their Western setting and progressively disseminated in societies around the globe—triggering the familiar agonies associated with "modernization." No matter how traditional and averse to Western modernity, no society today can for long escape the relentless onslaught of modern science, technology, and the forces of the global market.

The same onslaught also is bound to exert a profound impact on traditional forms of religion. Just as European Christianity had to confront and come to terms with the pressures of modernity—which were partly triggered by and partly a reaction to "the Reformation"—so today religions around the globe are constrained to regroup and to redefine their role vis-à-vis the inroads of global modernization. A crucial feature of modernity—implicit in the above account— is the rise of the modern "state" or "nation-state," a public regime predicated on rational construction and no longer monopolized by religious elites or anchored in commonly shared religious beliefs. Faced with this development, some Reformers in the sixteenth and seventeenth centuries were tempted by the lure of "theocracy" which would fuse religious autocracy with modern state structures. However, experiments of this kind were short-lived (and also marred by extensive violence).[4] Shunning theocratic fundamentalism, most Reformers chose instead a more "inward" or spiritual path, a path granting political rule to legally designated "secular" authorities while bestowing on religious believers the enormous modern gifts of "religious freedom" and "freedom of worship." Thus, by accepting the differentiation between public and private domains, between politics and faith, mainline Protestant churches in the West were able progressively to accommodate themselves to the pressures of secularizing modernity, including the dictates of the modern "liberal" state. With some retardation, the same accommodation was also reached by the Catholic Church whose medieval imperial position has been transformed into extra-political pastoral authority—with only the small Vatican State serving as a distant reminder of past imperial glory.[5]

Given the steady globalization of Western modernity, including its "Westphalian" system of nation-states, Islamic civilization cannot possibly escape the secularizing pressures of modern politics. Just as in the West the holistic unity of medieval Christendom cannot be maintained under modern auspices, attempts to restore the holistic or undifferentiated regime prevailing (presumably) during the Prophet's lifetime are bound to derail or be severely frustrated. At least since the end of the Caliphate in 1924, Islamic civilization is divided like the West into a series of (more or less autonomous) nation-states and bereft of an overarching, politically viable *umma*. Typically, attempts to revive the undivided holism of an earlier period lead to the creation of militant state-centered "theocracies"—marred by the same kind of violence that characterized millenarian movements in sixteenth- and seventeenth-century Europe. As has often been pointed out, fundamentalist Islamic movements today are characterized by a profound ambivalence: while celebrating a backward-looking and nostalgic traditionalism, such movements tend to employ the entire panoply of technological gadgets and political techniques provided by Western modernity and modernized state structures.[6] To avoid this ambivalence, and also the peril of massive coercion and violence, Islamic societies are constrained to follow more or less the path traveled at an earlier time by European Protestantism: the path toward greater inwardness or an inner-directed religiosity, which inevitably opens up the gates toward greater religious freedom and tolerance—the celebrated accomplishments of modern liberalism and liberal democracy.

For Muslim societies, to be sure, following this path is not without drawbacks or misgivings. For one thing, the reformist or "liberal" trajectory may appear as another form of Western imperialism or hegemonic domination. This suspicion is easily fueled by a certain missionary zeal often pervading Western liberalism. No doubt, especially in the wake of September 11, Western policy makers often proclaim it to be their avowed goal to spread the blessings of Western liberalism around the world, and particularly throughout the length and breadth of Islamic civilization. When backed up by military force or the threat of force, such proclamations are prone to be perceived as hostile not only to militant Islam but to the tradition of Islam as a whole. Confronted with this hostility, segments of Islamic societies unsurprisingly agitate in favor of an even greater militancy and a tightening of religious doctrines and practices. What is troubling in this situation is not only the likely upsurge of violence but the missed opportunity of a learning experience. Basically (or so it seems to me), what is involved here is not so much a "clash of civilizations" or a clash of (Western versus Islamic) ideologies, but rather an unavoidable structural constraint: the fact that under modern auspices, the traditional *umma* cannot be politically reclaimed, and that efforts to do so inevitably lead to a fusion of religion with modern state structures and hence to a contamination and possible corruption of religious faith by the prevailing model of international power politics.[7] Thus, it is not for the sake of pleasing Western liberals but rather to preserve the integrity of religious faith itself that Muslim societies are well advised to ponder—though not blindly to imitate—the inward path pursued by Western Reformers several centuries ago.

Seen from this angle, some kind of Islamic Reformation appears both likely and desirable. However, an important caveat needs to be added here. Although advised to head the example of European history, Muslim reformers may well face a more difficult or arduous task: basically, they are required to perform a double gesture or shoulder a double reformation. In many ways, Reformation in the West may have been too successful in liberalizing faith—and especially too successful in accommodating religion to the demands of secular modernity. Under the auspices of liberal Protestantism, faith has been radically consigned to the private sphere of inner individual life; to the extent that faith is allowed to surface in the social and public domains, it only serves as a glue of social cohesion (what is sometimes called "civil religion") and as a prop for dominant power structures. On this score, Muslim reformers may wish to dissent—and the lingering holistic aspirations of Islam may encourage them to dissent. For, entirely exiled from social and public domains, religion is reduced to a private pastime or to a personal "feel-good" therapy; at the same time, political power-holders and socio-economic oligarchies are freed of the requirement of social justice postulated by all major world religions, including the religion of Islam.[8]

This kind of license or immunity is particularly dangerous in the contemporary period. At a time when economic oligarchies control the fortunes and misfortunes of millions of people—a time when governments are in possession of unprecedented arsenals of coercive and destructive power—it is imperative for humankind to marshal all available reservoirs of moral conscience and transformative dissent. Some of these reservoirs are philosophical or ethical, stretching from the teachings of Aristotle to those of Kant and Albert Camus, from the lessons of Confucius to the practices of Gandhi. However, a particularly powerful resource is found in the teachings of the world's religions, given the tendency of genuine faith to rupture or transcend all totalizing or totalitarian forms of secular-political immanence in favor of a non-negotiable or "prophetic" demand. As Paul Ricoeur has reminded his readers (quoting Matthew 5, 13), religious faith is meant to be "the salt of the earth"—which means that, rejecting both world domination and world denial, "the salt is made for salting" in such a way that religion exists "for the sake of those outside itself" or the world that faith inhabits.[9] This insight was powerfully confirmed by Archbishop Oscar Romero in El Salvador when he stated shortly before his assassination by a government-sponsored death squad:

> Unfortunately, brothers and sisters, we are today the product of a spiritualized, individualistic education. We were taught: try to save your soul and don't worry about the rest. We told the suffering: be patient, heaven will follow, hang on. But no: that's not right, that is not salvation! That is not the salvation Christ

brought. The salvation Christ brings is a salvation from every bondage that oppresses human beings.[10]

Muslim reformers, intent on bringing religious freedom to Muslim societies, may wish to remember these words, translating them into their own Qur'anic language. Although religious reformation requires a certain internalization and a withdrawal from direct state control, Islamic faith also needs to remain the energizing and transformative "salt" of Muslim societies. Faced with both global hegemonic pressures and a host of indigenous tyrants and despots, Muslims must preserve the Qur'anic message, which is entrusted to them, as a critical restraint on economic and political elites and their rampant lust for power. In this way, the Qur'anic message can remain a leavening agent in society, a salt "made for salting," a light "made for illuminating" and not for blinding people. Here it may be appropriate to recall what the *Qur'an* calls the path of righteousness or the "path of the steep ascent" (*Sura* 90:12-17):

> How will you comprehend
> What the steep ascent is?—
> To free a neck
> (from the burden of debt or slavery),
> Or to feed in times of famine
> The orphan near in relationship,
> Or the poor in distress;
> And to be of those who believe,
> and urge upon one another to believe,
> and urge upon each other to be kind.

Notes

1. Roland H. Bainton, *The Age of Reformation* (Princeton, N.J.: Van Nostrand, 1956), 12. On the plural character of the European Reformation see also Felipe Fernández-Armesto and Derek Wilson, *Reformations: A Radical Interpretation of Christianity and the World* (New York: Scribner, 1996); Carter Lindberg, *The European Reformations* (Oxford: Blackwell, 1996).

2. Fernández-Armesto and Wilson, *Reformations*, p. xi. According to Alister E. McGrath, the European Reformation should be seen "primarily as an intellectual phenomenon" (where "intellectual" comprises the religious-spiritual dimension). See *The Intellectual Origins of the European Reformation* (Oxford: Blackwell, 1987), 4.

3. See Joseph C. McLelland, *The Reformation and Its Significance Today* (Philadelphia: Westminster Press, 1962), 6. McLelland also cites Friedrich Schleiermacher to the effect that "the Reformation must continue," and the ancient proverb: "Carry from the ashes of the past the fire, not the ashes."

4. Some chapters in the present volume deal in detail with the fortunes and misfortunes of millenarian experiments in Europe, especially the policies of Thomas Müntzer and the Anabaptists. Compare also Michael Walzer, *The Revolution of the Saints: A Study in the Origins of Radical Politics* (Cambridge: Harvard University Press, 1965).

5. Although formally a "state," the Vatican participates only minimally in inter-state or international politics in the modern sense.

6. Compare in this respect Roxanne L. Euben, *Enemy in the Mirror: Islamic Fundamentalism and the Limits of Modern Rationalism* (Princeton: Princeton University Press, 1999).

7. Compare on this point, e.g., Seyyed Vali R. Nasr, *Islamic Leviathan: Islam and the Making of State Power* (New York: Oxford University Press, 2001). As Nasr shows, the idea of an "Islamic state" is deeply problematic and even paradoxical.

8. See, e.g., Richard John Neuhaus, *The Naked Public Square: Religion and Democracy in America*, 2nd ed. (Grand Rapids, Mich.: Eerdmans, 1984).

9. Paul Ricoeur, *Political and Social Essays*, ed. David Stewart and Joseph Bien (Athens: Ohio University Press, 1974), 105.

10. See Oscar Romero, "Option for the Poor," 9 September 1979, www.bruderhof.com/articles/OptionForPoor.htm (30 May 2003). Compare also the statement of Thich Nhat Hanh articulating a critical Buddhist perspective: "A monk is much listened to by the people. In a time of elections, people ask his advice and his voice carries weight. But suppose he runs for office; he loses the respect people have from him. As a monk he speaks out of his wisdom, his spirituality. But when he runs for office . . . people cannot help thinking that he has [political] ambition. That changes the situation." See Daniel Berrigan and Thich Nhat Hanh, *The Raft is Not the Shore: Conversations Toward a Buddhist Christian Awareness* (Boston: Beacon Press, 1975), 86. In the words of Christopher S. Queen, critically engaged Buddhists "direct their energies toward social conditions over which the state has legal authority, if not control; but their objective is to influence the exercise of temporal power not to wield it. Sulak Sivaraksa [Thai Buddhist] is fond of contrasting 'capital-B Buddhists' who cultivate privileged relations with state power brokers, with 'small-B Buddhist' who change society by manifesting qualities of wisdom, compassion, and peace." See his "Introduction: The Shapes and Sources of Engaged Buddhism," in Queen and Sallie B. King, eds., *Engaged Buddhism: Buddhist Liberation Movements in Asia* (Albany: State University of New York Press, 1996), 19. In the same way, one may with to distinguish between "capital-M Muslims" who seek political domination and "small-M Muslims" whose faith acts as a critical barrier against domination and against oppressive construals of Islam (e.g., with regard to women).

Selected Bibliography

'Abd al-Karim, Khalil. *Quraysh min al-Qabila ila al-Dawla al-Markaziyya* (Quraysh from Tribe to Central State). Cairo: Sina, 1997.

——. *Mujtama' Yathrib* (The Society of Yathrib). Cairo: Sina, 1997.

——. *Shadw al-Rababa bi-Ahwal Mujtama' al-Sahaba: Muhammad wa al-Sahaba* (The Fiddle's Chants on the Ways of the Society of the Companions: Muhammad and the Companions), vol. 1. Cairo: Sina, 1997.

'Abd al-Rahman, Taha. *al-'Amal al-Dini wa Tajdid al-'Aql* (Religious Practice and the Renewal of Reason). Casablanca: al-Markaz al-Thaqafa al-'Arabi, 1997.

'Abduh, Muhammad. *The Theology of Unity*, translated by Ishaq Musa'ad and Kenneth Cragg. London: George Allen & Unwin, 1966.

al-'Aqqad, 'Abbas Mahmud. *'Abqariyyat Muhammad* (The Genius of Muhammad). Cairo: al-Maktabah al-Tijariyyah al-Kubra, 1942.

Abu Fakr, Saqir. "Trends in Arab Thought (Interview with Sadek Jalal al-Azm)." *Journal of Palestine Studies* 27 (1998): 68-81.

Abu Zaid, Nasr Hamid. "Divine Attributes in the Qur'an: Some Poetic Aspects." Pp. 190-211 in *Islam and Modernity: Muslim Intellectuals Respond*, edited by John Cooper, Ronald L. Nettler and Mohamed Mahmoud. London: I. B. Tauris, 1998.

Abu Zayd, Nasr Hamid. *Mar'ah fi Khitab al-Azmah* (Women in the Discourse of Crisis). Cairo: Dar al-Nusus, 1994.

——. *Mafhum al-Nass: Dirasah fi 'Ulum al-Qur'an* (The Concept of the Text: A Study of the Sciences of the Quran). Cairo: al-Hayat al-Misriyyat al-'Amma lil-Kitab, 1990.

——. *Naqd al-Khitab al-Dini* (Critique of Religious Discourse). Cairo: Sina lil-Nashr, 1992.

——. "The Qur'anic Concept of Justice." *Polylog. Forum for Intercultural Philosophizing* 2 (2001): 1-43.

——. *al-Tafkir fi Zaman al-Takfir: Didda al-Jahl wa al-Zayf wa al-Khurafah* (Thinking in the Age of Declaring Unbelievers: Against the Ignorance, Falsity and Superstition). Cairo: Sina lil-Nashr, 1995.

Abun-Nasr, Jamil. "The Salafiyya Movement in Morocco: The Religious Bases of the Moroccan Nationalist Movement." *St. Antony's Papers* 16 (1963): 90-105.

Adelkhah, Fariba. *Being Modern in Iran*. New York: Columbia University Press, 2000.

Afailal, Thami. "René Guénon: un modèle soufi du XXème siècle" (René Guénon: A Sufi Model of the 20th Century). *Demain* (1 July 2000).

Ahmad, Nazir. *Qur'anic and Non-Qur'anic Islam*. Lahore, Pakistan: Vanguard, 1997.

Akhavi, Shahrough. "Contending Discourses in Shi'a Law on the Doctrine of *Wilayat al-Faqih*." *Iranian Studies* 29 (1996): 253-59.

——. *Religion and Politics in Contemporary Iran: Clergy-State Relations in the Pahlavi Period*. Albany: State University of New York Press, 1980.

Akhunduf, Mirza Fath 'Ali. *Alifba-yi Jadid va Maktubat* (The New Alphabet and Letters). Baku, USSR: Nashriyat-i Farhangistan-i 'Ulum-i Jumhuri-yi Shuravi-yi Azarbayjan, 1963.

Anderson, Norman. *Law Reform in the Muslim World*. London: Athlone Press, 1976.

Anderson, Perry. *Lineages of the Absolute State*. London: Verso, 1979.

An-Na'im, Abdullahi Ahmed. "The Islamic Counter-reformation." *New Perspectives Quarterly* 19 (2002): 29-35.
——. *Toward an Islamic Reformation: Civil Liberties, Human Rights, and International Law*. Syracuse: Syracuse University Press, 1996.
Aras, Bülent. "Turkish Islam's Moderate Face." *Middle East Quarterly* 5, no. 3 (September 1998): 23-30.
Arjomand, Said Amir. "Iran's Islamic Revolution in Comparative Perspective." *World Politics* 38 (April 1986): 383-414.
——. *The Turban for the Crown: The Islamic Revolution in Iran*. New York: Oxford University Press, 1988.
Arkoun, Mohammed. *Essais sur la Pensée Islamique* (Essay on Islamic Thought). Paris: Maisonneuve et Larose, 1984.
——. *Rethinking Islam*. Boulder, Colo.: Westview Press, 1994.
——. *Rethinking Islam Today*. Washington D.C.: Center for Contemporary Arab Studies, Georgetown University, 1987.
——. *Tarikhiyyat al-Fikr al-'Arabi al-Islami* (The Historicity of Arab Islamic Thought). Beirut: Markaz al-Inma al-Qawmi, 1987.
——. *The Unthought in Contemporary Islamic Thought*. London: Saqi Books, 2002.
Armstrong, Karen. *The Battle for God*. New York: Alfred A. Knopf, 2001.
Arslan, Shakib. *Li-Madha Ta'akhkhara al-Muslimun wa li-Madha Taqaddama Ghayruhum?* (Why Did the Muslims Remain Behind and Why Did Others Progress?). Cairo: Matba'at al-Manar, 1930.
Arthur, Anthony. *The Tailor-King*. New York: St. Martin's Press, 1999.
Asad, Talal. *Genealogies of Religion: Discipline and Reasons of Power in Christianity and Islam*. Baltimore, Md.: The Johns Hopkins University Press, 1993.
——. *The Idea of an Anthropology of Islam*. Washington, D.C.: Center for Contemporary Arab Studies, Georgetown University, 1986.
al-Ash'ari, 'Ali ibn Isma'il. *Abu'l-Hasan 'Ali ibn Isma'il al-Ash'ari's al-Ibanah 'an Usul ad-Diyanah* (The Elucidation of Islam's Foundation), translated by Walter Conrad Klein. New Haven, Conn.: American Oriental Society, 1940.
al-'Ashmawi, Muhammad Sa'id. *al-Khilafa al-Islamiyya* (The Islamic Caliphate), 3rd ed. Cairo: Madbuli al-Saghir, 1996.
Ayalon, Ami. *Egypt's Quest for Cultural Orientation*. Tel Aviv: The Moshe Dayan Center for Middle Eastern and African Studies, 1999.
al-Azmeh, Aziz. "Barbarians in Arab Eyes." *Past and Present* 134 (1992): 3-18.
al-Bab, Ja'far Dik. "Asrar al-lisan al-'arabi" (Secrets of the Arabic Language). Pp. 741-819 in *al-Kitab wa al-Qur'an: Qira'a Mu'asira* (The Book and the Qur'an: A Contemporary Reading), by Muhammad Shahrour. Damascusa: al-Ahli lil-Taba'a wa al-Nashr wa al-Tawzi', 1990.
——. "Taqdim: al-Manhaj al-Lughawi fi al-Qur'an" (Preface: The Linguistic Method in the Qur'an). Pp. 19-27 in *al-Kitab wa al-Qur'an: Qira'a Mu'asira* (The Book and the Qur'an: A Contemporary Reading), by Muhammad Shahrour. Damascus: al-Ahli lil-Taba'a wa al-Nashr wa al-Tawzi', 1990.
Backus, Irene. *Historical Method and Confessional Identity in the Era of the Reformation*. Leiden: Brill, 2003.
Bainton, Roland Herbert. *Here I Stand*. New York: Abingdon-Cokesbury Press, 1950.
——. *The Age of Reformation*. Princeton, N.J.: Van Nostrand, 1956.
Bakhash, Shaul. *The Reign of the Ayatollahs*. New York: Basic Books, 1990.
Barber, Benjamin. *Jihad vs. McWorld*. New York: Ballantine Books, 1995.

Bayart, Jean-François. "Finishing with the Idea of the Third World: The Concept of the Political Trajectory." Pp. 51-71 in *Rethinking Third World Politics*, edited by James Manor. London: Longman, 1991.

Beedham, Brian. "It Is Now the Year 1415." *Economist* (6 August 1994): 14-16.

Berrigan, Daniel, and Thich Nhat Hanh. *The Raft is Not the Shore: Conversations toward a Buddhist Christian Awareness*. Boston: Beacon Press, 1975.

Bigiyef, Musa Jarullah. *Khalq Nazarïna Bir Nichä Mäs'älä* (Several Problems for Public Consideration). Kazan, Tatarstan, Russia: Äliktro-Tipografiyä Ümid, 1912.

Bloch, Marc. "Towards a Comparative History of European Societies." Pp.489-521 in *Enterprise and Secular Change: Reading in Economic History*, edited by Frederic C. Lane and Jelle C. Riemersma. Homewood, Ill.: R. D. Irwin, 1953.

Blunt, Wilfred Scawen. "The Future of Islam." *The Fortnightly Review* 30 (1881): 204-23, 315-32, 441-58, 585-602, and 31 (1882): 32-48.

———. *The Future of Islam*. London: Kegan Paul, Trench & Co., 1882.

———. *Secret History of the English Occupation of Egypt, Being a Personal Narrative of Events*. London: T. F. Unwin, 1907.

Böttcher, Annabelle. *Syrische Religionspolitik unter Asad* (Syrian Religious Politics Under Asad). Freiburg: Arnold-Bergsträsser-Institut, 1998.

Braudel, Fernand. "La Longue Durée." Pp. 41-83 in *Écrits sur l'Histoire* (Writings on History). Paris: Flammarion, 1985.

Brown, L. Carl. *Religion and State: The Muslim Approach to Politics*. New York: Columbia University Press, 2000.

———. "Review: Reason, Freedom, and Democracy in Islam." *Foreign Affairs* 79 (September/October 2000): 148.

Bruns, Gerald L. *Hermeneutics Ancient and Modern*. New Haven: Yale University Press, 1992.

Buaben, Jabal Muhammad. *Image of the Prophet Muhammad in the West: A Study of Muir, Margoliouth and Watt*. Leicester, England: The Islamic Foundation, 1996.

Burke, Edmund, III. "The Moroccan Ulama, 1860-1912: An Introduction." Pp. 95-123 in *Scholars, Saints, and Sufis: Muslim Religious Institutions in the Middle East Since 1500*, edited by Nikki R. Keddie. Berkeley: University of California Press, 1972.

Burrow, J. W. *The Crisis of Reason: European Thought, 1848-1914*. New Haven: Yale University Press, 2000.

Calder, Norman. *Studies in Early Muslim Jurisprudence*. Oxford: Clarendon Press, 1993.

Campbell, Colin. "The Cult, the Cultic Milieu and Secularization." Pp. 119-36 in *A Sociological Yearbook of Religion in Britain* 5, edited by Michael Hill. London: SCM Press, 1972.

Campo, Juan Eduardo. "The Ends of Islamic Fundamentalism: Hegemonic Discourse and the Islamic Question in Egypt." *Contention* 4 (Spring 1995): 168-75.

Casanova, Jose. "Civil Society and Religion: Retrospective Reflections on Catholicism and Prospective Reflections on Islam." *Social Research* 68 (2001): 1041-81.

Chambers, Richard L. "The Ottoman Ulema and the Tanzimat." Pp. 35-46 in *Scholars, Saints, and Sufis: Muslim Religious Institutions in the Middle East Since 1500*, edited by Nikki R. Keddie. Berkeley: University of California Press, 1972.

Choueiri, Youssef M. *Islamic Fundamentalism*. Boston: Twayne Publishers, 1990.

Clark, Peter. "The Shahrour Phenomenon: A Liberal Islamic Voice from Syria." *Islam and Christian-Muslim Relations* 7 (1996): 337-41.

Clement, W. R. *Reforming the Prophet: The Quest for the Islamic Reformation*. Toronto: Insomniac Press, 2002.

Cohn, Norman. *The Pursuit of the Millennium*. New York: Oxford University Press, 1970.

Cole, Juan. "Shi'i Clerics in Iraq and Iran, 1722-1780: The Akhbari-Usuli Conflict Reconsidered." *Iranian Studies* 18 (1985): 3-34.

Commins, David. *Islamic Reform: Politics and Social Change in Late Ottoman Syria*. New York: Oxford University Press, 1990.

Constitution of the Islamic Republic of Iran. Tehran: Islamic Propagation Organization, 1979.

Coulson, N. J. *A History of Islamic Law*. Edinburgh, Scotland: Edinburgh University Press, 1964.

Crecelius, Daniel. "Nonideological Responses of the Egyptian Ulama to Modernization." Pp. 180-205 in *Scholars, Saints, and Sufis: Muslim Religious Institutions in the Middle East Since 1500*, edited by Nikki R. Keddie. Berkeley: University of California Press, 1972.

Crone, Patricia. *Meccan Trade and the Rise of Islam*. Princeton: Princeton University Press, 1987.

——. *Slaves on Horses: The Evolution of the Islamic Polity*. Cambridge: Cambridge University Press, 1980.

Dajani, Zahia Ragheb. *Egypt and the Crisis of Islam*. New York: Lang, 1990.

Dallal, Ahmad. "Appropriating the Past: Twentieth Century Reconstruction of Pre-Modern Islamic Thought." *Islamic Law and Society* 7 (2000): 333-42.

——. "The Origins and Objectives of Islamic Revivalist Thought, 1750-1850." *Journal of the American Oriental Society* 113 (1993): 341-59.

Daniel, Norman. *Islam and the West: The Making of an Image*. Edinburgh, Scotland: Edinburgh University Press, 1960.

Davani, 'Ali. "Khaterat-e Hojjat al-Islam Aqa-ye 'Ali Davani" (Memoirs of Hojjat al-Islam Mr. 'Ali Davani). *Yad* (Memory) 8 (1987).

Dawes, Gregory W. *The Historical Jesus Question: The Challenge of History to Religious Authority*. Louisville, Ky.: Westminster John Knox Press, 2001.

Dekmejian, Hrair. "Islamic Revival: Catalysts, Categories and Consequences." Pp. 3-19 in *The Politics of Islamic Revivalism*, edited by Shireen Hunter. Indianapolis: Indiana University Press, 1988.

Dilthey, Wilhelm. "The Rise of Hermeneutics." Pp. 101-14 in *The Hermeneutic Tradition: From Ast to Ricoeur*, edited by Gayle L. Ormiston and Alan D. Schrift. Albany: State University of New York Press, 1990.

Eickelman, Dale F. "From Here to Modernity: Ernest Gellner on Nationalism and Islamic Fundamentalism." Pp. 258-71 in *The State of the Nation: Ernest Gellner and the Theory of Nationalism*, edited by John A Hall. Cambridge: Cambridge University Press, 1998.

——. "Inside the Islamic Reformation." *The Wilson Quarterly* 22 (1998): 80-89.

——. "Islam and the Languages of Modernity." *Daedalus* 129 (2000): 119-35.

——. "Islamic Liberalism Strikes Back." *MESA Bulletin* 27 (1993): 163-68.

——. "Islamic Religious Commentary and Lesson Circles: Is There a Copernican Revolution." Pp. 121-46 in *Commentaries = Kommentare: Aporemat* 4, edited by Glenn W. Most. Göttingen, Germany: Vandenhoeck & Ruprecht, 1999.

——. "Mass Higher Education and the Religious Imagination in Contemporary Arab Societies." *American Ethnologist* 19 (1992): 643-55.

——. "Muhammad Shahrour and the Printed Word." *ISIM Newsletter* 7 (2001): 15.

——. "The Coming Transformation of the Muslim World." *MERIA Journal* 3 (1999): 78-81.

Eickelman, Dale F., and Jon W. Anderson, eds. *New Media in the Muslim World: The Emerging Public Sphere.* Bloomington: Indiana University Press, 2003.

——. "Print, Islam, and the Prospects for Civic Pluralism: New Religious Writings and their Audiences." *Journal of Islamic Studies* 8 (1997): 43-62.

El-Affendi, Abdelwahab. "The Elusive Reformation." *Journal of Democracy* 14 (2003): 34-38.

Ernst, Carl W. *The Shambhala Guide to Sufism.* Boston: Shambhala, 1997.

Esposito, John L. *Islam: The Straight Path.* Oxford: Oxford University Press, 1998.

——. *The Islamic Threat: Myth or Reality?* New York: Oxford University Press, 1992.

Esposito, John L., and John Obert Voll. *Makers of Contemporary Islam.* Oxford: Oxford University Press, 2001.

Euben, Roxanne L. *Enemy in the Mirror: Islamic Fundamentalism and the Limits of Modern Rationalism.* Princeton: Princeton University Press, 1999.

Fadel, Mohammad. "The Social Logic of *Taqlid* and the Rise of the *Mukhatasar* [*sic*]." *Islamic Law and Society* 3 (1996): 193-233.

Fakhr, Saqir Abu. "Trends in Arab Thought (Interview with Sadek Jalal al-Azm)." *Journal of Palestine Studies* 27 (1998): 68-80.

al-Fasi, 'Allal. *Maqasid al-Shari'a al-Islamiyya wa Makarimuha* (The Purposes and Noble Traits of Islamic Law). Casablanca: Maktabat al-Ahda al-'Arabiyya, 1963.

Fernández-Armesto, Felipe, and Derek Wilson. *Reformations: A Radical Interpretation of Christianity and the World.* New York: Scribner, 1996.

Feyerabend, Paul. *Against Method.* London: Verso, 1975.

Findley, C. V. "Medjelle." Pp. 971-72 in *Encyclopedia of Islam,* edited by H.A. R. Gibb, et al., 2nd ed., vol. 6. Leiden: E. J. Brill, 1954-1971.

Finkelstein, Norman G. *Image and Reality of the Israel-Palestine Conflict.* London: Verso, 1995.

Fischer, Michael M. J. *Iran: From Religious Dispute to Revolution.* Cambridge: Harvard University Press, 1980.

Fouda, Faraj. *al-Haqiqa al-Gha'iba* (The Missing Truth). Cairo: Dar al-Fikr lil-Dirasat wa al-Nashr wa al-Tawzi', 1988.

Fukuyama, Francis, and Nadav Samin. "Can Any Good Come of Radical Islam?" *Commentary* 114 (September 2002): 34-38.

Fukuyama, Francis, Nadav Samin, et al. "Controversy: Modernizing Islam." *Commentary* 114 (December 2002): 17-21.

Fyzee, Asaf A. A. "The Reinterpretation of Islam." Pp. 188-93 in *Islam in Transition: Muslim Perspectives,* edited by John J. Donohue and John L. Esposito. New York: Oxford University Press, 1982.

Gadamer, Hans-Georg. *Truth and Method.* New York: Continuum, 1993.

Gellner, Ernest. *Muslim Society.* Cambridge: Cambridge University Press, 1983.

——. *Postmodernism, Reason and Religion.* London: Routledge, 1992.

Geoffroy, Eric. "Le traité de soufisme d'un disciple d'Ibn Taymiyya: Ahmad 'Imad al-Din al-Wasiti, m. 711/1311" (The Sufi Treatise of a Disciple of Ibn Taymiyya: Ahmad 'Imad al-Din al-Wasisti, d. 711/1311). *Studia Islamica* 82 (1995): 83-101.

Gershoni, Israel and James P. Jankowski, *Redefining the Egyptian Nation, 1930-1945.* Cambridge: Cambridge University Press, 1995.

——. "Print Culture, Social Change and the Process of Redefining Imagined Communities in Egypt." *International Journal of Middle East Studies* 31 (1999): 81-94.

al-Ghazali, Abu Hamid. *al-Mustasfa min 'Ilm al-Usul* (The Prime Selection from Islamic Legal Theory), edited by Hamza ibn Zubayr Hafiz. Jidda: Sharikat al-Madina al-Munawwara, 1993.

——. *Shifa al-Ghalil* (Quenching the Thirst), edited by Hamad 'Ubayd al-Kubaysi. Baghdad: Matba'at al-Irshad, 1971.

Gökalp, Ziya. *Turkish Nationalism and Western Civilization: Selected Essays of Ziya Gökalp*, edited and translated by Niyazi Berkes. London: George Allen and Unwin, 1959.

Goldberg, Ellis. "Smashing Idols and the State: The Protestant Ethic and Egyptian Sunni Radicalism." Pp. 195-236 in *Comparing Muslim Societies: Knowledge and the State in a World Civilization*, edited by Juan R. I. Cole. Ann Arbor: University of Michigan Press, 1992.

Goldziher, Ignaz. *Introduction to Islamic Theology and Law*, translated by Andras and Ruth Hamori. Princeton: Princeton University Press, 1981.

Gonzalez-Quijano, Yves. *Les Gens du Livre: Édition et Champ Intellectuel dans l'Égypte Republicaine* (People of the Book: Publishing and Intellectual Field in Republican Egypt). Paris: CNRS Éditions, 1998.

Goodson, Larry. *Afghanistan's Endless War*. Seattle: University of Washington Press, 2001.

Gouldner, Alvin W. *The Future of Intellectuals and the Rise of the New Class*. New York: Seabury Press, 1979.

Grell, Ole Peter, and Bob Scribner, eds. *Tolerance and Intolerance in the European Reformation*. Cambridge: Cambridge University Press, 1996.

Griffel, Frank. "Toleration and Exclusion: Shafi'i and Ghazali on the Treatment of Apostates." *Bulletin of the School of Oriental and African Studies* 63 (2001): 339-54.

Guénon, Rene. *The Crisis of the Modern World*. Ghent, NY: Sophia Perennis et Universalis, 2001.

——. *East and West*. Ghent, NY: Sophia Perennis et Universalis, 2001.

Guizot, François. *History of Civilization in Europe*. London: Penguin, 1997.

Haddad, Yvonne Yazbeck. *Contemporary Islam and the Challenge of History*. Albany: State University of New York Press, 1982.

Hafez, Sabry. *The Genesis of Arabic Narrative Discourse*. London: Saqi Books, 1993.

al-Hakim, Tawfiq. *Muhammad*. Cairo: Matba'at Lajnat al-Ta'lif wa al-Tarjamah wa al-Nashr, 1936.

Hallaq, Wael B. *A History of Islamic Legal Theories: An Introduction to Sunni Usul al-Fiqh*. New York: Cambridge University Press, 1997.

——. "On the Origins of the Controversy about the Existence of Mujtahids and the Gate of Ijtihad." *Studia Islamica* 63 (1986): 129-41.

Halperin, Charles J. *Russia and the Golden Horde*. Bloomington: Indiana University Press, 1985.

Hanafi, Hassan. *al-Din wa al-Thawra fi Misr: 1952-1981* (Religion and Revolution in Egypt). Cairo: Maktabat Madbuli, 1988.

——. "Islam and Revolution." Pp. 183-94 in *The Philosophical Quest: A Cross-Cultural Reader*, edited by Gail M. Presbey, Karsten J. Struhl, and Richard E. Olsen. Columbus, Ohio: McGraw-Hill, 2000.

——. *Islam in the Modern World: Volume I—Religion, Ideology and Development*. Cairo: Anglo-Egyptian Bookshop, 1995.

———. "Method of Thematic Interpretation of the Qur'an." Pp. 195-211 in *The Qu'ran as Text*, edited by Stefan Wild. Leiden: E. J. Brill, 1996.

———. "Phenomenology and Islamic Philosophy." Pp. 318-21 in *Phenomenology World-Wide: Foundations, Expanding Dynamisms, Life-Engagements—A Guide for Research and Study*, edited by Anna-Teresa Tymieniecka. Boston: Kluwer Academic Publishers, 2002.

———. *Religious Dialogue and Revolution: Essays on Judaism, Christianity, and Islam.* Cairo: Anglo-Egyptian Bookshop, 1977.

Hanafi, Hassan, and Muhammad 'Abid al-Jabiri. *Hiwar al-Mashriq al-Maghrib: Talih Silsila al-Rudud wa al-Munaqashat* (East-West Dialogue: Followed by a Series of Replies and Debates). Casablanca: Dar Tubqal, 1990.

Hanioglu, M. Sükrü. *Bir Siyasal Düsünür Olarak Doktor Abdullah Cevdet ve Dönemi* (Doctor Abdullah Cevdet: A Political Thinker and His Era). Istanbul: Üçdal Nesriyat, 1981.

Harbsmeier, Michael. "Introduction: European Media in the Eyes of 19th Century Muslim Observers." *Culture & History* 16 (1997): 8-12.

Hart, William D. *Edward Said and the Religious Effects of Culture.* Cambridge: Cambridge University Press, 2000.

Hashemi, Nader A. "From the Red Menace to the Green Peril: International Security and the Chimera of an 'Islamic Threat.'" M.A. Research Essay, Carleton University, 1995.

Hashmi, Sohail H. "Islamic Ethics in International Society." Pp. 148-72 in *Islamic Political Ethics: Civil Society, Pluralism, and Conflict*, edited by Sohail H. Hashmi. Princeton: Princeton University Press, 2002.

Haykal, Muhammad Husayn. *Hayat Muhammad* (Life of Muhammad). Cairo: Maktabat al-'Arab, 1935.

Heyd, Uriel. "The Ottoman 'Ulema and Westernization in the Time of Selim III and Mahmud II." Pp. 29-60 in *The Modern Middle East: A Reader*, edited by Albert Hourani. Berkeley: University of California Press, 1993.

Hillerbrand, Hans J. "Reformation." Pp. 244-54 in *The Encyclopedia of Religion*, vol. 12, edited by Mircea Eliade. New York: MacMillan Publishing Company, 1987.

Hirschkind, Charles. "Heresy or Hermeneutics?: The Case of Nasr Hamid Abu Zayd." *The American Journal of Islamic Social Sciences* 12 (1995): 465-69.

Hoffman, Valerie J. *Sufism, Mystics and Saints in Modern Egypt.* Columbia: University of South Carolina Press, 1995.

Horsch, John. *Mennonites in Europe.* Scottdale, Penn: Mennonite Publishing House, 1942.

Hourani, Albert. *Arabic Thought in the Liberal Age 1798-1939.* Cambridge: Cambridge University Press, 1983.

———. *A History of the Arab Peoples.* Cambridge: Harvard University Press, 1991.

Huff, Toby E. "Rethinking Islam and Fundamentalism (Review Essay)." *Sociological Forum* 10 (1995).

Huntington, Samuel P. *The Clash of Civilizations and the Remaking of World Order.* New York: Simon & Schuster, 1996.

Huq, Maimuna. "From Piety to Romance: Islam-oriented Texts in Bangladesh." Pp. 129-57 in *New Media in the Muslim World: The Emerging Public Sphere*, 2nd edition, edited by Dale F. Eickelman and Jon W. Anderson. Bloomington: Indiana University Press, 2003.

Husayn, Taha. *Ala Hamish al-Sira* (On the Margins of the Tradition of the Prophet). 3 vols. Cairo: Dar al-Ma'arif, 1946-1947.

Ibrahim, Saad Eddin. "Anatomy of Egypt's Militant Islamist Groups." *International Journal of Middle East Studies* 12 (1980): 423-53.

——. "From Taliban to Erbakan: The Case of Islam, Civil Society, and Democracy in the Arab World." Pp. 33-44 in *Civil Society, and Democracy in the Muslim World*, edited by Elisabeth Özdalgee and Sune Persson. Istanbul: The Swedish Institution, 1997.

International Journal of Politics, Culture, and Society. Special Issue on "Intellectuals in Post-Revolutionary Iran." 15 (Winter 2001).

Iqbal, Muhammad. "Islam as a Moral and Political Ideal." *The Hindustan Review* (July 1909): 29-38, 166-71. Pp. 304-313 in *Modernist Islam, 1840-1940: A Source-Book*, edited by Charles Kurzman. New York: Oxford University Press, 2002.

——. *The Reconstruction of Religious Thought in Islam.* Oxford: Oxford University Press, 1930.

Ismail, Salwa. "Confronting the Other: Identity, Culture, Politics and Conservative Islamism in Egypt." *International Journal of Middle East Studies* 30 (1998): 199-235.

——. *Rethinking Islamist Politics: Culture, the State and Islamism.* London: I. B. Tauris, 2003.

al-Jabiri, Muhammad 'Abid. *Nahnu wa al-Turath* (We and the Heritage). Casablanca: al-Markaz al-Thaqafi al-'Arabi, 1985.

John Zogby Group International, Inc. "American Attitudes towards Islam: A Nationwide Poll." *The American Journal of Islamic Social Sciences* 10 (Fall 1993): 403-7.

Jones, David Pryce. *The Closed Circle.* London: Paladin, 1990.

Jornier, J. Pp. 360-61 in *Encyclopedia of Islam*, edited by H.A. R. Gibb, et al., 2nd ed., vol. 6. Leiden: E. J. Brill, 1954-1971.

Kadivar, Mohsen. *Baha-ye Azadi: Defa'iyat-e Mohsen Kadivar dar Dadgah-e Vizheh-ye Ruhaniyat* (The Price of Freedom: Mohsen Kadivar's Defense Statement in the Special Clergy Court), 3rd printing, edited by Zahra Rudi. Tehran: Nashr-e Ney, 1999.

——. *Nazariyeh'ha-ye Dowlat dar Feqh-e Shi'a* (Theories of the State in Shi'i Jurisprudence). 4th printing. Tehran: Nashr-e Ney, 1998.

Kamil, 'Umar 'Abd Allah. *al-Ayat al-Bayyinat: li-ma fi Asatir al-Qimni min al-Dalal wa al-Khurafat* (The Clear Verses on the Deviation and Myths in Qimni's Legends). Cairo: Maktabat al-Turath al-Islami, 1997.

Kanlidere, Ahmet. *Reform within Islam: The Tajdid and Jadid Movements among the Kazan Tatars (1809-1917).* Istanbul: Eren, 1997.

Kaplan, Jeffrey. *Radical Religion in America: Millenarian Movements from the Far Right to the Children of Noah.* Syracuse: Syracuse University Press, 1997.

Kaplan, Robert D. "Reform Party: Can Turkish Islamists Save Islam?" *The New Republic* 227 (16 December 2002): 13.

Karim, Ben Driss. *Sidi Hamza al-Qadiri Boudchich. Le renouveau du soufisme au Maroc* (Sidi Hamza al-Qadiri Boudchich: The Revival of the Sufism in Morocco). Paris: Albouraq, 2002.

Keddie, Nikki R. *An Islamic Response to Imperialism: Political and Religious Writings of Sayyid Jamal ad-Din "al-Afghani."* Berkeley: University of California Press, 1983.

——. *Sayyid Jamal ad-Din al-Afghani: A Political Biography.* Berkeley: University of California Press, 1972.

Kepel, Gilles. *Les Banlieues de l'Islam: Naissance d'une Religion en France* (The Suburbs of Islam: Birth of a Religion in France). Paris: Éditions du Seuil, 1987.

Kerr, Malcolm H. *Islamic Reform: The Political and Legal Theories of Muhammad 'Abduh and Rashid Rida.* Berkeley: University of California Press, 1966.

——. "Rashid Rida and Islamic Legal Reform: An Ideological Analysis." *Muslim World* 50 (1960): 170-81.

Khallaf, 'Abd al-Wahhab. *Masadir al-Tashri' al-Islami fima la Nassa fih* (The Origins of Islamic Legislation When there is no Text). Kuwait: Dar al-Qalam, 6th ed. 1993.

Khomeini, Ruhollah. *Islam and Revolution: Writings and Declarations of Imam Khomeini*, translated by Hamid Algar. Berkeley: Mizan Press, 1981.

Koch, Jerry. "Reformation." Pp. 404-5 in *Encyclopedia of Religion and Society*, edited by William H. Swatos, Jr. Walnut Creek, Calif.: AltaMira Press, 1998.

Krämer, Gudrun. "Kritik und Selbstkritik: Reformistisches Denken im Islam" (Critique and Self Critique: Reformist Thought in Islam). Pp. 209-24 in *Der Islam im Aufbruch? Perspektiven der arabischen Welt* (Islam Bursting Forth? Perspectives in the Arab World), edited by Michael Lüders. München: Piper, 1992.

Kramer, Martin S. "Hizbullah: The Calculus of Jihad." Pp. 539-56 in *Fundamentalisms and the State: Remaking Politics, Economics, and Militance*, edited by Martin E. Marty and R. Scott Appleby. Chicago: University of Chicago Press, 1993.

——. "Islam vs. Democracy." *Commentary* 115 (January 1993): 35-42.

——. *Ivory Towers on Sand: The Failure of Middle Eastern Studies in America.* Washington, D.C.: Washington Institute for Near East Policy, 2001.

Kurzman, Charles. "Bin Ladin and Other Thoroughly Modern Muslims." *Contexts* 1, no.4 (2002): 13-20.

——. "Epistemology and the Sociology of Knowledge." *Philosophy of the Social Sciences* 24 (1994): 267-90.

——. *Liberal Islam: A Source-Book.* New York: Oxford University Press, 1998.

——. *Modernist Islam, 1840-1940: A Source-Book.* New York: Oxford University Press, 2002.

Knysh, Alexander. "Orthodoxy and Heresy in Medieval Islam: An Essay in Reassessment." *Muslim World* 83 (1993): 48–67.

Lambton, Ann K. S. "A Reconsideration of the Position of *Marja' al-Taqlid* and the Religious Institution." *Studia Islamica* 20 (1964): 115-35.

Lapidus, Ira M. *A History of Islamic Societies.* Cambridge: Cambridge University Press, 1988.

Lecler, Joseph. *Toleration and the Reformation*, translated by T. L. Westow. 2 vols. New York: Association Press, 1960.

Lemke, Wolf-Dieter. *Mahmud Šaltut (1893-1963) und die Reform der Azhar* (Mahmud Shaltut [1893-1963] and the Reform of al-Azhar). Frankfurt: Peter D. Lang, 1980.

Lerner, Daniel. *The Passing of Traditional Society: Modernizing the Middle East.* New York: Free Press, 1964.

Lewis, Bernard. *The Middle East and the West.* New York: Harper Torchbooks, 1964.

Lienhard, Marc. "Luther and Europe." Pp. 82-109 in *The Reformation*, edited by Pierre Chaunu. New York: St. Martin's Press, 1990.

Lindberg, Carter. *The European Reformations.* Oxford: Blackwell Publishers, 1996.

Luther, Martin. "Why the Books of the Pope and his Disciples Were Burned by Doctor Martin Luther" (1520). Pp. 379-95 in *Luther's Works*, vol. 31, edited by Harold J. Grimm. Philadelphia: Muhlenberg Press, 1957.

Mahmasani, Subhi Rajab. *Falsafat al-Tashri' fi al-Islam* (The Philosophy of Legislation in Islam), 3rd ed. Beirut: Dar al-'Ilm lil-Malayin, 1961.

Makdisi, George. "Ibn Taimiya: A Sufi of the Qadiriya Order." *American Journal of Arabic Studies* 1 (1973): 118-29.

Mallat, Chibli. *The Renewal of Islamic Law: Muhammad Baqer as-Sadr, Najaf and the Shi'i International.* Cambridge: Cambridge University Press, 1993.

Ma'oz, Moshe. "The 'Ulama and the Process of Modernization in Syria During the Mid-Nineteenth Century." *African and Asian Studies* 7 (1971): 79-84.

Marsot, Afaf Lutfi al-Sayyid. "The Ulama of Cairo in the Eighteenth and Nineteenth Centuries." Pp. 153-63 in *Scholars, Saints, and Sufis: Muslim Religious Institutions in the Middle East Since 1500,* edited by Nikki R. Keddie. Berkeley: University of California Press, 1972.

Martinussen, John. *Society, State and Market: A Guide to Competing Theories of Development.* London: Zed Books, 1997.

Marty, Martin E., and R. Scott Appleby, eds. "The Fundamentalism Project Series." *Volume 1: Fundamentalisms Observed* (1991); *Volume 2: Fundamentalisms and the State: Remaking Polities, Economies and Militance* (1993); *Volume 3: Fundamentalisms and Society: Reclaiming the Sciences, the Family and Education* (1993); *Volume 4: Accounting for Fundamentalism: The Dynamic Character of Movements* (1994); *Volume 5: Fundamentalisms Comprehended* (1995). Chicago: University of Chicago Press.

Masud, Muhammad Khalid. *Islamic Legal Philosophy: A Study of Abu Ishaq al-Shatibi's Life and Thought.* Delhi: International Islamic Publishers, 1989.

Matheson, Peter. *The Rhetoric of the Reformation.* Edinburgh: T & T Clark Ltd., 1998.

Mazower, Mark. *Dark Continent: Europe's 20th Century.* New York: Alfred A. Knopf, 1999.

Mazrui, Ali, and Alamin Mazrui. "The Digital Revolution and the New Reformation." *Harvard International Review* 23 (2001): 52-55.

McGrath, Alister E. *The Intellectual Origins of the European Reformation.* Oxford: Blackwell, 1987.

McLelland, Joseph C. *The Reformation and Its Significance Today.* Philadelphia: Westminster Press, 1962.

Melchert, Christopher. *The Formation of the Sunni Schools of Law, 9th-10th Centuries C.E.* Leiden: Brill, 1997.

Mir-Hosseini, Ziba. *Islam and Gender: The Religious Debate in Contemporary Iran.* Princeton: Princeton University Press, 1999.

———. "Stretching the Limits: A Feminist Reading of the *Shari'a* in Post-Khomeini Iran." Pp. 284-320 in *Feminism and Islam,* edited by Mai Yamani. Berkshire, England: Ithaca Press, 1996.

Mirsepassi, Ali. *Intellectual Discourse and the Politics of Modernization: Negotiating Modernity in Iran.* Cambridge: Cambridge University Press, 2000.

Mirza, Syed Kamran. "Why Critical Scrutiny of Islam Is an Utmost Necessity." *Free Inquiry* 22 (2002): 45-46.

Mottahedeh, Roy. *The Mantle of the Prophet: Religion and Politics in Iran.* New York: Simon and Schuster, 1985.

Motterlini, Matteo. *For and Against Method.* Chicago: University of Chicago Press, 1999.

Moosa, Ebrahim. "Introduction." Pp. 1-29 in *Revival and Reform in Islam: A Study of Islamic Fundamentalism,* by Fazlur Rahman. Oxford: Oneworld, 2000.

Muruwwa, Husayn. *al-Naza'at al-Madiyya fi al-Falsafa al-'Arabiyya al-Islamiyya* (The Materialist Tendencies in Arab Islamic Thought). 2 vols. Beirut: Dar al-Farabi, 1978-1979.

Nasr, Seyyed Vali R. *Islamic Leviathan: Islam and the Making of State Power.* New York: Oxford University Press, 2001.

Neuhaus, Richard John. *The Naked Public Square: Religion and Democracy in America,* 2nd ed. Grand Rapids, Mich.: Eerdmans, 1984.

Nuri, 'Abdollah. *Shukran-e Eslah: Defa'iyat-e 'Abdollah Nuri be Peyvast-e Ra'ye Dadgah-e Vizheh-ye Ruhaniyat* (The Hemlock of Reform: 'Abdollah Nuri's Defense Statement Together with the Opinion of the Special Clergy Court), 3rd printing. Tehran: Entesharat-e Tarh-e No, 1999.

Opwis, Felicitas. "Maslaha: An Intellectual History of a Core Concept in Islamic Legal Theory." Ph.D. thesis, Yale University, 2001.

Ostle, Robin. "The Printing Press and the Renaissance of Modern Arabic Literature." *Culture & History* 16 (1997): 145-49.

Peacock, James L. *Muslim Puritans: Reformist Psychology in Southeast Asian Islam.* Berkeley: University of California Press, 1978.

Peters, F. E. "Jesus and Muhammad: A Historian's Reflection," *The Muslim World* 86 (1996): 334-41.

Peters, Rudolph. "*Idjtihad* and *Taqlid* in 18th and 19th Century Islam." *Die Welt des Islams* (The World of Islam) 20 (1980): 131-44.

——. "The Islamization of Criminal Law: A Comparative Perspective." *Die Welt des Islams* (The World of Islam) 34 (1994): 246-74.

Piscatori, James. *Islam in a World of Nation-States.* Cambridge: Cambridge University Press, 1986.

Platt, Katie. "Island Puritanism." Pp. 169-86 in *Islamic Dilemmas,* edited by Ernest Gellner. Berlin: Mouton Publishers, 1985.

Qasim, 'Abd al-Hakim. *Ayyam al-Insan al-Sab'a* (The Seven Days of Man). Cairo: Dar al-Kitab al-'Arabi, 1969.

al-Qimni, Mahmud Sayyid. *al-Hizb al-Hashimi wa Ta'sis al-Dawla al-Islamiyya* (The Hashemite Faction and the Foundation of the Islamic State). Cairo: Madbuli al-Saghir, 1996.

Queen, Christopher S. "Introduction: The Shapes and Sources of Engaged Buddhism." Pp. 1-44 in *Engaged Buddhism: Buddhist Liberation Movements in Asia,* edited by Christopher S. Queen and Sallie B. King. Albany: State University of New York Press, 1996.

Qustas, Ahmad. *Nibras al-Murid fi Tariqa al-Tawhid* (The Lamp of the Novice in the Order of Unity). Fez: al-Murid, 1993.

Rahman, Fazlur. "A Survey of Modernization of Muslim Family Law." *International Journal of Middle East Studies* 2 (1981): 451-65.

——. "Revival and Reform in Islam." Pp. 30-68 in *The Cambridge History of Islam,* edited by P. M. Holt, Ann Katharine Swynford Lambton, and Bernard Lewis. Cambridge: Cambridge University Press, 1970.

Raja'i, Gholam-'Ali. *Bar-dasht'hayi az Sireh-ye Emam Khomeini* (Selections from the Life of Imam Khomeini). 3 vols. Tehran: Mo'aseseh-ye Chap va Nashr-e 'Oruj, 1997-1998.

Ramadan, Tariq. *To Be a European Muslim.* Markfield, England: The Islamic Foundation, 1998.

Rashid, Ahmed. *Taliban: Militant Islam, Oil, and Fundamentalism in Central Asia.* New Haven: Yale University Press, 2000.

Reid, Donald M. *Cairo University and the Making of Modern Egypt.* Cambridge: Cambridge University Press, 1990.

Rida, Muhammad Rashid. "Renewal, Renewing, and Renewers." Pp. 77-85 in *Modernist Islam, 1840-1940: A Source-Book,* edited by Charles Kurzman. New York: Oxford University Press, 2002.

———. *Yusr al-Islam wa Usul al-Tashri' al-'Amm* (Islam's Facility and the Sources of General Legislation). Cairo: Maktabat al-Salam al-'Alamiyya, 1984.

Ricoeur, Paul. *Political and Social Essays,* edited by David Stewart and Joseph Bien. Athens: Ohio University Press, 1974.

———. "The Model of the Text: Meaningful Action Considered as a Text." In *Understanding and Social Inquiry,* edited by Fred R. Dallmayr and Thomas A. McCarthy. South Bend: University of Notre Dame Press, 1977.

Roberson, Barbara Allen, ed. *Shaping the Current Islamic Reformation.* London: Frank Cass, 2003.

Roberts, J. M. *The Penguin History of the World.* New York: Penguin, 1990.

Robertson, Roland, and JoAnn Chirico. "Humanity, Globalization, and Worldwide Religion Resurgence: A Theoretical Exploration." *Sociological Analysis* 46 (1985): 219-42.

Robinson, Francis. "Technology and Religious Change: Islam and the Impact of Print." *Modern Asian Studies* 27 (1993): 233-50.

Rodinson, Maxime. "A Critical Survey of Modern Studies on Muhammad." Pp. 23-85 in *Studies on Islam,* edited and translated by Merlin L. Swartz. New York: Oxford University Press, 1982.

———. *Marxism and the Muslim World,* translated by Jean Matthews. New York: Monthly Review Press, 1981.

Rouadjia, Ahmed. *Grandeur et Décadence de l'État Algérien* (Grandeur and Decadence of the Algerian State). Paris: Karthala, 1994.

Roy, Olivier. "Has Islamism a Future in Afghanistan?" Pp. 199-211 in *Fundamentalism Reborn?: Afghanistan and the Taliban,* edited by William Maley. New York: New York University Press, 1998.

Ruhani, Hamid. *Shari'at-Madari dar Dadgah-e Tarikh* (Shari'at-Madari in the Court of History). Qom, Iran: Daftar-e Entesharat-e Eslami, 1982.

Sabanegh, E. S. *Muhammad, le Prophète: Portraits Contemporains, Égypte 1930-1950* (Muhammad, The Prophet: Contemporary Potraits, Egypt 1930-1950). Paris: Librairie J. Vrin, 1981.

Sadowski, Yahya. "The New Orientalism and Democracy Debate." Pp. 33-50 in *Political Islam: Essays from Middle East Report,* edited by Joel Beinin and Joe Stork. Berkeley: University of California Press, 1997.

Safi, Louay M. "Editorial: Overcoming the Cultural Divide." *American Journal of Islamic Social Sciences* 18, no. 1 (2002): v-x.

Said, Edward. *Orientalism.* New York: Vintage Books, 1978.

Sa'idzadeh, Mohsen. "Bandi Digar: Defa' az Hoquq-e Zanan Mamnu'!" (Another Subsection: Defense of the Rights of Women Banned!). *Zanan* (Women) 42 (1998): 6-7.

Schacht, Joseph. *Introduction to Islamic Law.* Oxford: Clarendon Press, 1964.

Schirazi, Asghar. *The Constitution of Iran: Politics and the State in the Islamic Republic,* translated by John O'Kane. London: I. B. Tauris, 1997.

Schulze, Reinhard. *Islamischer Internationalismus im 20. Jahrhundert: Untersuchungen zur Geschichte der Islamischen Weltliga* (Islamic Internationalism in Twentieth Century: Investigations in the History of the Islamic World League). Leiden: E. J. Brill, 1990.

——. "The Birth of Tradition and Modernity in 18th and 19th Century Islamic Culture—the Case of Printing." *Culture & History* 16 (1997): 31-58.

Schweitzer, Albert. *The Quest for the Historical Jesus: A Critical Study of its Progress from Reimarus to Wrede.* New York: Macmillan, 1961.

Sedgwick, Mark. "Sects in the Islamic World." *Nova Religio* 3 (2000): 195-240.

——. "Establishments and Sects in the Islamic World." In *New Religious Movements: The Future of New Religions in the 21st Century,* edited by Phillip Lucas and Thomas Robbins. New York: Routledge, 2003.

——. *Saints and Sons: The Making and Remaking of the Rashidi Ahmadi Sufi Order, 1799-2000.* Leiden: Brill, forthcoming.

Setton, Kenneth M. *Western Hostility to Islam, and Prophecies of Turkish Doom.* Philadelphia: American Philosophical Society, 1992.

al-Shahrastani, Muhammad ibn 'Abd al-Karim. *Muslim Sects and Divisions: The Section on Muslim Sects in "Kitab al-milal wa 'l-nihal,"* translated by A. K. Kazi and J. G. Flynn. London: Kegan Paul International, 1984.

Shahrour, Mohammad. "The Case against Modernity." *Islam21* 5. August 1996. www.islam21.net/pages/keyissues/key1-4.htm (30 March 2003).

——. *Dirasat Islamiyya al-Mu'asira fi al-Dawla wa al-Mujtama'* (Contemporary Islamic Studies on State and Society). Damascus: al-Ahali lil-Taba'a wa al-Nashr, 1994.

——. "The Divine Text and Pluralism in Muslim Societies," *Muslim Politics Report of the Council on Foreign Relations* 14 (July-August 1997): 3-4, 7-9.

——. "Islam and the 1995 Beijing World Conference on Women." Pp. 139-42 in *Liberal Islam: A Source Book,* edited by Charles Kurzman. New York: Oxford University Press, 1998.

——. *al-Kitab wa al-Qur'an: Qira'a Mu'asira* (The Book and the Qur'an: A Contemporary Reading). Damascus: al-Ahli lil-Taba'a wa al-Nashr wa al-Tawzi', 1990.

——. "Proposal for an Islamic Covenant." *Islam21.* May 2000. www.islam21.net/pages/charter/may-1.htm (30 March 2003).

——. "Reading the Religious Text—A New Approach." *Islam21* 21 (December 1999): 2-3.

Shari'ati, 'Ali. *Man and Islam,* translated by Fatollah Marjani. Houston: Free Islamic Literature, 1981.

——. *What Is to Be Done?* edited and translated by Farhang Rajaee. Houston: Institute for Research and Islamic Studies, 1986.

Sharpe, Eric J. "Religious Studies, the Humanities, and the History of Ideas." *Soundings* 71 (1988): 245-58.

Siedentop, Larry. "Introduction." Pp. vii-xxxvii in *The History of Civilization in Europe,* by François Guizot. London: Penguin, 1997.

Siddiqi, Mazheruddin. *Modern Reformist Thought in the Muslim World.* Islamabad, Pakistan: Islamic Research Institute, 1982.

Skali, Faouzi. *La Voie Soufie* (The Sufi Way). Paris: Albin Michel, 1993.

Skøvgaard-Petersen, Jakob. "Fatwas in Print." *Culture & History* 16 (1997): 73-86.

Smith, Charles D. "The 'Crisis of Orientation': The Shift of Egyptian Intellectuals to Islamic Subjects in the 1930's." *International Journal of Middle East Studies* 4 (1973): 382-410.

——. "'Cultural Constructs' and Other Fantasies: Imagined Narratives in Imagined Communities; Surrejoinder to Gershoni and Jankowski's 'Print Culture, Social Change and the Process of Redefining Imagined Communities in Egypt.'" *International Journal of Middle East Studies* 31 (1999): 95-102.

Sonn, Tamara. "Bandali al-Jawzi's *Min Tarikh al-Harakat al-Fikriyyat fi 'l-Islam*: The First Marxist Interpretation of Islam." *International Journal of Middle East Studies* 17 (1985): 89-107.

Soroush, Abdolkarim. "Keynote Address." Center for the Study of Islam and Democracy 2nd Annual Conference, Georgetown University. 7 April 2001. www.islam-democracy.org/SoroushAddress.shtml (15 May 2003).

——. *Reason, Freedom, and Democracy in Islam: Essential Writings of Abdolkarim Soroush*, edited by Mahmoud Sadri and Ahmad Sadri. New York: Oxford University Press, 2000.

Southern, R. W. *Western Views of Islam in the Middle Ages*. Cambridge: Harvard University Press, 1962.

Stark, Rodney, and Williams Bainbridge. *The Future of Religion: Secularization, Revival and Cult Formation*. Berkeley: University of California Press, 1985.

Starr, Paul. *The Social Transformation of American Medicine*. New York: Basic Books, 1982.

Stork, Joe and Joel Beinin. "On the Modernity, Historical Specificity and International Context of Political Islam." Pp. 3-25 in *Political Islam: Essays from Middle East Report*, edited by Joel Beinin and Joe Stork. Berkeley: University of California Press, 1997.

Spitz, Lewis W. *The Renaissance and Reformation Movements*. Chicago: Rand McNally, 1971.

Sultanate of Oman. *Statistical Year Book, 1996*. Muscat, Oman: Ministry of Development, 1997.

Tabataba'i, Mohammad Hossein et al. *Bahsi Dar-bareh-ye Marja'iyat va Ruhaniyat* (A Discussion of Religious Leadership and Religious Scholars). Tehran: Sherkat-e Sehami-ye Enteshar, 1962.

Tabawi, A. L. "English-Speaking Orientalists: A Critique of their Approach to Islam and Arab Nationalism, Part I." *Islamic Quarterly* 1-2 (1964): 25-45.

al-Tahtawi, Ahmad. *Ahwal al-Qubur wa Ma Ba'd al-Mawt* (The Terrors of the Grave, or What Follows Death). Cairo: Dar al-Bashir, 1987.

Tavakoli-Targhi, Mohamad. "Frontline Mysticism and Eastern Spirituality." *ISIM Newsletter* 9 (January 2002): 13, 38.

Taylor, Charles. "Modernity and the Rise of the Public Sphere." Pp. 203-60 in the *Tanner Lectures on Human Values*, vol. 14, edited by Grethe E. Peterson. Salt Lake City: University of Utah Press, 1993.

——. *The Malaise of Modernity*. Concord, Ontario: Anansi Press, 1991.

Tozy, Mohammed. "Le Prince, le Clerc et l'Etat: La Restructuration du Dhamp Religieux au Maroc" (The Prince, the Cleric, and the State: The Reconstruction of the Religious Field in Morocco). Pp. 71-90 in *Intellectuels et Militants de l'Islam Contemporain* (Intellectuals and Militants in Contemporary Islam), edited by Gilles Kepel and Yann Richard. Paris: Du Seuil, 1990.

Trofimov, Yaroslav. "As Taliban Falls Inside Afghanistan, So Do Islamic Rules Beyond Order." *Wall Street Journal* (31 December 2001): A10.

UNESCO. *Statistical Yearbook, 1998*. Latham, Md.: UNESCO Publishing and Bernan Press, 1998.

Vatin, Jean-Claude. "Popular Puritanism Versus State Reformism: Islam in Algeria." Pp. 98-121 in *Islam in the Political Process*, edited by James P. Piscatori. Cambridge: Cambridge University Press, 1983.

Voll, John Obert. *Islam: Continuity and Change in the Modern World*, 2nd edition. Syracuse, N.Y.: Syracuse University Press, 1994.

Waardenburg, Jean-Jacques. *L'Islam dans le Miroir de l'Occident: Comment Quelques Orientalistes Occidentaux se Sent Penchés sur l'Islam et se Sont Formés une Image de Cette Religion* (Islam in the Mirror of the West: How Several Western Orientalists Felt Inclined Toward Islam and Formed an Image of that Religion). Paris: Mouton & Co., 1963.

——. "The Puritan Pattern in Islamic Revival Movements." *Schweizerische Zeitschrift für Soziologie* (Swiss Journal of Sociology) 3 (1983): 687-702.

Walzer, Michael. *Revolution of the Saints: A Study in the Origins of Radical Politics*. Cambridge: Harvard University Press, 1965.

——. *The Revolution of the Saints: A Study in the Origins of Radical Politics*. Cambridge: Harvard University Press, 1965.

Watt, W. Montgomery. *Muhammad: Prophet and Statesman*. Oxford: Oxford University Press, 1964.

——. *A Short History of Islam*. Oxford: One World, 1996.

Weber, Max. *The Protestant Ethic and the Spirit of Capitalism*. London: Routledge, 1992.

Wiederhold, L. "Blasphemy against the Prophet and his Companions (Sab al-Rasul wa Sab al-Sahaba): The Introduction of the Topic into Shafi'i Legal Literature and its Relevance under Mamluk Rule." *Journal of Semitic Studies* 63 (1997): 39-73.

Weiss, Bernhard. *The Search for God's Law: Islamic Jurisprudence in the Writings of Sayf al-Din al-Amidi*. Salt Lake City: University of Utah Press, 1992.

Weissman, Itzchak. *Taste of Modernity: Sufism, Salafiyya, & Arabism in Late Ottoman Damascus*. Leiden: Brill, 2001.

White, Jenny B. *Islamist Mobilization in Turkey: A Study in Vernacular Politics*. Seattle: University of Washington Press, 2002.

Wiebe, Donald. *The Politics of Religious Studies: The Continuing Conflict with Theology in the Academy*. New York: St. Martin's Press, 1999.

Williams, George Huntston. *The Radical Reformation*, 3rd edition. Kirksville, Mo.: Sixteenth Century Journal Publishers, 1992.

Williams, George. *The Radical Reformation*. Philadelphia: The Westminster Press, 1962.

Wilson, Samuel Graham. *Modern Movements among Moslems*. New York: Fleming H. Revell Company, 1916.

Wittfogel, Karl. *Oriental Despotism: A Comparative Study of Total Power*. New Haven: Yale University Press, 1957.

World Bank. *Knowledge for Development: World Development Report, 1998-1999*. New York: Oxford University Press for the World Bank, 1999.

Wright, Robin. "Iran's New Revolution." *Foreign Affairs* (January-February 2000): 133-45.

——. "Islam and Liberal Democracy: Two Visions of Reformation." *Journal of Democracy* 7 (1996): 64-75.

——. *The Last Great Revolution: Turmoil and Transformation in Iran.* New York: A. A. Knopf, 2000.

——. "Two Visions of Reformation." *Journal of Democracy* 7 (1996): 64-75.

Zahedi, Dariush. *The Iranian Revolution Then and Now.* Boulder, Colo.: Westview Press, 2000.

Zaman, Muhammad Qasim. *The Ulama in Contemporary Islam: Custodians of Change.* Princeton: Princeton University Press, 2002.

Zebiri, Kate. *Mahmud Shaltut and Islamic Modernism.* Oxford: Clarendon Press, 1993.

Zilfi, Madeline C. *The Politics of Piety: The Ottoman Ulema in the Postclassical Age (1600-1800).* Minneapolis, Minn.: Bibliotheca Islamica, 1988.

Zubaida, Sami. *Islam, the People and the State: Political Ideas and Movements in the Middle East.* New York: I. B. Tauris, 1993.

Zurayq, Burhan Khalil, ed. *Nasr Hamid Abu Zayd bayn al-Takfir wa al-Tanwir: Hiwar, Shahadat, Watha'iq* (Abu Zayd Between Unbelief and Enlightenment: Interviews, Testimonies and Documents). Cairo: Markaz al-Mahrusah, 1996.

Index

About the Contributors

Michaelle Browers is an Assistant Professor of Political Science at Wake Forest University. Her areas of teaching and research are political theory, Arab and Islamic political thought, cross-cultural encounters, democratic theory, and political ideologies. She has published articles in *Political Studies* and *Environmental Ethics*, and chapters in *New Approaches to Comparative Politics: Insights from Political Theory*, ed. Jennifer S. Holmes (Lexington Books, 2003) and *Handbook of Political Theory*, ed. Gerald Gaus and Chandran Kukathas (Sage Publications, forthcoming May 2004). She has recently completed a book manuscript entitled *Democracy and Civil Society in Arab Political Thought: Transcultural Possibilities*.

Fred Dallmayr is the Packey J. Dee Professor of Political Theory and a Professor of Philosophy at the University of Notre Dame. He is a specialist in modern and contemporary European thought and has a growing interest in comparative philosophy, particularly non-Western political thought (focusing on Islam, Hinduism, Buddhism, and Confucianism), cross-cultural dialogue, and global human rights. In addition to his many articles, he has authored twelve books, including *Beyond Orientalism: Essays on Cross-cultural Encounter* (SUNY, 1996), *Alternative Visions: Paths in the Global Village* (Rowman and Littlefield, 1998), *Achieving our World: Toward a Global and Plural Democracy* (Rowman and Littlefield, 2001), and *Dialogue Among Civilizations: Some Exemplary Voices* (Palgrave, 2002).

Dale F. Eickelman is the Ralph and Richard Lazarus Professor of Anthropology and Human Relations at Dartmouth College. His publications include *New Media in the Muslim World: The Emerging Public Sphere*, 2nd ed., coedited with Jon W. Anderson (Indiana University Press, 2003), *The Middle East and Central Asia: An Anthropological Approach*, 4th ed. (Prentice Hall, 2002), and *Muslim Politics*, coauthored with James Piscatori (Princeton University Press, 1996).

Nader A. Hashemi is a Ph.D. Candidate in the Department of Political Science at the University of Toronto. He is working on a dissertation entitled "Rethinking the Relationship between Religion, Secularism and Democracy: Toward a Democratic Theory for Muslim Societies."

Salwa Ismail is a Senior Lecturer in the Politics Department at Exeter, having previously held posts at McGill University in Canada and the Australian National University. She is part of an international panel of the Middle East Studies Association planning the future of research on the city of Cairo. Her own research covers Islamist politics, state-society relations in the Arab world, Arab and Islamic thought, space and everyday-life politics in urban settings, and identity politics (both local and global), and she has conducted extensive fieldwork in various parts of the Middle East. She has published articles in *Comparative Studies in Society and History*, *Annuaire de l'Afrique* *du Nord, Critique, International Journal of Middle East Studies, Arab Studies Journal* and *Arab Studies Quarterly*, as well as a book entitled *Rethinking Islamist Politics: Culture, the State and Islamism* (I. B. Tauris, 2002).

Charles Kurzman is an Associate Professor of Sociology at the University of North Carolina at Chapel Hill. He is editor of the anthologies *Liberal Islam: A Source-Book* (Oxford, 1998) and *Modernist Islam, 1840-1940: A Source-Book* (Oxford, 2002). He is author of several articles on recent Iranian history and the forthcoming monograph *The "Unthinkable" Revolution in Iran* (Harvard).

Felicitas Opwis is an Adjunct Professor of Religion at Wake Forest University. Recently, she was a Visiting Lecturer on Islamic Law at Yale School of Law. Her dissertation (2001) at Yale's Department of Near Eastern Languages and Civilizations Department was entitled *"Maslaha: An Intellectual History of a Core Concept of Islamic Legal Theory."* She has published in *Die Welt des Islams* and *International Journal of Middle East Studies.*

Mark Sedgwick is an Assistant Professor of Middle East History at the American University in Cairo who is currently working on the Islamic Reformation. His publications include articles in *Nova Religio: The Journal of Alternative and Emergent Religions,* as well as *Sufism: The Essentials* (AUC Press, 2000) and *Against the Modern World: Traditionalism and the Secret Intellectual History of the Twentieth Century* (Oxford, forthcoming 2004).

Ernest Tucker is an Assistant Professor of History at the U.S. Naval Academy who principally focuses on early modern Iran and the Ottoman Empire. He is currently editing and translating a nineteenth-century Arabic-language account of Imam Shamil from Dagestan.